NEIGHBOURS IN ARMS

ADVANCE PRAISE FOR THE BOOK

'Like most Indians, I was long familiar with the Pressler Amendment and it was therefore a pleasant surprise when, on moving to Washington, I discovered that Senator Larry Pressler was our neighbour. A person of grace and modesty, Larry Pressler became a personal friend from whom I heard about his struggles to foster closer ties between the US and India. This book is a fascinating account of the struggle and also a recent history of US–India relations. While the proposed economic sanctions in the amendment were never fully tested, as the Pressler Amendment was sabotaged by forces within the Pentagon, its lessons as a template for economic sanctions remain with us'—Kaushik Basu, former chief economic adviser, Government of India

'I have known Senator Larry Pressler since our days together at Oxford University as Rhodes Scholars in 1964. In fact, we spoke together at one English public school in those days. We were both idealistic twenty-two-year-olds then, and now we write as seventy-five-year-olds, semi-retired, battle-scarred veterans of public life. Senator Pressler's work illustrates the significant role a member of the United States' Congress can constructively play in the formulation of foreign policy. Our nations continue to face many of the same issues of sanctions to reduce the spread of nuclear weapons, and Senator Pressler's book deserves serious consideration by anyone trying to understand how foreign policy is made'—Montek Singh Ahluwalia, former deputy chairman, Planning Commission, Government of India

'Larry Pressler has written a remarkable book. In telling the tragic story of the Pressler Amendment, which would have prevented Pakistan from taking the nuclear weapons route, he also explains the forces at work that first circumvented the amendment legislated by the US Congress and approved by the US President, and later rolled it back. The description of these power circles by Pressler as the "Octopus" is most appropriate. With its numerous tentacles and a common centre, the Octopus is a frequently used metaphor for a powerful and manipulative system that can strangulate and be lethal. This extant system in Washington is a tremendous upgrade of the military-industrial complex that President Eisenhower had warned of many decades ago. Indians would do well to understand how this species works, if relations between the world's strongest and largest democracies have to progress'—Vikram Sood, former head, Research and Analysis Wing, Government of India

'Senator Pressler has been a true friend of India, and has been my friend for many years. He served on the board of directors of Infosys for some years. He has a unique interest in India. Whenever he came to board meetings in India, he would make an extra effort to visit a site of historical significance. He is a true Indophile. Fundamentally, this book introduces the real Larry Pressler to India'—N.R. Narayana Murthy, founder, Infosys

'Senator Pressler has invested considerable effort in affirming America's non-proliferation goals in Pakistan. Without his efforts, I have little doubt that the nuclear situation in South Asia would be far worse than it already is. We are not offering gifts, bribes or charity—we are offering a proposal that would create some concrete incentives for Pakistan to honor its non-proliferation commitments'—Senator John Glenn, chief author of the United States' Nuclear Non-Proliferation Act of 1978

'Senator John Glenn and Senator Larry Pressler co-sponsored the Pressler Amendment (or the Glenn–Pressler Amendment as it was known while the Democrats were in control) which tried to keep nuclear weapons out of both India and Pakistan. The two did a wonderful job in keeping the US Senate informed of nuclear proliferation in the subcontinent'—Senator Bob Dole, Republican nominee for President of the United States in 1996

'I served in the US Senate with Larry Pressler for many years. I always admired Larry for several reasons, not the least of which is his stunning education—Rhodes Scholar, Harvard Law. He's proved to be a real patriot; he's served two tours of duty in Vietnam in the US Army and the US Foreign Service. John Glenn and Larry Pressler worked on ways to stop the proliferation of nuclear weapons. Some of the most significant work on this issue during the last thirty years has been Pressler and Glenn trying to limit nuclear proliferation through the Glenn–Pressler Amendment. In spite of their tireless work, Pakistan developed a robust nuclear weapons program. The two senators' efforts did result in the US–India nuclear agreement which is in effect today. Senator Pressler's new book is an insight into the influence of lobbying on foreign policy and the difficulty in developing sound foreign policy'—Senator Harry Reid, former Democratic majority leader, US Senate

'I have been aware of Senator Pressler's long interest and activity in the nuclear non-proliferation field; as a fellow member of the US Senate's Foreign Relations Committee, I joined in his and Senator Glenn's struggle to prevent the spread of nuclear weapons in the Indian subcontinent. Although he admits he was not successful in keeping nuclear weapons out of Pakistan, his efforts had a number of positive results. In this book, Senator Pressler also discusses the growing role of law and lobbying firms in the formulation of foreign policy, and brings us up to date on the current US–India nuclear deal'—Senator Richard Lugar, president, Lugar Center

'Internationally, Larry Pressler is known and respected for his efforts on nuclear non-proliferation'—Senator Trent Lott, former Republican majority leader, US Senate

'Throughout his time in Congress, US Senator Larry Pressler provided deft and steady leadership in foreign policy. As the author of the "Pressler Amendment" aimed at keeping Pakistan from acquiring nuclear weapons, he has been one of our nation's leading thinkers in matters of foreign relations, with a particular expertise in nuclear non-proliferation policy. In this insightful and eye-opening new book, Senator Pressler adroitly describes how foreign policy is actually formulated in Washington today, advocating for a stronger, more active role for the legislative branch. He favors the use of Congressional hearings and actions over involvement of lobbyists and consulting firms. This is a must-read story for every student of foreign policy and anyone interested in getting a glimpse of the behind-the-scenes process of policymaking'—Senator Mike DeWine, attorney general of Ohio

'Senator Pressler tells an important story of an insider who battled what he calls the "Octopus" from both political parties who represent financial interests, much to the detriment of sound policymaking. This book provides an eyewitness account of the virtually unchecked power of law firms and lobbying firms which usurp the State Department's and the Congress's role in making foreign policy, of the unseen money flow that lubricates the entire process, and the real-world damage caused by it all'—Danielle Brian, executive director, Project On Government Oversight

NEIGHBOURS IN ARMS

An American Senator's Quest for Disarmament in a Nuclear Subcontinent

LARRY PRESSLER

PENGUIN
VIKING

An imprint of Penguin Random House

VIKING

USA | Canada | UK | Ireland | Australia
New Zealand | India | South Africa | China

Viking is part of the Penguin Random House group of companies
whose addresses can be found at global.penguinrandomhouse.com

Published by Penguin Random House India Pvt. Ltd
7th Floor, Infinity Tower C, DLF Cyber City,
Gurgaon 122 002, Haryana, India

First published in Viking by Penguin Random House India 2017

Copyright © Larry Pressler 2017
Foreword copyright © Shashi Tharoor 2017
Introduction copyright © Husain Haqqani 2017

10 9 8 7 6 5 4 3 2 1

ISBN 9780670089314

Typeset in Bembo Std by Manipal Digital Systems, Manipal
Printed at Thomson Press India Ltd, New Delhi

www.penguin.co.in

To the people of India, who have paid dearly for the nuclear race in the subcontinent, and to the hope that the US–India nuclear agreement will lead to a better quality of life for you. To all the men and women in the United States of America who are wrestling with the military-industrial state, the Octopus. To all those working tirelessly for political reform and a more transparent, accountable and ethical government, I salute you. And to the late senator John Glenn, who fought fiercely with me side by side for the Pressler Amendment. We lost the battle, but we advanced the cause of nuclear non-proliferation. We were right with history. Rest in peace, John.

Contents

Acknowledgements

This book all started with a pleasurable and chance meeting I had with Swati Chopra, my commissioning editor at Penguin Random House, in Delhi. She had the vision for this book and has encouraged me all along this journey. To her, I am eternally grateful. I also want to thank Taylor Baldwin Kiland for her tireless assistance in the production of this book. Much appreciation also is given to Dr Shashi Tharoor and Ambassador Husain Haqqani for contributing their beautiful prose and encouraging words to this book. And, finally, I thank my lovely wife, Harriet, for tolerating the countless hours I spent away from her to create *Neighbours in Arms*.

Foreword

The term 'nuclear' is one that was transformed, in a very short space of time, from a scientific marvel of unimaginable potential to one characterized by uncontrollable, looming horror. The world, it seemed, had ended one terrible war, but unleashed in the process a weapon that threatened not merely nations, but humanity itself. India, as a young country emerging into this new world after centuries of colonial rule, was cognizant from the start of both the nuclear opportunity as well as the implications of a nuclear disaster.

Without a doubt, it was a formidable achievement for a young nation, waging everyday battles against poverty, unemployment and food insecurity to announce, without warning, its arrival into the nuclear club in May 1974, from a sleepy village deep in the desert in Rajasthan. But for the most part, India's achievements in the nuclear space—and the responsibility with which India has acted in this regard—have been overshadowed by its relationship with its most immediate and traditionally unfriendly neighbour, which also acquired nuclear strength in due course, notwithstanding its inherent volatility.

As a country, India is aware that beyond its frontiers lies an uneasy state that exemplifies not only the danger of nuclear power falling into the wrong hands, but one where even the right hands might not hesitate to take decisions that hold calamitous consequences for the subcontinent and the world beyond. As I have argued in the past, in working with Pakistan, we are compelled to deal with two decision-making bodies—the country's civilian government and also, more significantly, its military complex that stands on quite a different page from the official face of the state.

In *Neighbours in Arms*, Larry Pressler has shown convincingly that employing a recipe that exploits American paranoia about Islamic terrorism combined with projecting itself as the best bulwark against fundamentalist terror, Pakistan has succeeded in extracting large sums of money from the United States to feed the appetites of its own military complex—which has then funded and wielded the very terrorism it claims to be a shield against. It has also successfully sought aid and assistance from a sophisticated lobby—'the Octopus'—that is available for hire at a price, buying favour in the capital of the world's greatest power, winning support ostensibly to fight terror but really to satisfy its own peculiar interests.

As the first veteran of the Vietnam War to be elected to the United States Senate and member of its Foreign Relations Committee, Pressler brings a unique perspective to his investigation of how United States' foreign policy in the nuclear realm is crafted. We learn of who the actors in the process are and of the relationships and entrenched interests involved around the globe, all of which influence decisions taken in the White House. Pressler takes us on a disturbing but revealing journey through the murky waters dominated by the Octopus, exposing the far reach of its tentacles and the often violent (and amoral) implications of its services.

The concept of allegiance and morality is alien to a lobbyist and it is the highest bidder who dictates the outcome of its insidious efforts. As Pressler startlingly shows, the same individuals and groups, under various disguises, often operate on both sides of the fence, driven more by profit to peddle certain narratives over others than by correctness, shaping foreign policy in a way that can often cross the bounds of accountability, responsibility and even reason. Pressler is, of course, famous for his 1985 Pressler Amendment that sought to challenge this state of affairs by forbidding assistance to Pakistan unless the US administration certified it was not developing nuclear weapons. Regrettably, political and administrative expediencies meant the amendment was watered down instead of being invoked when it should have been, and Pakistani nuclear proliferation was overlooked to shore up support for other geopolitical interests.

Senator Pressler will always have a place of honour for his contributions to fighting proliferation. But more significantly, his voice in calling out the actions of a rogue state despite the disproportionate influence it could command through money and lobbying, will ensure a place for him as a voice of reason—and a voice of what is right—in the history of global nuclear politics.

I met Larry Pressler a few times at the United Nations and always found him a remarkably open, candid and principled individual. Pressler, to me, is a friend of India. But he is also a friend of peace, of responsibility and of international integrity. I wish this book and its author all success.

New Delhi   Shashi Tharoor
May 2017

Introduction

Amid concern about the nuclear weapons programmes of Iran and North Korea, it is important to remember the role of Pakistan's Dr A.Q. Khan as one of the world's most reckless proliferator of weapons of mass destruction. Pakistan's own clandestine nuclear programme was enabled by the United States' mistaken policy of looking the other way as long as Pakistan served as a partial ally in containing the threat from the Soviet Union. Senator Larry Pressler was one of very few Americans who realized that preventing nuclear proliferation was more important than fulfilling through Pakistan some tactical needs of the US military and intelligence services. This book is his account of his efforts to limit nuclear proliferation in South Asia and beyond. Had those efforts succeeded, the world would also have not faced the threat posed by Dr A.Q. Khan's onward proliferation to Iran and North Korea.

Senator Pressler was the author of the 1985 Pressler Amendment to the US Foreign Aid Act, which required certification by the President of the United States that Pakistan did not possess nuclear weapons as a precondition to providing US economic or military assistance to Pakistan. The restrictions on aid prescribed in the Pressler Amendment went into effect after President George H.W. Bush refused certification in 1990. As aid to Pakistan, which ran into almost a billion dollars a year at the time, was suspended, Senator

Pressler was demonized in Pakistan as the man who undermined US–Pakistan relations. Even some Americans joined the chorus about the 'ill-advised' sanctions on Pakistan, completely ignoring the fact that the sanctions were the result of Pakistan breaking its promises to the US (albeit out of its own concerns about its national security).

As Pakistan's ambassador to the United States under a civilian government, and later as author of *Magnificent Delusions: Pakistan, United States and an Epic History of Misunderstanding*, I have often heard ill-informed comments about how the Pressler Amendment turned Pakistanis against the US, led Pakistan into alliances with global jihadis and the Taliban, and interrupted the close personal ties between US and Pakistani military officers that had worked well during the Cold War and the US-backed guerrilla war against the Soviets in Afghanistan. The reality is quite different from the myths about the origins and consequences of the Pressler Amendment.

Pakistan's national interest, as defined by its overbearing military leaders, does not always overlap with American interests. For seven decades, the transactional relationship based on Pakistan doing specific favours to the US in return for military aid inevitably used against India has benefited neither the US nor the Pakistani people. The series of transactions defining the US–Pakistan relationship has only empowered the military in Pakistan in addition to perpetuating conflict with India. On the US side, the greatest advocates of a transactional alliance is what Senator Pressler describes as 'the Octopus', the vast interconnected network of special interests that makes money from aid and ties with governments abroad without regard for any real benefit for the people of those countries or for Americans.

It is important to recall the history of the Pressler Amendment. Beginning in 1978, a year before the Soviets sent in their troops to Afghanistan, Pakistan and the Central Intelligence Agency (CIA) were arming and training mujahideen who fought the pro-communist Afghan government. That 'jihad' escalated after the induction of Soviet troops and was seen by Americans as an opportunity to create a situation for the Soviets similar to the one faced by the Americans in

Vietnam. Pakistan's military dictator General Zia-ul-Haq leveraged the Afghan jihad to secure vast amounts of US military and economic aid, including the purchase of F-16 fighter aircraft for the Pakistan Air Force on concessional terms. Pakistan also secretly persisted with its efforts to build nuclear weapons while promising the US, in return for aid, that it would not do so.

By 1985 the United States had completed disbursement of a $3.2-billion aid package, and Pakistan sought assistance for a further five years. Pakistan and the Reagan administration were forced to address Congress's nuclear proliferation concerns before approving additional aid. Pakistani diplomats as well as officials in the Reagan White House supported an amendment to the Foreign Aid Bill that would help get around the restrictions of the Symington and Glenn Amendments that forbade aid to countries with unsafeguarded nuclear programmes.

Pressler, who had recently been elected as the Republican senator from South Dakota, authored what became the Pressler Amendment to enable the flow of aid to Pakistan as long as the US President certified on an annual basis that Pakistan did not possess a nuclear explosive device. The Pressler Amendment helped Pakistan get around the provisions of the Symington and Glenn Amendments for several years. Contrary to propaganda in Pakistan, Senator Pressler did not 'victimize' Pakistan as part of some plot to help India. He only stood for the principle of non-proliferation. The reason why the proliferation sanctions hurt Pakistan more relates to Pakistan's dependence on US aid; India had pursued nuclear weapons without making specific commitments to the United States because it did not accept conditional aid as Pakistan had done.

Sanctions under the Pressler Amendment should not have surprised Pakistani leaders. In a 1984 letter to Zia that praised his contribution to the war against the Soviets, Reagan had warned of 'serious consequences' if Pakistan enriched uranium beyond 5 per cent. The hopes expressed by a former secretary of state, Alexander Haig, that the US-provided advanced conventional weapons would stop Pakistan from continuing with a nuclear programme had, by then, proved futile.

Within months of the Pressler Amendment's adoption, the US Defense Intelligence Agency reported that Pakistan had produced an atomic weapon in October 1985 'with on-site technical assistance' from China. The US intelligence community believed that Pakistan was producing enough highly enriched uranium for at least one atomic weapon. But still the administration committed itself to providing $4.02 billion in aid to Pakistan over the next six years, including additional F-16 aircraft.

The White House presumed that Pakistan would hold its uranium enrichment levels below 5 per cent to continue qualifying for US assistance. This gave Pakistan the capability for going nuclear later but enabled the US President to certify that Pakistan did not, as of yet, possess nuclear weapons. Each year, from 1986 to 1988, Reagan signed the certificate required under the Pressler Amendment to keep the aid flowing. His successor, George H.W. Bush, did the same in 1989.

With Pakistan's help, the United States had succeeded in bleeding the Soviet Union in Afghanistan. Soviet casualties in Afghanistan included 13,310 dead and 35,478 wounded while the United States lost no soldiers in its proxy engagements. But the war in Afghanistan had two direct consequences, neither of them good for America's longer-term interest. First, it popularized the idea of an Islamic Holy War and the volunteers from several Arab and Muslim countries who flocked to Pakistan to fight alongside the Afghans constituted al-Qaeda and its associated terrorist groups after the collapse of the Soviet Union. Second, Pakistan was able to advance its nuclear weapons programme while receiving US aid at the same time.

By the time President Bush refused to certify that Pakistan did not possess nuclear weapons, triggering the sanctions under the Pressler Amendment, Pakistan had already expanded support to radical Islamist groups fighting India in Jammu and Kashmir while continuing the fight in Afghanistan, eventually leading to the rise of the Taliban there. Ironically, most American officials took years to recognize that their singular focus on Afghanistan, while ignoring other aspects of Pakistan's policy, was mistaken.

Even though the Soviets were driven out of Afghanistan, the US did not really win there either. The country became the home of al-Qaeda and the base from which the 9/11 attacks were launched. Robert Oakley, who served as US ambassador in Islamabad from 1988 to 1991, admitted years later that 'the United States made a mistake in continuing to support the largely ISI-driven Pakistan policy on Afghanistan'. Richard Armitage, assistant secretary of defense for international security affairs at the time, said, 'We drifted too long in 1989 and failed to understand the independent role that the ISI was playing.'

The costliest mistake, however, was the failure to prevent Pakistan from acquiring nuclear weapons. In fact, had non-proliferation been taken as seriously as Senators Stuart Symington, John Glenn and Larry Pressler had advocated, both India and Pakistan would have been discouraged from going nuclear and South Asia would not persistently face the spectre of nuclear conflict.

Senator Pressler did a great service in 1985 by continuing the tradition of Senators Symington and Glenn in making nuclear non-proliferation an important element of US foreign policy. He has done us all another favour by writing an account of his battle within the American political system against special interests that enable major foreign policy catastrophes such as the spread of nukes.

Washington, D.C.   Husain Haqqani
May 2017

Author's Note

This book is part autobiographical and part a tale of the famous 'Pressler Amendment', which was aimed at deterring Pakistan from acquiring nuclear weapons. It also tells the story of how we have progressed to the present state of US–India relations. I find that many Indians have only a vague idea of who I am, so this is my attempt to tell an Indian and an international audience about the man behind the eponymous Pressler Amendment.

The formulation of foreign policy is a complex and byzantine process in the United States. I have struggled to craft foreign policy as a soldier, a foreign service officer, a United States senator, a professor, and a member of the Council on Foreign Relations. I have also taught students and policymakers how to do it as a Fulbright professor in Europe and Asia, at Sciences Po in Paris, at St. John's at the Vatican, at the Indian Law School in Bangalore, at seven Chinese universities, and at other academic institutions around the world.

This is a tale of my country's conflicted relationship with South Asia, and of my experiences, challenges, and lessons learnt while helping to formulate US foreign policy in that region from a seat in Congress, specifically in the area of nuclear arms control. Members of Congress, regardless of what state or district they represent, have to balance the need to address domestic issues with the demand for setting and overseeing American foreign policy. It might seem surprising that a young senator from a small, rural state like South Dakota would go on to play a leading role in arms control initiatives, but this is what happened in my career.

This book is drawn from my memory and observations over the last fifty years. I have recounted the events and experiences to the best of my memory. I will be seventy-five years old when this book is published, so let me say that I consider myself a seasoned professional, and this book is drawn from my many experiences.

I should emphasize that this is not an academic book. It is a memoir full of my observations. It is not footnoted, but I have referenced my sources in the text of this book where necessary so that readers can research more about the topic for themselves.

At the heart of it, this is a book of recollections of a veteran legislator and a wise statesman (I hope!) who worked for several decades to prevent the global spread of nuclear weapons throughout South Asia and to foster a closer US–India alliance.

1

Growing Up in the Nuclear Age

Plus ça change, plus c'est la même chose. (The more things change, the more they remain the same.)—French proverb

While sitting at my desk at St. Anne's, the Catholic grade school I attended in the early 1950s in the small town of Humboldt in South Dakota, my studies would be interrupted once a month by a piercing siren. Similar to the air raid sirens that blared across many European cities during World War II, this shrill noise could be heard for miles. But this alarm did not warn of an impending air assault by a bomber aircraft. It was designed to signal an incoming nuclear missile attack from the Soviet Union. In this case, the monthly siren was just a drill.

As we had been trained to do, my classmates and I would immediately crawl under our desks for several minutes—sometimes for up to an hour. Or, we were herded into what was called a 'nuclear fallout shelter', an underground chamber the school had created. It was made of cement and was windowless, but was dry and warm. We would huddle together, talk in a whisper and play cards or jacks. If we were hungry or had to go to the bathroom, we had to wait. As schoolchildren, we were probably oblivious to the threat that had

1

prompted these drills and they soon became somewhat rote. During the Cold War–era, drills like these were conducted in schools all over the United States.

At the height of this conflict with the Soviet Union, South Dakota was home to the 44th Missile Wing, one of the largest nuclear missile installations in the United States, as well as to long-range bombers at Ellsworth Air Force Base in the western part of the state. Traffic was sometimes halted to allow nuclear Minuteman missiles to be trucked from one silo to another. It was part of our daily life. We knew that in the event of a nuclear war with the Soviet Union, we would be the primary target. The threat was real and it was in our collective backyard.

Children in the United States today live with the threat of terrorist attacks and deranged gunmen. School campuses are put on 'lockdown', where teachers hide the students in their classrooms until the threat is eliminated. It is a sad fact of life in my country. For Americans now over the age of fifty, however, the threat of a Soviet nuclear attack was always at the back of their minds when they were children. The monthly drills we experienced instilled in us a certain fear—probably not unlike the fears American children have today of gun violence and terrorists. Consequently, it is probably not surprising that I am, and always have been, a vehement advocate of nuclear non-proliferation. My career and my relationship with South Asia have always focused on controlling the speed of nuclear weapons acquisition.

Soon after he assumed office, President Donald Trump announced that he might renew the nuclear arms race and spend whatever is necessary to outdistance Russia. I think this would be a great mistake. I hope he will use his apparent friendship with Russian President Vladimir Putin to continue the arms reduction programme under the Nunn–Lugar Act, a 1991 piece of legislation that I co-sponsored. It was aimed at reducing nuclear, biological and chemical weapons stockpiles in the former Soviet republics.

At the same time, perhaps ironically, I am also a strong proponent of nuclear energy and the peaceful use of nuclear material. The impact nuclear power could have on the quality of life, health and productivity of the Indian people could be transformative for the country. At least that is what President George W. Bush and Prime Minister Manmohan Singh stated in 2005, when they unveiled the landmark India–United States Civil Nuclear Agreement (or the 'US–India nuclear agreement'). However, reconciling those two issues has proven to be a vexing challenge.

When I became a United States senator for the first time in 1979, I was assigned to the Senate Foreign Relations Committee and, through an unusual set of circumstances, was given the chairmanship of the Arms Control Subcommittee. This chairmanship was a powerful position, especially for a junior senator.

In this role, I immersed myself in arms control issues, and started to study the countries that were on the brink of obtaining nuclear weapons, including Brazil, South Africa and Pakistan. I was what you might call a nuclear non-proliferation 'purist'. I saw the issue in black-and-white terms: the more countries that obtained nuclear weapons, the worse off the world would be. Nuclear weapons in the hands of unstable governments like those in Iraq and Iran worried me. Nuclear weapons in the hands of unstable Pakistan terrified me. In my new job as a US senator, I felt I could do something about this potential world threat.

But I also knew then that the United States viewed Pakistan as an important ally. I understood why Hans Morgenthau's classic textbook on international relations, *Politics Among Nations*,[1] provided a key rationale for the United States' reasoning for embracing a small, corrupt country like Pakistan. Morgenthau's book was first published in 1948 and I initially read it in college. It had a profound impact on me and sparked a lifetime of interest in foreign policy. My friend Henry Kissinger later put into practice Morgenthau's theory of 'political realism', but sometimes disagreed with Morgenthau on issues such as the Vietnam War. I worked in Kissinger's State Department in the Office of the Legal Adviser, and felt that Kissinger used Morgenthau's foreign policy approach with India, Pakistan and Bangladesh.

Morgenthau introduced the concept of 'political realism', which recognizes that the opposing interests and conflicts of the world are inevitable. It also acknowledges that power plays a larger role than ethics or morality, a fact that took me a long time to recognize. Morgenthau demonstrated how large countries like the United States have historically allied themselves with smaller countries adjacent to their geopolitical enemies or rivals. Our long-time alignment with Taiwan against China is an example. President Trump most recently courted Taiwan in December 2016 in an apparent attempt to compel China to behave more favourably to the United States. Our historic alignment with Pakistan is another example. We wanted to counter the looming Soviet influence over India, despite India's record as a responsible democracy. The Soviet threat was a higher priority.

The proliferation of nuclear weapons, of course, has made this argument about smaller states somewhat obsolete. A small country with nuclear weapons, like Pakistan, can be just as threatening and powerful as a large country. Despite this fact, when I saw Kissinger at a private retreat in California in 2016, he told me that he feels Morgenthau's theories are still relevant.

Aside from the nuclear threat that Pakistan poses, the problem with the United States' historic alignment with Pakistan is that our relationship with this country has been purely militaristic. The alliance is controlled by the Pentagon and Pakistan's intelligence agency, the Inter-Services Intelligence (ISI). I was suspicious of this relationship when I first arrived at the Senate in January 1979. As the first Vietnam veteran elected to the Senate, I questioned the size and influence of the US military-industrial complex. My service in Vietnam made me very anti-war for a time, and made me disagree with my country's knee-jerk impulse to put 'boots on the ground'. But my military service also reinforced a truth for me: so many people glorify war until they actually have to go to war. Young people who have not witnessed combat say they want to go to war. They enthusiastically write about war and they celebrate war at military parades. But, in reality, when people actually get into combat and witness death in combat, their attitude changes. I am reminded of the American Civil War–era poet Walt Whitman's words in 'When Lilacs Last in the Dooryard Bloom'd':

> I saw battle-corpses, myriads of them,
> And the white skeletons of young men, I saw them,
> I saw the debris and debris of all the slain soldiers of the war,
> But I saw they were not as was thought,
> They themselves were fully at rest, they suffer'd not,
> The living remain'd and suffer'd, the mother suffer'd,
> And the wife and the child and the musing comrade suffer'd,
> And the armies that remain'd suffer'd.

When I became the chairman of the Arms Control Subcommittee, I was certainly an advocate of a strong military, but I supported reform of certain weapons systems, reform of the United Nations, and reform in the North American Treaty Organization (NATO) in order to achieve our foreign policy goals. My stand on these issues put me in a good light with many midwestern, Republican, moderate conservatives, who generally opposed using ground forces abroad. Being more of an economic Republican, I was interested in stimulating investment and encouraging job growth through wise taxation policies. In my heart, I really wanted to be an Independent, as I felt the national Republican and Democratic parties had become too quick to deploy troops in support of overseas wars.

I knew I wanted to develop a close relationship with the new President, Ronald Reagan. His support on my arms control initiatives would be critical. Critics have said that Reagan was a passive, incurious President who glossed over details. On the contrary, Reagan knew the arcane details of arms control like nobody else in Washington. He and I saw eye to eye on arms control from the very start of my chairmanship and his presidency. In fact, it was high on his personal agenda.

Reagan seemed to like my plain speaking, or 'plains speaking' as we say on the South Dakota prairie, where I was born and raised. Some of Reagan's national security team could not understand why Reagan liked me; they viewed me as a foreign policy neophyte. In truth, they wanted me to go away.

When I discovered that our policy to support the Afghan resistance against the Soviet Union was actually helping Pakistan finance a nuclear weapons programme, I shared this intelligence with him and he appeared genuinely shocked. I certainly supported US assistance to the Afghan rebels, but baulked at the prospect of US taxpayer dollars fuelling a nuclear arms race in South Asia. With his encouragement, I worked on an amendment to the Foreign Assistance Act, and this was called the Pressler Amendment. This amendment to the 1960s' piece of legislation that I sponsored banned all US economic and military assistance to Pakistan unless the President could certify to Congress that Pakistan did not possess a nuclear device and that it had not progressed in the previous year in its attempt to obtain nuclear weapons. If the President could not make such a certification, the Pressler Amendment placed a trade embargo on Pakistan, blocked the delivery of certain fighter jets and military equipment, and cut off joint military operations and training.

The Reagan administration's attention, frustratingly, was not on Pakistan but on the resistance forces fighting the Soviets in neighbouring Afghanistan. Our fight against communist expansion trumped many policy issues, and that included potential nuclear proliferation in Pakistan. Incredulously, for several years after the Pressler Amendment became law, US intelligence agencies felt that they were able to certify that Pakistan wasn't making progress on building a nuclear device. By the time President George H.W. Bush came into office in January 1989, the evidence that Pakistan was aggressively pursuing nuclear weapons was becoming widespread public knowledge. Moreover, US and Pakistani public officials' statements and media reports were confirming the obvious. More importantly, the Cold War was over.

Without the required certification, President George H.W. Bush enforced the Pressler Amendment. He quickly ran into opposition from the 'Octopus', a new term I coined to add to the international political dialogue. Over time, I have come to suspect that President Reagan was opposed by this 'creature' as well.

The Octopus is the great-grandchild of the 'military-industrial complex', the pestiferous beast that President Eisenhower named in his farewell address to the American people in 1961. In that historic speech, Eisenhower warned, 'In the councils of government, we must guard against the acquisition of unwarranted influence, whether sought or unsought, by the military-industrial complex. The potential for the disastrous rise of misplaced power exists and will persist.'

That 'complex' started out as a relatively simple organism, but it has mutated and evolved over the five decades of my time in Washington into a true monster with multiple tentacles. Most nations in the world today have an Octopus of their own and only these nations' small ruling elite enjoy the benefits that flow from it. As soon as the Pressler Amendment was enforced, the Octopus went to work. The Octopus and its allies in Pakistan used every tactic they could find to weaken and circumvent the Pressler Amendment. Eventually, they succeeded in killing it.

The Pressler Amendment was one of those rare instances since World War II where Congress took a leading role in foreign policy. It had usually been the President who set the foreign policy agenda, and Congress just appropriated the monies for it; in short, Congress played a supporting role. For instance, it was President Harry Truman's secretary of state, George C. Marshall, who called for massive American assistance to rebuild Europe after World War II. This was later called the Marshall Plan. President Truman also led the effort to assist South Korea after communist forces from North Korea invaded, calling for a deployment of US air and naval forces to aid South Korea in repelling the invasion. Congress approved the action. Likewise, it was President Lyndon Johnson—not Congress—who pushed for an expansion of the Vietnam War with the infamous 'Gulf of Tonkin' resolution. It was based on faulty intelligence that the North Vietnamese attacked US Navy forces in the Gulf of Tonkin and this demanded retaliation. Again, Congress almost unanimously approved the resolution, but did not lead the effort.

The Pressler Amendment turned that tradition on its head. It also made me a household name in foreign policy circles around the world. Its impact was much greater than many laws and presidential declarations. It became the cornerstone of the annual foreign policy debates on the floor of Congress for nearly a decade. Because the Pressler Amendment used a cut-off in US foreign and military assistance to achieve a critical public policy goal, the dispensers of that assistance—the Pentagon and the State Department—strongly opposed it. (I might add that many of the career foreign services officers at the State Department supported it, but the politicians at the top fought it.) But many defence and foreign policy experts today laud the Pressler Amendment.

If the US government stood firm in its enforcement of the Pressler Amendment, Pakistan would have been forced to yield in its development of a nuclear bomb and we might have potentially made progress deterring India from further investing in its nuclear weapons programme. Many foreign policy experts have noted that the Pressler

Amendment also had an important side effect: the threat of a US aid cut-off helped deter other countries from pursuing nuclear weapons programmes as well.

In more detail, this book will tell the story of 'the making' of the Pressler Amendment; the worldwide impact of its 1990 enforcement against Pakistan; how the Pressler Amendment was weakened and repealed; the evolution of the US–India relationship over the last thirty years; my predictions for the US–India nuclear agreement; the massive Octopus labyrinth that now controls the purse strings in Washington; the total control of lobbyists in Washington and, to some extent, India; and, finally, my recommendations for a new 'super US–India alliance' that would set our countries on a different diplomatic trajectory in the twenty-first century.

As Hans Morgenthau advocated in *Politics Among Nations*, countries that have synergy between each other should form an alliance. There is no better example of that than India, the world's largest democracy, and the United States, the world's oldest democracy. The United States should be closer to India than any other ally in the world. Instead, the United States just continues to trade in arms with both India and Pakistan. The Indian government, to my great disappointment, seems to have totally accepted this apparent paradox.

What are the ethical considerations of this contradiction in foreign affairs? What is the future of my nation's relationship with South Asia? How do we simultaneously fight the War on Terror and conduct an ethical foreign policy in the region? Why has India accepted the fact that our nations' relationship is almost entirely a military one? And why does the US continue to tolerate Pakistan's lies?

Time and again over the course of our fifteen-year War on Terror in the region, Pakistan has said one thing and done another. Just as it did during the Cold War, it has sought the best of two worlds. The country's military leaders happily take US taxpayer assistance and say they are using it to root out terrorists hiding inside Pakistan. Evidence shows otherwise. They are most likely not using US aid for its intended purposes. In my opinion, it's just Pakistan up to its old tricks again. It played the same game with us when the country's leaders denied that they were using US resources to develop nuclear weapons during the Cold War. They lied then and they lie now. *'Plus ça change, plus c'est la même chose.'* The more things change, the more they remain the same.

I have not given up on my country or my dedication in fighting the Octopus. From my current bully pulpit as a former US senator, a professor and lecturer, a columnist, a member of the Council on Foreign Relations, and a lawyer, I frequently speak about the nation's yearning for political reform, and distrust of the Octopus. The Octopus has come to totally dominate US politics where candidates seem to be totally controlled by it. The democratic government in India seems to face similar problems. Meanwhile, the US Congress—both the House of Representatives and the Senate—does little to affect foreign policy. Why? The United States' founding fathers intended that Congress would lead on issues of foreign policy, but today's politicians leave the job to the Octopus.

2

The Octopus

This conjunction of an immense military establishment and a large arms industry is new in the American experience. The total influence–economic, political, even spiritual—is felt in every city, every State house, every office of the Federal government. We recognize the imperative need for this development. Yet we must not fail to comprehend its grave implications. Our toil, resources and livelihood are all involved; so is the very structure of our society. In the councils of government, we must guard against the acquisition of unwarranted influence, whether sought or unsought, by the military-industrial complex. The potential for the disastrous rise of misplaced power exists and will persist.

—President Dwight Eisenhower, 17 January 1961[1]

Just days before he left the White House, President Dwight Eisenhower delivered a dire warning to the country. He spoke out against the growing influence of a large and permanent arms industry in the United States. A retired five-star army general, he had presided over an immense military force during World War II as well as the Allies' successful D–Day invasion. His farewell speech was a surprising one. But he saw the fierce arms race that was developing as a result of the Cold War with the Soviet Union. He witnessed the fact that the Pentagon had maintained a large standing army after the Korean War. He watched the defence industry become richer and more powerful. He was worried about how this 'military-industrial complex', a term he coined in that speech, might come to dominate and corrupt the United States. Fox News anchor Bret Baier told me that Eisenhower called it 'the military-industrial-congressional-scientific state' in an earlier draft of the speech. Baier is the author of *Three Days in January: Dwight Eisenhower's Final Mission*, published in 2017.[2]

How prophetic President Eisenhower was. His fears about the military-industrial complex, a term that is still used today, were spot on. Eisenhower spoke of the horrors of war and a burgeoning defence industry that threatened American democracy. He was concerned that civilians would lose control of this carnivorous creature. However, the speech was a bit ironic coming from Eisenhower, given what a large role he played in creating and institutionalizing the military-industrial complex. He also offered no solutions to this threat that he outlined so memorably.

Eisenhower would not recognize our democracy today. The United States has become a nation *run* by the monster I call the Octopus. Its tentacles are long and its grip is strong. Its shape is without solid form. It can lurk in nooks and crannies. It can change its appearance to hide from predators and strike at prey. If confronted, it can conjure up a cloud of silt and ink, camouflaging itself. It slowly strangles its enemies to death.

There are other names for the Octopus. My friend, Andrew J. Bacevich Sr., a professor at Boston University, is one of the most respected American military historians today and has published numerous books on foreign policy. In 2010, he wrote a book titled *American Rules*.[3] In it, he gave another name to the Octopus. In shorthand, he called it 'Washington' or 'the Military Industrial State' and he provided a more comprehensive definition:

As used here, Washington (the Military Industrial State) is less geographic expression than a set of interlocking institutions headed by people, who, whether acting officially or unofficially, are able to put a thumb on the helm of state. Washington (the Military Industrial State), in this sense, includes the upper echelons of the executive, legislative, and judicial branches of the federal government. It encompasses the principal components of the national security state—the Departments of Defense, State, and more recently, Homeland Security, along with various agencies comprising the intelligence and law enforcement communities. Its rank extends to select think tanks and interest groups. Lawyers, lobbyists, fixers, former officials, and retired military officers who still enjoy access are members in good standing. Yet Washington (the Military Industrial State) also reaches beyond the Washington 'Beltway' to include big banks and other financial institutions, defense contractors, and major corporations, and television networks ... With rare exceptions, acceptance of the Washington (the Military Industrial State) rules forms a prerequisite for entry into this world.

I agree. Professor Bacevich does a formidable job of articulating how many tentacles the Octopus has and the extent of its reach. He went on to add to his definition elite news publications like the *New York Times* and even quasi-academic entities like the Council of Foreign Relations and Harvard's Kennedy School of Government. His theory was that these entities are also beholden to their corporate benefactors and this underwriting affects their independence. I would add one more tentacle to the definition: labour unions. The Octopus makes it difficult for any military equipment and weapons to be built without union labour. Thus, labour unions and their Democratic Party base give unquestionable support for increased defence spending in the United States.

All these factions swirl around Washington, D.C., looking for ways to influence policy, lawmaking and elections—both directly and indirectly. Money drives them all. There is very little centralized oversight of this whirling dervish and there are few restrictions on its behaviour. The United States Constitution allows it to cloak its activities and call it 'freedom of speech'. The Octopus operates virtually unfettered.

But, of all the Octopus tentacles, by far the most pervasive is the lobbying industry. For the Indian reader, trying to describe the US lobbying industry is challenging and could take several books to thoroughly understand. If you are teaching political science in the United States, you would not hear much about this underbelly of the US political process. But what are lobbyists and what do they do? The term was allegedly coined in Britain, referring to the men who loitered in the lobbies of the Houses of Parliament, where they waited for members to emerge so that they could engage with them and promote a particular piece of legislation.

Another piece of folklore says that Ulysses S. Grant, who was US President from 1869 to 1877, would be greeted in the evening by political advocates in the lobby of Washington's famous and lavish Willard Hotel. Frequently, these 'lobbyists' offered gifts—or bribes—for specific votes, something that is now prohibited by US law. It is this type of behaviour that earned lobbyists their poor reputation. Simply put, they are professionals who are paid to advocate on behalf of an individual, a company, an organization or a country for specific legislation or public policy. Over the course of the last century, several regulations have been put in place to control the undue influence of lobbying—or at least to make their activities more transparent to the public.

The regulation of lobbying activities began in the United States in the 1940s, when the Federal Regulation of Lobbying Act first required that lobbyists register if they spent more than 50 per cent of their time lobbying with the federal government. That requirement was tightened in the 1990s with the passage of the Lobbying Disclosure Act, which required registration for anyone who spends at least 20 per cent of his time lobbying. In 2007, Congress passed the Honest

Leadership and Open Government Act, which strengthened the rules surrounding the gifts legislators on Capitol Hill can receive from lobbyists. However, any of these rules can be easily circumvented.

Also, since 1938, the Foreign Agents Registration Act (FARA) has required that all American citizens working on behalf of foreign governments register with the Department of Justice (DOJ) every six months. These lobbyists are called 'foreign agents'. These agents are also required to submit copies to the Justice Department of all of their communications with two or more people—within forty-eight hours of the activity. This law was originally intended to track Nazi propaganda efforts in the US during World War II. Revealing the correspondence, communications tactics, and relationships between registered lobbyists and legislators is supposed to provide some oversight and transparency in lobbyists' activities. It is also intended to prevent legal lobbying from straying into the illegal activity of bribery and coercion.

However, the line between lobbying and bribery is a fine one. In a review of 2012 filings conducted by the US non-profit organization Project on Government Oversight (POGO), researchers found that some lobbying firms made political contributions to the campaigns of members of Congress *on the same day* these firms were lobbying these same members of Congress on behalf of a foreign government.[4] So, while foreign governments like Pakistan are prohibited by US law from making campaign contributions, they can pay a lobbying firm to make a contribution for them.

Violation of the FARA rules are common. POGO's research determined that 46 per cent of the required filings were done late. Of these, 15 per cent were filed more than thirty business days after they were distributed, and 12 per cent were filed more than 100 business days after they were distributed. In many cases, the filings did not reveal a date indicating when the communications were distributed, making it difficult to determine its tardiness. Surprisingly, including a distribution date on the documents registered with the DOJ is not a FARA requirement.

FARA has become a farce. The Justice Department is just trusting that the foreign agents are going to willingly identify themselves and voluntarily file copies of every communication they have engaged in with two or more people, on a timely basis. Incidentally, this is allegedly why President Trump's national security adviser, General Michael Flynn, is in trouble: he apparently registered with the DOJ retroactively for work he performed on behalf of the Turkish government.

FARA infractions are also not very well enforced. FARA keeps paper records which are only open for public inspection at their offices for four hours a day, so access is very limited. Their records are not online. When infractions are revealed, punishment is rare. It appears that only occasionally does the Justice Department use a court injunction—the enforcement option available to them. In my judgement, much tougher penalties are needed. The late Rhode Island Republican senator John Chafee and I tried to legislate FARA enforcement reforms, but we were unsuccessful.

There is a reason that the US government should be wary of foreign agents. Sometimes unsavoury characters working as lobbyists have shamelessly taken money from dictators, tyrants and human rights abusers around the world—all for a buck. Take the case of Edward von Kloberg III. A self-styled aristocrat who added the 'von' to his name because he thought it sounded more sophisticated, he donned black capes to social functions and hosted elaborate soirées where he would mix with State Department diplomats, politicians and reporters. He agreed to represent almost any despot who would pay him. As he told a newspaper in 2003, 'Shame is for sissies.'[5] Among his clients were Saddam Hussein of Iraq, Nicolae Ceaușescu of Romania, Samuel K. Doe of Liberia, and Mobutu Sese Seko of the former Zaire.

He also seemed to have no qualms about switching his allegiance when it was financially beneficial to him. He served as a lobbyist for the Government of Pakistan for several years.[6] When that tie was severed, he shot off a letter in 2003 to the *Washington Times* about

Pakistan's alleged missile purchase from North Korea. In this letter, he criticized Pakistan as a 'so-called ally' of Washington and reprimanded the country for 'systematically deceiv[ing] and [lying] to the United States by engaging in its fight against terrorism'.[7] It was revealed in the media that he had subsequently become a foreign agent of India. Apparently, his allegiance was for sale.

There is no indication that he made political contributions to lawmakers on behalf of India or Pakistan. His lobbying activities were apparently legal. But his willingness to represent anyone who would pay him demonstrates the seedier side of the lobbying industry.

And then there is the case of Jack Abramoff. He was a registered lobbyist who was convicted of grossly overcharging his Native American clients and illegally giving gifts and campaign donations to members of Congress in return for favourable votes for those he represented. Abramoff charged his Native American clients exorbitant fees—reportedly several million dollars. At the same time, he was lobbying state governments to shut down Native American casinos and then charging them a fee to lobby Congress to keep them open! He was working with both sides of the gaming issue—in order to keep the money flowing from the Native American tribes to him and his colleagues. He also reportedly had the tribes directly pay his colleague, Michael Scanlon, millions of dollars in public relations fees, which Scanlon shared with Abramoff. Because these fees were going to a public relations firm not registered as a lobbying entity, their activities were not reported.

Abramoff bribed lawmakers with sports and concert tickets, trips, drinks and dinners. His shady lobbying practices were rampant. He was a registered lobbyist for the Government of Pakistan from 1995 to 1997 to help overturn sanctions imposed on Pakistan by the Pressler Amendment standards. Without disclosing the fact that he was on the Pakistani government's payroll, he led a Congressional delegation to Pakistan in 1997. Those who accompanied Abramoff on the trip and the non-profit sponsor of the trip, the now-defunct National Security Caucus Foundation, said they were unaware of Abramoff's affiliation with Pakistan and felt 'deceived', according to a 2005 *New York Times* article.[8] It is unclear if the Government of Pakistan knew that Abramoff was being less than honest about his affiliation.

Abramoff's activities for the Government of Pakistan were typical behaviour for him, but it was hardly the most egregious. The Native Americans probably suffered the most at the hands of Abramoff. He was eventually convicted of fraud, tax evasion and conspiracy, along with several other lawmakers. He was sentenced to almost six years in prison. Foreign countries doing business in the US need to be much more vigilant when hiring lobbyists. For India, this became a critical issue when the milestone US–India nuclear agreement was announced in 2005.

3

India Learns to
Use Washington's Revolving Door

'[The US–India nuclear agreement] has been a coming-out party
of sorts for the India lobby.'

—Robert Hoffman, a lobbyist for Oracle, in an interview
with the *International Herald Tribune* in 2006[1]

It was not surprising that many American companies who stood to
gain financially from the US–India nuclear agreement and the opening
of trade between the US and India rallied behind it and employed
their own lobbyists to help. They recognized the trade potential of the
world's eleventh-largest economy. What was unexpected was the new
sophistication of the Indian-American business community's and the
Indian government's lobbying efforts to get the bill passed.

While countries like Israel have had well-oiled lobbying
machines in the United States for decades, the Indian government
and the Indian-American community in the US are relative novices.
Many Indian Americans have said they wanted to emulate the Israeli
lobbying machine in the US as it is very powerful.[2] Unlike other

immigrant populations in the US, Indians were late to arrive on the scene. The US Immigration Act of 1990 provided a path of entry to skilled professionals, prompting large numbers of educated and English-speaking Indians to come to the US for jobs. According to the US Census Bureau, the number of Indian immigrants in the US increased ten times between 1980 and 2013 and today more than 2 million Indians call America their home.[3]

Indians are one of the most highly educated and affluent immigrant groups in the US, so when they wanted to advocate on behalf of India for this nuclear deal, they had the means to do it. They rightly saw this deal as the start of a warmer and closer relationship between their home country and their adopted one—and they were eager to nurture this relationship. They also wanted to establish their political clout and use it. They created several organizations to galvanize their efforts: the US–India Friendship Council, the Indian-American Security Leadership Council, the US–India Political Action Committee (USINPAC), the Indian-American Leadership Initiative (IALI), and the Indian-American Republican Council (IARC).

They went to work, diligently and relentlessly pressing for the approval of this deal. They called members of Congress, attended the members' congressional district meetings, and made donations to the members' campaign coffers. As the world's largest democracy, India had become a popular cause on Capitol Hill. Congressmen and senators did not want to look like Cold War relics—holding grudges against India for its historical ties to the Soviet Union.

The Indian government did even more. In 2005, it hired two top Washington lobbying houses: Venable, and Barbour Griffith and Rogers (BGR Group). India paid the BGR Group more than $1 million between 2005 and 2007.[4] Why would India's leaders spend so much cash on lobbyists? Why wouldn't they spend their time and money with the diplomats at the State Department or engage with Capitol Hill or the White House directly? Why use these proxies?

For one, the BGR Group had some employees with powerful connections—including Robert Blackwill, a former US ambassador to India. The Indian government was essentially buying the influence that Blackwill and other former government officials have with Capitol Hill. Blackwill had built a big coterie of friends on Capitol Hill, friends he made while serving as India's ambassador, in his role as President George W. Bush's deputy national security adviser, and over the course of decades of government service. In the US, this move from a seat of power (in the executive or legislative branches of the US government) to a seat of influence (lobbying) is called 'the revolving door'. This portal is a well-travelled path in Washington. People frequently shuffle back and forth between government jobs and lobbying firms, consulting firms, public relations firms and think tanks. Government officials can make a lot of money in the private sector from the relationships they build while serving in the public sector.

According to published media articles at the time, Blackwill was not the only former government official who was taking advantage of the revolving door, literally cashing in on the relationships he built while working as a public official. Thomas Pickering, another former ambassador to India, reportedly was hired by the Boeing Company, a defence contractor that builds both commercial and military aircraft. Boeing was probably salivating over the potential aviation business that would open up if the US–India nuclear agreement was passed.

Another former ambassador to India, Frank Wisner, was vice chairman at the insurance and financial services firm American International Group (AIG) at the time. The nuclear agreement would have opened up possible new business opportunities for the international insurer, including the potential to insure contracts between military contractors and the Indian government.

Wisner's brother, Graham Wisner, was a lawyer and lobbyist at Squire Patton Boggs, and was also reportedly being paid by the US–India Business Council to secure the passage of the nuclear agreement. It was all very incestuous.[5]

While Pickering and the Wisner brothers were not being paid by the Indian government, they were clearly doing the Indian government's bidding by lobbying for the nuclear deal's passage. In my judgement, their employers and the Indian government both stood to profit if the deal passed.

Today, it is evident that one of the first things a new Indian ambassador to Washington, D.C. does is review the lobbying contracts the Indian government has and draw up new ones. They also frequently hire new lobbying firms at the outset of a new presidential administration. They want a lobbying firm on retainer that has the closest relationships with the incoming President. In this era, this is much more important than developing relationships at the State Department, on Capitol Hill, and in the White House. The lobbying firms can do the hard and dirty work that diplomats used to do. It is almost as if the work of diplomats has been privatized. The perception of a quid pro quo for financial donations from the lobbying firms to legislators—sometimes on the same day they are conducting their influencing tactics—is unseemly. It feels like a bribe.

4

Lobbying 'Light': The Increasing Influence of Public Relations Firms and Think Tanks

'This is thinly disguised lobbying, but lobbying nonetheless.'

—Massachusetts Democratic Senator
Elizabeth Warren, in the *New York Times*
on the activities think tanks are paid to perform
for corporations, 7 August 2016[1]

While lobbying firms have been in the business of influence peddling for a long time, public relations agencies and think tanks are relative newcomers to the scene. The Octopus has only recently embraced them, but their ranks are growing.

When Prime Minister Narendra Modi was chief minister of the state of Gujarat, he hired APCO Worldwide, an international public relations powerhouse with offices all over the world. Modi is savvy—I met him once before he was prime minister. As a pro-business and free enterprise advocate, he reminded me of an American Republican state governor. He put Gujarat on the world map. How did he do it? He knew how to put the Octopus to work for him.

APCO's contract was executed with the Industrial Extension
Bureau (iNDEXTb), which was the state government's agency for
investments. APCO's stated goal was to transform Gujarat's annual
investment meeting, Vibrant Gujarat, into the Davos of India. I have
attended and spoken at both Vibrant Gujarat and Davos. Davos is
a premier international conference held each winter in the city of
Davos, Switzerland. It convenes business executives, media, academia,
scientists and politicians to discuss world issues.

Until APCO was hired in 2009, Vibrant Gujarat was a small show
attracting only regional attendees and modest investment: $14 billion,
$20 billion and $152 billion in the first three years. With APCO's
involvement and promotion, investment promises for the region
skyrocketed over the next two years to $253 billion and $450 billion.[2]

While this event significantly boosted the profile of Gujarat, it
also enhanced the reputation of Modi, who had big ambitions and a
tarnished image after the 2002 Gujarat riots and allegations of anti-
Muslim violence. As a global public relations firm, APCO has vast
expertise in polishing tainted reputations. One of the ways the agency
can do this is by controlling access to its clients and managing their
media appearances. Indeed, while APCO publicly claimed it did not
speak for Modi, media requests for interviews with him about Vibrant
Gujarat were directed to APCO for approval, not his office.[3]

Is APCO lobbying? You might call it 'lobbying light', as it does not
involve exerting direct influence on a particular piece of legislation, but
rather on 'educating' and 'communicating' the benefits of investing in
Gujarat and, indirectly, giving a stamp of approval to the leadership of
Modi. APCO's work clearly helped elevate Modi's stature in India and
the United States. When he became prime minister, he wasn't even
able to get a visa to visit the US. But by May 2016, he was addressing
a joint session of the US Congress. What a long way he has come!
Incidentally, I thought it was unfair and quite an embarrassment to
initially refuse to give Modi a US visa. It was pure political nonsense.
When he ran for prime minister, I offered to publicly support him in
the US and India.

APCO has credited much of its company's success to its International Advisory Council (IAC), which is chock-full of corporate executives, former politicians and former government bureaucrats—both American and Indian.[4] It includes a former Indian diplomat, Lalit Mansingh, and a former US ambassador to India, Tim Roemer. APCO can access the IAC members' extensive contacts for its 'education' and 'communications' efforts without calling themselves lobbyists. Instead, APCO calls them 'advisors'. Public relations agencies have become as integral to the Octopus as the lobbyists. Indeed, many firms have both lobbying and public relations divisions under the same roof.

But the most recent and increasingly worrisome Octopus tentacle are the think tanks. Traditionally non-partisan and academic in their mission, these organizations are focused on research and public policy issues. Most are non-profit entities, which means they have a tax-exempt status. They publish articles, papers, books and studies. They host events, forums and fundraisers that convene a variety of experts to debate public policy issues. They have a reputation of being neutral and objective. But, increasingly, they are being given money by foreign countries, with implicit instructions to produce research with favourable conclusions—to advance these countries' foreign policy goals in the US. Researchers at organizations like the influential Brookings Institution, the Atlantic Council and the Center for Strategic and International Studies (CSIS) have long claimed to be impartial, but their hunt for ever-dwindling sources of research grant money has led them to accept foreign donations. And that has come with an apparent quid pro quo.

Some Indian officials have admitted as much. In September 2007, the New York Times reported that an organization of Indian software companies, the National Association of Software and Service Companies (NASSCOM), had begun an aggressive lobbying campaign in the US.[5] They hired a number of US firms to help them, including the Brookings Institution and the Heritage Foundation think tanks. Their campaign was aimed at countering an effort by organized labour to stop 'outsourcing'. Through this practice, many US corporations have sent their software development, engineering, and call centres to India where the labour force is less expensive. The Indian trade group, formed in the run-up to the 2008 presidential election specifically to lobby in favour of outsourcing, insists that the practice keeps consumer prices low for Americans and provides jobs for Indians. But the export of these jobs to India had incensed many Americans and continues to be contentious.

In addition to hiring lobbyists, NASSCOM also 'collaborated' with the Brookings Institution and the Heritage Foundation, and made donations of about $10,000–$15,000 to each of them. The president of this trade group at the time, Kiran Karnik, told the *New York Times* that the donations were 'symbolic'. Karnik's trade group armed the think tanks with data on the outsourcing industry: '... [M]aybe that enables someone to write a good paper on the global trade in services.' Are these think tanks lobbying for Karnik and his association? Of course, they are.

Carol Browner, President Bill Clinton's Environmental Protection Agency (EPA) administrator for eight years and then President Barack Obama's 'energy czar' from 2009 to 2011, now works for a company called Nuclear Matters. In addition, she serves on the board of directors of the Center for American Progress (CAP), a think tank formed in 2003 that grew exponentially during the Obama administration. Having spent the majority of her career working as an environmentalist, she was probably one of the least likely individuals to embrace nuclear energy—given its unpopularity with many clean energy advocates.

However, since leaving the Obama administration in 2011, she appears to have become a surprisingly vocal advocate for nuclear energy. She has said publicly that she never considered herself pro-nuclear power until she began to understand the implications of climate change. At that point, she decided that it was 'irresponsible' not to consider nuclear energy as part of the solution, according to an article published in the *Hill* in 2014.[6] Of course, it probably helps that her new employers receive support from the nuclear power industry.

Nuclear Matters is the nuclear industry's domestic advocacy organization. Its spokesperson insists it does not lobby, but instead 'educates'. It receives funding from many major nuclear suppliers, including Westinghouse, the company poised to build six nuclear reactors in India. CAP's donors include Pacific Gas and Electric, General Electric and Lockheed Martin.[7] General Electric Hitachi Nuclear Energy builds nuclear reactors. Lockheed Martin is the massive defence contractor that manufactures the F-16 fighter jet. While Nuclear Matters and CAP are not registered as lobbying organizations, both of them are definitely performing some of the same activities that registered lobbyists do for their clients.

CAP was founded by John Podesta, a former chief of staff to President Bill Clinton and manager of Hillary Clinton's 2016 presidential campaign. A chief source of early support for CAP was John Podesta's brother, Tony, a high-profile Democratic operative and fundraiser and the founder and chairman of the influential lobbying firm, the Podesta Group. (His former sister-in-law and Tony Podesta's ex-wife, Heather Podesta, also runs her own government relations shop called Heather Podesta & Partners. There are lots of Podesta lobbyists in Washington!) CAP is one of the think tanks that is decidedly partisan—with left-leaning, progressive roots and opinions. (The Heritage Foundation, equally as prominent as CAP, is a right-of-centre think tank. Many other think tanks have oblique or more overt partisan leanings.) The Podesta Group has been on the lobbying payroll of Lockheed Martin for many years, helping them with their enormous defence and aerospace business.

The Podesta Group has to register its lobbying activities for Lockheed Martin with the secretary of the Senate and the clerk of the House of Representatives. The think tank CAP, which also receives money from Lockheed Martin, does *not* have to register its activities. Both organizations benefit from the work of John and Tony Podesta. They are talented and skilled professionals, and all of the work they do for their clients appears to be totally legal; but many of the activities that the Podesta Group and CAP do for Lockheed

Martin are strangely similar. In my view, this is another instance of the Octopus at work.

In their relentless pursuit of ever-dwindling private donations, think tanks and their executives have increasingly turned to corporations, which are some of the most deep-pocketed donors. But these donations have come with strings attached: many of these corporations are looking for research that will support their business objectives. The *New York Times*[8] and the *Washington Post*[9] have been reporting on this disturbing trend for a few years. In August 2016, the *New York Times* published an analysis of think tanks and their cosy relationships with their corporate donors. The articles outlined some of the more egregious conflicts of interest—what you might call 'pay for play'. The report focused most notably on the Brookings Institution, which is headed by Strobe Talbott, a former deputy secretary of state during the Clinton administration and a renowned expert in foreign policy, nuclear arms control, and South Asia.

The report demonstrated that Brookings, which is a tax-exempt, non-profit organization, systematically engages in a strategy of what it calls 'high impact philanthropy'. This means that it seeks out corporate donors and finds ways to offer them maximum returns on their corporate donations. Brookings will offer their corporate donors the opportunity to review the think tank's research reports—in advance of publication. It will engage public relations experts to promote the results of the research, most of which dovetails with the research underwriter's business or political objectives. It will also secure meetings and host events with elected officials for the corporate donors. This so-called academic research and these promotional activities sound much more like market research and classic marketing communications. The supposed education sounds much more like lobbying. The difference between what think tanks do and what lobbying and public relations firms do has become quite murky.

These think tanks have 'experts' on staff or people paid as outside consultants who trek to Capitol Hill to testify before Congress on issues, and frequently use their think tank titles—'Resident Fellow' or

'Senior Advisor'—when making statements that advocate a particular policy viewpoint. What they frequently fail to disclose is that many of them testifying on the Hill are also being retained by corporations to lobby on some of these same issues. But they don't identify themselves that way. In other words, these experts have several business cards they can pass on, depending on the audience they are addressing.

Public officials frequently make appearances and speak at events sponsored by think tanks. It is getting harder and harder to trust the objectivity of these forums and their speakers. In July 2014, CAP launched an initiative, kicked off by President Obama's last secretary of state, John Kerry, called 'India 2020'.[10] Secretary Kerry gave a long speech at CAP about the importance of the relationship between the US and India. In it, he focused on the urgency of finding new, clean energy sources for the people of India. He said:

> I know Prime Minister Modi understands the urgency. . . . The United States has an immediate ability to make a difference here, and we need to eliminate the barriers that keep the best technology out of the Indian market. And the United States can help India find and develop new sources of energy through renewable technologies and greater export capacity for liquefied natural gas.
>
> Already, we've brought together more than $1 billion in financing for renewable energy projects. And with this funding, we helped to bring India's first 1,000 megawatts of solar power online. But we need to build on the U.S.–India Civil Nuclear Agreement, so that American companies can start building and can start providing clean power to millions in India. And we need to build on the $125 million investment that we've made in a Joint Clean Energy Research and Development Center.
>
> Prime Minister Modi has also made a commitment to electrify every home in India by 2019. With fewer limits on foreign technology and investment in India's green energy sector, we can help make clean power more cost-effective and more accessible at the same time. We can provide 400 million Indians with power

without creating emissions that dirty the air and endanger public
health. And by working together to help an entire generation of
Indians leapfrog over fossil fuels, we can actually set an example to
the world.

All of this sounds good and positive and in the best interests of
Indians. But, how can we know if CAP, which hosted the venue where
Secretary Kerry gave this speech and whom Secretary Kerry lauded
at the outset of his speech, has a purely educational and community
interest objective? CAP and its donors, including several in the energy
industry, stand to benefit financially from selling renewable energy and
an increase in nuclear power in India.[11] What happens when public
interest conflicts with the interest of CAP's donors? How will CAP
react when the Indian people reject the building of a nuclear reactor
in their backyard? What will CAP say when their donors are pushing
to build these reactors or other renewable energy infrastructure that
Indians might oppose?

I am not the first person to notice this conflict of interest. There
has been a steady drumbeat of criticism raised in the US mainstream
media about the increasing corporate influence of think tanks in
America. India's think tanks are starting to create some of the same
problems.

Brookings set up an affiliate organization in India in 2013, run
by Vikram Singh Mehta, former chairman of the Shell Group of
Companies. The Brookings affiliate in India was funded by an initial
group of donors called the 'Brookings India Initiative Founders
Circle'. According to the Brookings India website, the Founders
Circle 'believes in the importance of independent policy research
at this critical juncture in India's history'.[12] This group comprises
twenty-four corporations and individuals who coughed up the seed
funding to create Brookings's Indian outpost. (Brookings also has the
Brookings Doha Center in Qatar and the John L. Thornton Center
in Beijing. Brookings India is a stand-alone company, registered as a
not-for-profit organization.)

In an interview with the Indian newspaper *DNA* in March 2013, Mehta said that his aim was to replicate in India the successful Brookings Institution model of the US: 'If you look at Brookings in the U.S., 80–85 percent of its projects get funded by outside sources— not by the American government or by anyone with a particular point of view. It's funded because the issues are relevant to the society.... Businessmen are interested in funding because our research becomes the basis of their information and course of action. So it's altruistic to that extent.'[13]

These outside sources that Mehta refers to are most likely corporations looking for access to and influence with the many former government officials employed by think tanks. These former government officials, in turn, have access to and influence with the government. It is hard for the Indian reader to comprehend the extent to which the American 'revolving door'—the door between the public and private sector—benefits individuals who jump in and out of public service throughout their careers. It is ubiquitous in Washington. Anyone who has held a position of influence in the US government can quickly transition to the private sector—a lobbying firm, law firm, think tank or public relations firm—and cash in on his relationships and offer introductions and influence to any client who hires him.

Unlike the United States, Mehta explained, government officials in India usually spend their entire career in government. They are not allowed to move back and forth between the government and the private sector. Remaining in their silos, these Indian bureaucrats can become somewhat isolated from the private sector's opinion on public policy.

Over time, Mehta said, the Indian government has become increasingly open to outside input on policy on a variety of issues, including energy. 'People in government don't have the time to study every issue in the depth that is required. They need to draw on outside support.' Mehta envisions that think tanks are going to play an increasingly important role in policy formulation in India.

When the journalist Raj Nambisan asked Mehta how much each of these Founders Circle members ponied up, he replied, 'I won't be able to divulge that.' So much for transparency! I predict think tanks in India will begin to look more and more like think tanks in the United States. That is to say, as lobbyists.

5

F-16 Jousting: How One Firm
Worked for Both India and Pakistan

'... I am still very troubled that the Pakistani government maintains
a relationship with the Haqqani network. After years of pressuring
the Pakistanis on this point, the Haqqani terrorists still enjoy
freedom of movement, and possibly even support from the Pakistani
government. . . . For now, if [the Pakistanis] wish to purchase this
military equipment, they will do so without a subsidy from the
American taxpayer.'

—Tennessee Republican senator Robert Corker protesting the
taxpayer-subsidized sale of F-16s to Pakistan in February 2016[1]

Andrew Bacevich's definition of what I call the Octopus does
not elaborate on the massive homeland security and intelligence
machine that has mushroomed since the 11 September 2001 attacks.
In response to the terrorist attacks on the World Trade Center
and the Pentagon, the Octopus has created an army of top-secret
intelligence agencies, analysts, specialists, and building complexes—
phalanxes, really—devoted to identifying, spying on and rooting out

33

terrorists both domestically and around the world. In addition, it has spawned a whole cottage industry of large and small companies that provide people with new expertise in sophisticated data analysis of emails and phone calls, social media monitoring and manipulation, body scanners, air marshals, and the thousands of security guards at airports that make up the new Transportation Security Administration (or TSA). Then, there are the legions of people who recruit and train them. Plus, there are the people who conduct background investigations on this population in order to qualify for security clearances.

A two-year investigation conducted by the *Washington Post* that was published in 2010 reported that 'some 1,271 government organizations and 1,931 private companies work on programs related to counterterrorism, homeland security and intelligence in about 10,000 locations around the United States'. That does not include the overseas locations.[2]

A large majority of this homeland security and intelligence apparatus actually comprises individuals who do not work for the US government directly. They are employees of private sector companies who are hired by the government to do these jobs, and are known as 'contractors'. Most government agencies use contractors to augment their workforce. According to the *Washington Post*, 'At the Department of Homeland Security (DHS), the number of contractors equals the number of federal employees. The department depends on 318 companies for essential services and personnel, including nineteen staffing firms that help DHS find and hire even more contractors. At the office that handles intelligence, six out of ten employees are from private industry.'[3]

While these contractor companies and their employees can come to the job well trained and equipped with highly specialized expertise that the Octopus needs to fight the War on Terror, these companies are often publicly traded corporations. They have obligations to their shareholders and their bottom line. They are profit-driven, presenting an inherent conflict of interest. Their executives and leadership are part of the Octopus. These contractors can buy influence on Capitol Hill using lobbyists and campaign contributions.

On any given issue facing scrutiny by the US Congress, these agencies and their contractors will hire subcontractors—smaller contractor companies, law firms, public relations agencies or consulting firms—to assist them. With all these layers of contractors, subcontractors and outside consultants, it is sometimes difficult to know exactly how many people are actually working on behalf of any of these government agencies.

Many of these individuals and organizations claim that they are not officially lobbying, like think tanks, public relations agencies and political action committees (PACs). Or they claim they are not really lobbyists because they avoid direct contact with the lawmakers. Instead, they send their subordinates to Capitol Hill to do the heavy lifting— the cajoling of members of Congress and their staffs. Or they claim that they spend less than 20 per cent of their time lobbying. This legal threshold is what allowed former South Dakota Democratic senator Tom Daschle to lobby for more than a decade without registering as a lobbyist. Senator Daschle was my former colleague in the Senate and I have known him for more than thirty years. By limiting his lobbying activities, he was not subject to lobbying regulations. While he was adhering to the letter of the law, he most certainly was skirting the spirit of the law. This evasion tactic is actually nicknamed and widely referred to as the 'Daschle loophole'.

But make no mistake. Such lobbyists are getting paid well and, in many cases, are raising a lot of money for lawmakers' campaigns to influence votes, legislation and policy. In some cases, the organizations these lobbyists work for are lobbying for both sides of an issue— thereby, making money off adversaries.

Let us take the case of the issue of the sale of F-16 fighter jets to Pakistan in 2016. Ever since the 11 September 2001 terrorist attacks on the United States, the US government has provided Pakistan with a steady stream of military assistance—to the tune of $25 billion since 2002 (as of 2012)—on the grounds that Pakistan is a willing ally in our counterterrorism efforts in the region and cooperates with us in Afghanistan.[4]

Islamabad had been pushing to resume its purchases of the United States' advanced F-16 fighter jets ever since 1990. This was the year the Pressler Amendment was enforced, preventing Pakistan from getting twenty-eight of the F-16s they had agreed to buy in the early 1980s. Forced to pay for storage fees as the unused F-16s collected dust in a boneyard in the Arizona desert, the Pakistanis were incensed.

During my service in the US Senate, there were a number of efforts by the Pakistani government to take possession of the F-16s. President Bill Clinton initially tried to convince Congress to waive the Pressler Amendment to allow the F-16s to be transferred to Pakistan. I vehemently opposed that effort. In addition to being a gross violation of the spirit and intent behind the Pressler Amendment, the F-16s would have served to advance Pakistan's nuclear posture, since F-16s are capable of carrying a nuclear payload.

However, after 9/11, Pakistan upped its advocacy campaign and convinced the George W. Bush administration to sell them the fighter jets—to 'exorcise the bitter pill of the Pressler Amendment' and to forge new relations with Islamabad.[5] The United States determined it was critical to placate Islamabad in order to get its cooperation in the war against the terrorists. Consequently, the Bush administration announced in 2005 its intent to once again sell F-16 fighter jets to Pakistan—as many as Pakistan wanted to buy.

How did Pakistan convince the Bush administration and, later the Obama administration, to continue to give it more and more military aid? According to the DOJ's FARA database,[6] Pakistan has not paid a registered lobbying firm since 2013, when they opted not to renew their annual lobbying contract with Locke Lord Strategies, the lobbying arm of the full service international law firm Locke Lord, which employs more than a thousand lawyers around the world and is one of the fifty largest US law firms. This is misleading, as everyone knows full well that Pakistan continues lobbying in Washington. The ISI just finds other *unregistered* individuals and organizations to do it.[7]

However, the manufacturer of the F-16—the massive defence corporation Lockheed Martin—with $47 billion in annual revenue in 2016, also has a labyrinthine lobbying operation. According to the Center for Responsive Politics' Open Secrets database, the company has been spending more than $10 million on it annually since 2006.[8] In addition to their in-house lobbyists, they have amassed an army of outside companies to assist them with their lobbying efforts: law firms, public relations agencies, consultants. By far the largest amount of Lockheed Martin's lobbying budget is paid out to the Podesta Group, the powerful firm headed by the super-lobbyist, Tony Podesta. Lockheed Martin paid the group $550,000 in the years 2014, 2015 and 2016. Most of the issues the Podesta Group advocated for on behalf of Lockheed Martin were defence and aerospace issues. It is highly likely that they assisted in the overall effort to push through the sale of F-16s to Pakistan!

In February 2016, the State Department and the Department of Defense announced that they were approving a sale of eight more F-16s to Pakistan, clearly a victory for Lockheed Martin. Under the terms of this new deal, however, the sale of these additional F-16s was to be *subsidized by the US government*. In a move to make these deals even sweeter, the government sometimes uses what is called Foreign Military Funds (FMFs). FMF is a bucket of taxpayer money that is used to subsidize sales of military equipment to foreign countries. (Under the US Arms Control Export Act, the President is authorized to finance—with taxpayer dollars—the procurement of defence articles and services for certain partner nations. Pakistan is considered one of these partner nations.) Although the full cost of these eight fighter jets is close to $700 million, under this deal Pakistan would only have to pay $270 million. US taxpayers would offset the difference.

The Defense Security Cooperation Agency (DSCA), the government body responsible for managing and overseeing the sales of military equipment to foreign governments, issued a press release on the action in February 2016.[9] It contained standard language and stated, 'The proposed sale improves Pakistan's capability to meet current and future security threats. . . . The proposed sale of this equipment and support will not alter the basic military balance in the region. . . . There will be no adverse impact on U.S. defense readiness as a result of this proposed sale.'

The DSCA and the State Department probably hoped the announcement would not attract much notice, since they distributed the press release on a Friday afternoon. The Indian government immediately and publicly protested both the sale and the subsidy, causing quite a hiccup for the US government. India's leaders recognized the jets for what they were: a nuclear-capable force projection that could be used against them. The Indian foreign secretary, S. Jaishankar, immediately summoned Richard Verma, the US ambassador to New Delhi, to express his displeasure. And then the Pakistani government publicly feigned surprise over the Indians' complaints.

The Indian embassy in Washington summarily deployed their army of lobbyists to block the deal. So, who has been lobbying on their behalf since 2010? Once again, the Podesta Group. According to their FARA filings, the Podesta Group was paid $700,000 by the Government of India for work they performed in 2016.[10]

Conventional wisdom says that a firm that is representing India cannot very well represent Pakistan at the same time. But in the world of the Octopus, the same firm represents competing interests and it is all legal. The Octopus's tentacles can be very long and hard to untangle. Representation for a defence contractor who happens to be promoting a weapons' sale that benefits Pakistan is one step removed from direct representation for Pakistan's government. Many of the lobbyists working for these firms and contractors are decent citizens who see a chance to make some real money—and probably feel they have the nation's best interests at heart. Nothing they are doing is illegal. But I find it duplicitous. The Octopus and its convoluted and powerful infrastructure just make it too easy for lobbyists to profit.

The power and pressure of the Indian embassy's lobbying firm produced results. A week after the State Department's announcement of the planned subsidized F-16 sale to Pakistan, Kentucky Republican senator Rand Paul introduced a joint resolution to halt the sale. In his press announcement, he asserted, 'The U.S. and Pakistani relationship has been a troubled one. Though the government of Pakistan has been considered America's ally in the fight on terrorism, Pakistan's behavior would suggest otherwise.'[11] The next month, Senator Paul forced a vote on the Senate floor by invoking the Arms Export Control Act of 1976, which allows any senator 'to secure a floor vote to disapprove an arms sale law'.

Senator Paul went on to say, 'We have to borrow money from China to send it to Pakistan. Such a policy is insane and supported by no one outside Washington.' (Paul was referring to the fact that China invests heavily in the American bond market, which means that China owns a significant amount of US debt.) Senator Paul's resolution was debated on the floor of the Senate and a vote was called, but the resolution was scuttled in what is called a 'tabling motion'. In a seventy-one to twenty-four vote, the Senate voted to 'table' the resolution, which effectively killed the effort. Senator Paul received some bipartisan support for this resolution, but not enough.

The sale, however, did not go through as planned. The chairman of the Senate Foreign Relations Committee, Tennessee Republican senator Robert Corker, said at the time of the vote, 'Prohibiting a taxpayer subsidy sends a much-needed message to Pakistan that it needs to change its behavior, but preventing the purchase of U.S. aircraft would do more harm than good by paving the way for countries like Russia and China to sell to Pakistan while also inhibiting greater cooperation on counterterrorism.'[12] As the chair of the Senate Foreign Relations Committee, Senator Corker had the individual power to prevent taxpayer funds from being used for the sale.

I know both Senators Paul and Corker. They, along with Pennsylvania Democratic senator Bob Casey, are the most likely legislators to take up the arms control mantle that the late Ohio Democratic senator John Glenn and I carried during the 1980s and 1990s. They are the most hopeful figures in the Senate who share

the passion for nuclear arms control that Senator Glenn and I did.
However, all three have presidential ambitions, so I fear they will
always try to walk the political tightrope and placate advocates on
both sides of the issue.

The sale was approved but without the FMF subsidies, and now
Pakistan says it cannot afford to pay full freight for the eight fighter
jets. Lockheed Martin also complained about the news, saying that
it would not be able to afford to keep its F-16 production line in
operation without the sale. It also said, incredulously and ironically,
that it planned to move the entire F-16 production line from Texas
to India.[13] Indeed, the vice president of Lockheed's F-16 programme,
Susan Ouzts, said in an interview with reporters from the Pakistani
English-language daily, the *Nation,* that Prime Minister Narendra
Modi had expressed interest in the planes.[14] The *Nation* article even
alleged that India may have lobbied to place on hold an India F-16
deal to disrupt the Pakistan F-16 one.

Some Pakistani newspaper columnists blamed the collapse of the
deal on the lack of sophistication of the Pakistani lobbying efforts in
the United States. In a March 2016 editorial in the *Express Tribune,* a
Pakistani newspaper that partners with the *New York Times,* columnist
Hussain Nadim asserted:

> While technology changed diplomacy, lobbying and narrative-
> building, Pakistan continued with its traditional style of running
> diplomatic missions and releasing press releases as a primary method
> of communications.... On the other hand, while India pumped
> money into think tanks, academia, and enhanced its presence in
> Washington, DC, let alone setting up new endowments, Pakistan
> had even its professorial chairs comparatively empty in the US and,
> in most cases, continues to do so. It is startling to note that while
> Pakistan was taking billions of dollars in aid from the US to fight
> a long bloody war in the region, it completely missed the fact that
> it would require an extraordinary level of presence in think tanks,
> academia, and policy circles in the US to ensure the right message

goes out globally. In other words, Pakistan went to fight a war without a story in mind and without a medium to tell that story.[15]

As cosy a relationship as Pakistan has with the Pentagon, apparently it forgot that the Octopus has many, many tentacles that would need to be choreographed.

This case study is just one example of the corruptive—*but thoroughly legal*—behaviour of the Octopus. It will sink its suctioned feet into any client that will pay it. Everyone and everything is sullied with money. No transaction or representation is completely transparent. Nowhere is that more evident than in the case of the US–India nuclear agreement, inked in 2005 and approved in 2008. Almost a decade later, the only beneficiaries of this deal are arms traders. No nuclear power plant has even broken ground. I blame the Octopus for this.

6

The Untapped Potential of the India–United States Civil Nuclear Agreement

'Almost a tenth of India's economy was being murdered in the dark, strangled by power shortages. And then George W. Bush said, "Let there be light."'

—*International Herald Tribune*, in a March 2006 article
describing the historic US–India nuclear agreement[1]

When I first visited India in 1965, I was enthralled by the people, the food, the heat and the colours. The plight of its poor moved me. As a graduate student in the Rhodes Scholar programme at Oxford University in England, I was looking for material to complete a doctorate in philosophy and made a brief visit to New Delhi. There, I spent three to four days during a term break in December.

On a low budget, I travelled by rail. The trains were crowded and the passengers were noisy and boisterous. It was such a contrast to the quiet and subdued cross-country train rides in the United States. I ate whatever my modest budget allowed, and remember enjoying my first taste of idli in southern India. Enveloped by the country's spirit, I found the whole experience exhilarating.

But I also witnessed the long-term impact of foreign occupation and the devastating effects on its poverty-stricken people. I later saw the same negative impact of long-term foreign intervention in Vietnam. In India, there didn't seem to be as strong a sense of national pride as I have witnessed in many other countries. At the time, I blamed it on colonialism. But, fifty years later, I also wonder if extreme poverty, corruption and the burden of the old caste system play a large role as well. Of course, the country's lack of reliable electricity also keeps the population in a type of permanent Dark Ages—pun intended.

Consequently, I was highly encouraged when I learnt that, along with members of the US Congress, President George W. Bush and Prime Minister Manmohan Singh had agreed in July 2005 to a nuclear deal to bring electricity to the mass population. The US–India nuclear agreement would allow the United States to supply India with nuclear fuel for civilian power generators. In exchange, India agreed to institute international safeguards on its nuclear reactors to prevent them from being used for military purposes. The negotiations, surprisingly, had been conducted in almost total secrecy. Highly controversial, the agreement ended the United States' three-decade ban on nuclear trade of any kind with India without requiring the country to join the Nuclear Non-Proliferation Treaty (NPT) or to dismantle its nuclear weapons programme.

An idealist, especially in the field of international development, might look at this deal as a great victory for the people of India, as the mass population would finally get reliable and clean electricity. In a country where 300 million of its citizens have no electricity and millions more have unreliable electricity, the US–India nuclear agreement—if implemented—could significantly improve the quality of life for more than a billion people.[2]

Currently, India fulfils only about 2 per cent of its energy needs using nuclear power, compared to a whopping 60 per cent of its needs from coal.[3] India's overuse of coal to produce electricity has contributed to extremely high levels of pollution throughout the country. According to a study published in 2016 in the *Geophysical Research Letters* journal, the outdoor air pollution in India contributed to more than 500,000 premature deaths in 2011.[4] The country has some of the highest rates of particulate matter in its outdoor air in the world. In addition, there are myriad accidents caused by the extraction of coal from mines and the distribution process required to move coal to electrical plants via ship, rail and truck. Combine that with the long-term health problems coal workers suffer and you have a country dependent on a very dirty and dangerous energy source. In contrast, nuclear energy is one of the cleanest sources of energy in the world, as it is emissions-free. It is also one of the cheapest.[5] Thus, the US–India nuclear agreement, if fully implemented, would help solve India's energy shortages, pollution problems and associated health issues.

Nuclear power will not solve all of India's air pollution problems, a good portion of which comes from the extensive use of open fires for cooking, as well as the operation of cars with less than strict emissions controls. This problem is not unique to India. Many developing countries around the world have pollution challenges stemming from the widespread practice of open fires for cooking, trash burning and brush clearing. First World countries do too. Americans love their roaring wood fireplaces. When attending environmental fundraisers in the wintertime in affluent homes in the Georgetown neighbourhood of Washington or the Upper East Side of New York City, the hosts frequently have decorative fireplaces with fires burning all winter long. To me, it seems so inconsistent that we are asking developing countries to give up their open fires when we are so fond of ours.

India has attempted to develop some clean energy sources. As I have observed on my more recent trips to India, there are solar panels all over the country. Being near the equator allows India to access a huge amount of solar energy. At the moment, India gets about 15 per cent of its energy needs from solar and other renewable sources (not including hydroelectric dams).[6] Solar power can be effective for lighting homes, but it will not be enough to satisfy the demand for commercial and industrial power in India.

A responsible energy policy would include utilizing all the clean sources of power available. That means bringing nuclear power in line with other renewables. Nuclear energy, as has been proven in France, can supply an abundant amount of electricity for industrial use. France could be a model for India. In fact, France exports a huge amount of electricity to a number of other countries, in particular Italy. India might be able to market some of its surplus energy to its neighbour Bangladesh, for example, and possibly even to Pakistan. However, the need for more electricity in India alone is so overwhelming that the country will probably use most of the electricity produced in the nuclear reactors within its borders.

To development specialists, the US–India nuclear agreement could be a godsend. Nearly 30 per cent of India's population lives below the poverty line and 75 per cent earns less than 5000 rupees per month.[7] The residents of the state of Bihar are among the most impoverished people in the world, with more than 70 per cent of its population suffering in extreme poverty.[8] An ample and reliable supply of electricity will increase productivity in states like Bihar. More light in homes and in workplaces results in greater activity. This increased productivity will lift up those living in the most abject poverty in India. That is what proponents of the nuclear agreement must state as its main objective. It is a worthy humanitarian goal. But, thus far, the architects of this deal and its advocates have failed to reinforce it.

I have visited some of the remotest parts of India, and the more populated ones—like where the Golden Temple is located— some of these with my friend, the late parliamentarian Murli Deora. Deora and I first met at an inter-parliamentary meeting in London in 1980, where we befriended each other. I know that he was a controversial figure to some, but he recognized my interest in India early on. He always helped me when I needed introductions.

He set up several meetings for me with both Sonia and Rajiv Gandhi. Deora's constituents lived in one of the poorest areas of Mumbai and he was always searching for creative ways to help the poor. He took me on street and market tours of his district. There, I saw the faces of people with nothing to live for except more of the worst type of poverty and eventual death at a young age. It reminded me of my experience visiting poverty-stricken, rural parts of Vietnam on my army deployments during the Vietnam War.

My parents' socio-economic status was what is now defined as poverty, or 'rural poor', because we did not have indoor plumbing or electricity until I was in high school. But my modest upbringing can hardly be compared to what the impoverished population of India faces on a daily basis. It would not be considered severe poverty by world standards. My family lived on about 64 hectares in the beautiful, safe and pristine state of South Dakota in the midwestern plains region of my country. There, we have vast open spaces and huge rivers. Life in South Dakota is in stark contrast to life in India. I realize that if an Indian family owns one hectare, they are considered well off. Despite these differences, I have always felt a spiritual connection between my state's sense of independence and patriotism and the energetic and proud culture of India. I experience the same wonderful optimism both when I stand near the Missouri River in Vermillion, South Dakota, and when I travel on the scenic and open road between Bengaluru and Mysuru in India.

South Dakota is the home to Mount Rushmore, the massive sculpture carved into the side of a mountain of Presidents George Washington, Thomas Jefferson, Theodore Roosevelt and Abraham Lincoln. It is a major tourist attraction and is featured on our state licence plates and our drivers' licences. As a result, since I was a very young boy, I always felt a connection with our presidents who served in faraway Washington, D.C. My participation in my local '4-H' club, a national agricultural youth organization administered by the US Department of Agriculture, enabled me to travel to the National 4-H Club Conference in Washington, D.C., in 1959, my first trip to

Washington. It is quite an experience to visit the nation's capital for the first time, probably not unlike the sense of wonder an Indian might feel upon seeing the Taj Mahal for the first time or experiencing the urban splendours of New Delhi.

For most of the developed world, reliable electricity is a given. The businesses in these countries would not function without it. Some Indian economists have said that the increased and reliable nuclear energy that the Indo-US nuclear deal envisions could even further improve India's gross domestic product, as production would not be hampered by power outages that are embarrassing for Indian businesses.

For six years, I served on the board of directors of Infosys Technologies, now called Infosys Limited (NYSE: INFY), a multinational Indian corporation that provides information technology and business consulting services. We would frequently experience flickering lights or intermittent blackouts at our offices in Bangalore, although Infosys did have sophisticated backup generators that kicked in almost automatically. Infosys experienced two or three of these blackouts during one meeting with President Vladimir Putin. I personally experienced short blackouts during an Infosys meeting with a Chinese foreign minister and while a delegation of US senators, including my friend, the Georgia Republican senator Johnny Isakson, was touring the facility. It does not inspire a whole lot of confidence in a high-tech company when the power goes out. Reliable electricity could also improve the perception about the capabilities of India's private sector industries.

Surprisingly, however, during my last year on the board of Infosys, I was amazed at how little public debate there was among the business community about the nuclear agreement. Hatched in total secrecy, it was not widely discussed outside of the US and Indian governments and their associated lobbyists. The public just was not engaged and galvanized behind it. I think my colleagues at Infosys and others in the private sector saw the nuclear agreement as just another unfulfilled promise. They are probably right.

My love for India and its people is heartfelt. That is why I am so passionate about the transformative effects nuclear power can have on its citizens. If properly implemented, the US–India nuclear agreement could bring electricity, an improvement in the standard of living, and some level of dignity for many poor Indians. The poor are the ones who need the nuclear agreement the most, but so far this deal has just been a shuffling of millions of dollars between governments, arms dealers, consulting firms and lobbyists. Almost a decade after the deal was approved, not one nuclear power plant has even started construction.

Why hasn't this happened? Importantly absent from the deal was a requirement forcing India to join the NPT and adhere to all its requirements. The Nuclear Non-Proliferation Treaty, enacted in 1970, extracted a bargain between nuclear weapons states and non-nuclear weapons states. Nuclear weapons states promised to use their nuclear capability only for peaceful purposes in exchange for a promise from non-nuclear weapons states not to pursue nuclear weapons in any form. The US–India nuclear agreement essentially gave India a waiver from the NPT, in an attempt to build a closer relationship with India and counter the rising threat of its powerful neighbour, China. This has antagonized many nuclear non-proliferation advocates, who see this move as a type of 'nuclear double standard'.[9] Many foreign policy experts claim that the special exemptions the US is giving India have done irreparable damage to global non-proliferation efforts. I tend to agree that we have executed an 'about face' on non-proliferation, but I believe it is necessary to get nuclear power for the Indian people.

Our nuclear agreement with India proves that we do whatever we wish on a country-by-country basis and find some way to legitimize it—even if it contradicts our previously stated public policy. I started my career as a young foreign service officer in 1971 writing legal memoranda—official and supposedly objective legal opinions on various policy proposals. Believe it or not, some days we would get word from the White House that the administration was going to reverse itself on some previous position, such as invading a country.

We would be ordered to produce a legal memorandum justifying the reversal, and we produced it! We did not have the choice to be objective—it felt like we were required to provide a legal opinion to support the administration or we would not get our next promotion. Even though I think this exemption for India was necessary, the US–India nuclear agreement was a startling policy reversal for the region.

It took nearly three years for both countries to approve the final agreement, which was signed by the then Indian external affairs minister, Pranab Mukherjee, and his counterpart, the then secretary of state, Condoleezza Rice, on 10 October 2008. Since it is not a treaty and merely an exchange of statements, we must accept the fact that it is not enforceable. Both sides are depending on the goodwill of the other for implementation. The publicly stated purpose of the agreement is to build nuclear plants in India to supply electricity to the country.

In actuality, the United States' primary goal with this deal was, selfishly, an economic one. The US–India nuclear agreement was primarily an arms trade deal. While it certainly was intended to allow nuclear suppliers entry into India, it also opened up vast new trade opportunities between the United States and India for many other industries. According to the US Census Bureau, trade between our two countries grew more than 100 per cent between 2006 and 2014—from \$32 billion to \$67 billion.[10] Likewise, according to the Office of the US Trade Representative, US exports to India increased by 339 per cent between 2003 and 2012. And herein you might spy the tentacles of the Octopus slithering out of the water, feeling and grasping for opportunities to offload more weapons—gorged at the expense of civil development in India.

So far, the defence industry is the only industry that has enjoyed significant gains from the nuclear deal. This was not a quid pro quo, but the deal did open the doors wide for significantly more arms deals, notably C-130 and C-17 transport aircraft, and joint military exercises with India. This deal is simply a pathway to justify an escalation in arms sales between the two countries. Indeed, Stephen

Cohen, a Senior Fellow from the Brookings Institute and an India expert, said that India will be 'one of the largest markets for defense equipment in the coming two decades'.[11]

President Obama continued the trend started by President Bush and further opened up arms trade between our two countries. In 2009, the Boeing Company won a contract for a $2-billion order for P-3 Orion maritime reconnaissance aircraft. Lockheed Martin secured a $1-billion contract for more C-130 transport aircraft. In 2010, President Obama pledged $5 billion of military equipment to India, making the US one of India's top three military suppliers.

Further efforts were made to loosen antiquated restrictions on technology transfer and to relieve onerous oversight controls. In 2013, the then secretary of defense, Ashton Carter, announced that India would be admitted into the coveted 'Group of Eight', the US allies that share the most sensitive technology details—without any export controls.[12]

In 2014, analysts from the military trade publication *Jane's Defense* said that India had become the largest foreign buyer of US weapons (only to be outbought by the Saudis in 2015).[13] And, in 2015, President Obama and Prime Minister Modi announced new partnerships between our countries to jointly develop military jet engine technology and aircraft carrier design. President Obama said publicly that forging deeper ties between our two nations was a primary foreign policy objective for his administration. What he did not say is that these deep ties are mostly military ones.

The US–India nuclear agreement was a good first step towards making India a key global ally. However, the deal has not even begun to achieve its full potential. I fear it never will. Domestic support for the deal in both countries is lacking. But I believe the on-again, off-again support the US continues to give to Pakistan prevents the US–India alliance from reaching its full potential. We need only look back at the history of our complicated relationship—and lingering Cold War attitudes—to understand why.

7

The Obstacles to the Nuclear Agreement and the Complicated History between the US and India

'For the first time since the signing of the Treaty of Westphalia in 1648, the single largest concentration of international economic power will be found not in Europe—not in the Americas—but in Asia. This, of course, has profound global implications ... Where better today to stress that point in Asia than in democratic India.'

—Robert Blackwill, US ambassador to India, on 27 January 2003[1]

Although India and the United States are both large and successful democracies, we have been at political cross-purposes for most of the decades since India became independent in 1947. Indian economic policy was determinedly socialist; it discouraged foreign investment and trade, and attempted to erect high tariff walls. The United States in the 1950s wanted all newly independent countries to become its military allies against communism. Pakistan quickly did so joining the Central Treaty Organization (CENTO) and the Southeast Asia

Treaty Organization (SEATO), but India resisted. This created some acrimony and some distrust towards India among Americans.

I can recall many informal conversations in the 1950s and '60s with my fellow Americans about India. They viewed India as part of the Soviet bloc. In those days, the Soviet Union supplied India with weapons and ships. The rhetoric in India was decidedly anti-American and the rhetoric in the United States was very anti-India, despite the shared democratic and entrepreneurial traditions in both countries. World maps posted in US classrooms in the 1950s and 1960s highlighted American allies. Pakistan was always listed as an ally and India was not.

In the run-up to the 1971 war with Pakistan over Bangladesh, it appeared to me that India faced the danger of a war on two fronts: Pakistan as well as China. At the time, Prime Minister Indira Gandhi signed a treaty for mutual security cooperation with Moscow. This proved effective in keeping China out of the 1971 war, and formed a strong foundation for growing Indo-Soviet cooperation in military and economic affairs. However, I saw that it further alienated the United States and it made our diplomats wary of dealing with India. I was working at the State Department at that time and the distrust between India and the US was at an all-time high. When President Richard Nixon paid an official visit to Prime Minister Indira Gandhi earlier that year, the tension between the two of them was evident—even in still photographs. They detested each other and Prime Minister Gandhi made her feelings clear to President Nixon that day. It was a stunning and stinging snub of an American President.

I noted warily Pakistan's role in assisting the United States' efforts to open diplomatic doors to China in 1971 and, later, as a facilitator of aid to the Afghan resistance fighters against the Soviet occupation in the 1980s. As a result, the US effectively looked the other way when it came to Pakistan's nuclear programme and the assistance it obtained from China for its missile and nuclear programmes. That is, until the Pressler Amendment was enacted and enforced.

All of these events, of course, have coloured the relationship between India and the US. India's nuclear test in 1974 did not help matters. The United States saw this move as irresponsible, but what I think Americans failed to understand was that India wanted to be recognized as a mature power with a nuclear deterrent against a nuclear-armed adversary, China, which it had always considered its biggest rival and threat. India also wanted to offset the unpredictable Pakistan next door. We still treated India as a colonial stepchild and continued to punish the country for its Russian affiliation. It seems to me that any measure India took to defend itself against other nuclear powers like China—and, later, Pakistan—was a legitimate right.

The United States acted like a two-faced ally to India. We acknowledged India's fears of a nuclear-armed Pakistan and gave lip service to this threat, but did nothing about it. We continued to fund Pakistan's military to support the goal of fighting the spectre of communism anywhere in the world at the expense of furthering our nuclear non-proliferation goals in South Asia. Now, once again, we are funding the rogue Government of Pakistan because we need their questionable help in fighting the terrorists in Afghanistan. This move risks the use of US taxpayer money for purposes contrary to our interests.

To my mind, it seems befitting that India and the US should be the closest of allies—more so than they are currently. We should have a 'super alliance'. As the largest democracy in South Asia, India is more like the United States than any other country in that region. However, other than advancements largely in information technology and intellectual property, a large proportion of the Indian people are so impoverished that they are essentially oppressed. Weapons and arms— that has been the principal focus between our two governments, and that saddens me.

I strongly believe we need to do more to promote India's interests worldwide. We tout England and Israel as our closest allies, yet India's democratic government, location, brain trust, and trade synergies make it a natural and potentially more important economic and

geopolitical ally for the future. We should decisively choose India
and stop pretending that India and Pakistan are diplomatically equal.
We must downgrade Pakistan and treat it as it is: an irresponsible,
dishonest, rogue state.

As we continue to root out terrorists worldwide, it is important
that we stand by our friends around the world who reflect our faith
in democracy, entrepreneurship, human rights and religious freedom.
India is the biggest of these friends. We must make the alliance
between the democracies of India and the United States a robust
economic one, built on a foundation of trust, shared democratic values
and mutually beneficial trade and knowledge-sharing. India should
be granted a special relationship with the United States, one that
gives it a preferred status in trade, knowledge-sharing, intelligence-
sharing, immigration and defence. Part of that defence should include
defending India against China.

I recognize that defence officials view China as America's biggest
potential threat in the world today. At least one of the historical
motivations for continuing aid to Pakistan was to prevent it from
becoming a client state of China's. The Obama administration quietly
started executing its 'Pacific Pivot' strategy, which has been turning
our diplomats' and our navy's focus to Asia, and more specifically,
to China. Perhaps to amplify this threat, the Octopus provokes and
pokes China. When I was in Cambodia in 2010, for instance, the
US sailed big warships into Cambodian ports, allegedly bringing in
medical supplies. But my State Department contacts told me it was
actually a show of force to irritate the Chinese—and to reinforce
the importance of maintaining open sea lanes for international trade.
Naval manoeuvres like these are strictly a way for the Octopus to
taunt the Chinese and remind them that the US is in control and
committed to keeping international waters free and open—especially
in the South China Sea.

This strategy involves the cooperation of India as well. Over the
course of my lifetime, I have witnessed India migrate from a pro-Russian
country with an anti-American prime minister to a pro-American

country and one of our closest allies in the region. I recall in the 1950s listening to very anti-American remarks from V.K. Krishna Menon, the legendary Indian ambassador to the United Nations. Now Prime Minister Modi says just the opposite of what Menon said—a 180-degree shift. It seems to me that both India and the US see the other as important allies in containing the geopolitical influence of China.

In my recent discussions with current and former senior navy officials, I have learnt that the United States is on the verge of a massive effort to help build up the Indian Navy, and outfit its navy ships with nuclear weapons. The Indian Navy's ship inventory is being significantly modernized. Most notable was the secret commissioning in August 2016 of its first nuclear ballistic missile submarine (SSBN), the INS *Arihant*, and the January 2017 test of a long-range nuclear-capable submarine-launched ballistic missile from an underwater pontoon.[2]

The Chinese are posturing aggressively against the US Navy in the Philippines and the Spratly Islands, a disputed group of islands in the South China Sea near Vietnam. This archipelago is situated in the middle of important air and sea navigation routes. Free access to the South China Sea is critical for international trade and travel. In addition, there are oil and gas reserves there. We really do not want a naval war with China. It would be costly to defend a place like the Spratly Islands. But we can send China a devastating message by strengthening the Indian Navy. An Indian Navy that has the capability of delivering nuclear weapons would cause China great concern. In fact, if we actually outfitted the Indian Navy with nuclear weapons, China might back down from its antagonistic stance in the region.

In addition to upgrading the Indian Navy, the United States and India should develop an intense 'soft-power' relationship. That is to say, we should work on promoting more non-military relationships like those fostered by the Millennium Challenge Corporation, an independent and somewhat entrepreneurial US government agency that invests in developing countries around the world fighting poverty, but only in those nations that have sound governance and economic freedom.

We should also host many more academic, business and charitable exchanges between our two nations to increase the number of India's small businesses, which can improve the lives of many of the poor. What India represents, overall, is economic potential. The economic potential for both our countries is much larger than just arms trade. In 2003, I proposed to the Asia Society the creation of an India Institute that would capitalize on the goodwill generated by India's generous assistance in counterterrorism efforts in South Asia. As I said at the time, 'The fall of the Soviet Union should have resulted in a better bilateral relationship between the world's largest democracy and the world's oldest living democracy.'

To some extent, I feel that my India Institute proposal was adopted in the form of President Obama's US–India Strategic and Commercial Dialogue (S&CD), kicked off in January 2015.[3] This annual forum is aimed at strengthening the bilateral relationship between our two countries with business, educational, cultural, familial and people-to-people exchanges. Bilateral trade—albeit military in nature—between our two countries has grown exponentially in the twenty-first century: from $19 billion in 2000 to more than $100 billion in 2014. Exports to India topped $38 billion in 2014 and Indian investment in the US was $28 billion.

In addition, we should liberalize visas for students and workers from both countries to lubricate the flow of talent between our two nations. Canada and India have a model for this. Indians are one of the largest immigrant groups in Canada and bring highly skilled talent to the country. In the United States, the technology sector boasts a large number of highly skilled Indians. These immigrants have significantly contributed to the strong entrepreneurial culture in the technology sector. Why can't we expand this trend to other industry sectors?

Finally, I firmly believe in the traditional channels of diplomacy—the ones the Octopus has skirted. We could start by getting the India caucuses in the House of Representatives and the Senate more involved. We have significant, functioning inter-parliamentary groups with the United Kingdom, Germany and Canada, but not India. Why not? We should also revive the art of 'statecraft' that is being taught at schools like John Lenczowski's Institute of World Politics, on which I volunteer on the board of advisers. This graduate school decries today's reliance on 'arms, money, and the diplomacy concerning them'.[4] The institute instead emphasizes the range of statecraft that diplomats must use—economic, corporate, cyber—as well as traditional and public diplomacy. It also tries to engender a spirit of public service and moral leadership in the practice of diplomacy.

India and the US really need to think about statecraft when working on their relationship. We need to develop a customized educational programme—with a holistic statecraft approach—for diplomats serving in India because India is such a complicated country. US diplomats who serve in India, especially mid-career officers, need to have much better training on the intricacies of India.

By putting to bed the remnants of our two nations' Cold War–era adversarial relationship, we invited India into the nuclear 'tent'. In return, we were hopeful that India would assist us in bolstering our defences against a rising and threatening China.

The US–India nuclear agreement has other obstacles to overcome. An enhanced diplomatic and trade relationship between our two countries will not be enough to satisfy the widespread suspicion and fears—albeit misplaced—about nuclear power.

A great fear also persists in the US that a large amount of nuclear material flowing to India will somehow be intercepted by terrorists who will take the material and upgrade it to 'weapons grade' and use it in small weapons, wherever they might want to do so. From talking to many of my Indian friends, I'm convinced that the average Indian citizen is suspicious of the level of nuclear safeguards that their government can provide.

The nuclear suppliers themselves are voicing one of the more vexing obstacles: nuclear liability. The Bhopal Gas Tragedy frightened US corporations looking to do business in India. These corporations cannot and will not build nuclear reactors until India gives them limited liability. The 2010 Civil Liability Act passed by the Indian Parliament further intimidated these companies. President Obama announced in 2015 that he and Prime Minister Modi had reached a 'breakthrough understanding' on the liability issue in the form of a non-binding legal memorandum. If it is non-binding, it is not enforceable.[5]

India must provide limits on civil liability for damages that might occur at US plants in India in order for US suppliers to build in India. US corporations eager to invest in India for this deal are scared off by the potential liability. These companies' top executives are also hesitant, as they know that the Union Carbide chief executive officer endured death threats against him and his family after the Bhopal disaster. India has joined the International Atomic Energy Agency's (IAEA's) Convention on Supplementary Compensation for Nuclear Damage (CSC). India, the United States and other countries really need to do much more on limiting nuclear damage liability. The United States' Price-Anderson Nuclear Industries Indemnity Act could be a model. This Act requires non-military nuclear plants in the US to obtain the maximum amount of insurance against nuclear-related incidents and contribute to an industry fund that pays for damages above the insured amount.

This problem of limiting nuclear liability really should be a United Nations initiative. It is the sort of project the UN was created to tackle. But in my opinion, the UN totally avoids these types of challenges because they are difficult. As a result, the UN is becoming a wasteland. I twice served as a delegate to the UN and witnessed how ineffective it actually is. Sometimes I wonder how long this institution would have survived if its headquarters were located in a developing country instead of cushy New York City, and if its food relief organization were located in a city that suffers from hunger instead of Rome.

Trial lawyers, one of the most powerful lobbying groups in the United States, are also strongly opposed to any reform of our litigation system, which leads to endless lawsuits that benefit no one except attorneys. We will have to do a lot of internal domestic political work to get the trial lawyers to change their position. India will also have to do a lot of domestic groundwork to overcome obstacles to the deal. So, while the nuclear deal has been a boon for the US defence industry and the Octopus, there doesn't seem to be any tangible move by US nuclear power companies to begin construction.

8

Galvanizing Grass-roots Support for the US–India Nuclear Agreement

'Of the 25 million who live in zones of conflict, 23 million could be accessed through their religious communities.'

—William Vendley, secretary general of World Religions for Peace, addressing a UNESCO conference in Paris in 2005[1]

I always tell students of foreign relations that a good formulation of foreign policy requires a lot of domestic groundwork in advance, or the effort will fail. Private sector support from higher education, religious institutions and humanitarian organizations must be galvanized, as they have influence over enormous constituencies. A historic example is President Woodrow Wilson's failure to secure the support of the American Congress for the Covenant of the League of Nations, due in part to his making the deal in Europe without really laying the groundwork on the domestic front. The League of Nations was a forerunner to the United Nations and was created after World War I to maintain world peace, to avoid a worldwide arms race, and to settle international disputes. It was an effort to prevent another world war. However, even though President Wilson barnstormed the country afterwards to make his case directly to the American people, he was too late. He never secured the support he sought and the League of Nations was created without the participation of the United States—a fact that is often cited as one of the main reasons why it failed to stop the occurrence of another world war.

Likewise, the US–India nuclear agreement was made almost entirely without domestic input from universities, religious institutions or humanitarian organizations in either India or the United States. These groups have a strong history in formulating foreign policy and advocating for political and societal changes that benefit a nation's population. Without their support, I fear the agreement will never be fully implemented.

Universities in the United States, particularly the Ivy League and the great state universities, have a substantial history of contributing to the formulation of foreign policy. In the 1950s, Secretary of State John Foster Dulles had regular advice from universities—and many newsworthy foreign policy events happened at universities. For example, Winston Churchill gave his famous 'Iron Curtain' speech at Westminster College in Fulton, Missouri, at the request of the college. Universities were very active in opposing the Vietnam War. Students marched, professors lectured on the fruitlessness of the war, and university publications were filled with anti-war literature. The effort was largely successful in influencing the debate over the war.

President John F. Kennedy hired many university professionals such as Walter Heller, his economic adviser, who came from the University of Minnesota. His speechwriter, Ted Sorenson, came from the University of Nebraska. And, of course, John Kenneth Galbraith, his ambassador to India, started his career as a professor of agricultural economics at Harvard. We just do not seem to have the same quality of national advisers coming out of our nation's universities today.

Even the prestigious Hoover Institution, an organization housed on the campus of Stanford University, some of whose fellows serve on the Pentagon's Defense Policy Board, has become more of a research centre and archive library than an incubator of policy ideas. Universities used to be at the epicentre of foreign policy debates, hosting all sorts of wide-ranging discussions, but our schools are now so politically correct that they will not do it any more.

I'm what is called a 'C-SPAN junkie', and you can find me watching this public affairs channel at all hours of the night. C-SPAN airs these forums regularly, where I have occasionally served as a panellist. While they always used to be sponsored by universities, they are now almost always sponsored by think tanks. Indeed, new foreign policy ideas now seem to originate almost exclusively from the think tanks.

Indeed, with the mushrooming size of the think tank industry in Washington and the exponential rise in its fundraising and influence within the world of politics in the United States, the impact of academics in the world of foreign policy has faded from its past glory. Universities have been sidelined, to a degree, I feel, by the ranks of former government officials filling up think tanks and lobbying firms. These executives have, by definition, closer relationships with policymakers in Washington and can capture their attention more readily than obscure professors can, even though academics could be just as well qualified to provide policymaking advice. So, it was not surprising to me that the US–India nuclear agreement had very little input from our universities and academia. In fact, the universities were not even asked for, nor did they offer any comments. This is a great flaw in the process and one that needs to be corrected.

The same is true of churches and charitable groups whose mission it is to alleviate poverty. While religious differences and religious intolerance have certainly been *the cause* of major conflicts throughout history, there are many examples worldwide from the twentieth century, of churches acting as *positive* forces in reaching foreign policy goals—*and doing so peacefully*. Religious institutions in India could and should be playing an important role in the successful execution of the US–India nuclear agreement.

The goals of religious institutions are usually aligned with a need to promote social and economic justice within a country, but in many instances they were instrumental in forcing a change in national policy or national leadership. India's leaders should look at some of these cases as a model for the US–India nuclear agreement. In the 1994 book, *Religion: The Missing Dimension of Statecraft*, authors Douglas Johnston and Cynthia Sampson make the case that religious leaders and institutions have played a significant role in shaping public policy and improving diplomatic relations within and between nations. Some examples they cite could apply to India.

For example, they cite the Roman Catholic Church's role in ousting President Ferdinand Marcos from the Philippines in 1986. The Church changed its view of its role in the world following the adoption of the Second Vatican Council ('Vatican II') in the early 1960s, which renewed the Church's commitment to human rights, freedom and social justice. It would be hard to imagine the College of Cardinals coming out in support of nuclear energy, but this is the type of action that is needed to get the US–India nuclear agreement implemented.[2]

When President Marcos imposed martial law in 1972, the Catholic Church was forced to cease its work with labour and peasant groups, and this led to widespread human rights violations. As a result, its leaders decided to step outside its traditional purview and publicly criticize the Marcos regime. And when former Philippine senator Benigno Aquino was assassinated in 1983, the Church's leaders went a step further. They publicly aligned themselves with the political opposition and began publishing a series of 'pastoral letters' condemning the Marcos regime for having lost its moral legitimacy to govern. During the three-day revolution that ousted President Marcos in February 1986, the Church assisted the coup by galvanizing the faithful population to assemble and protect the coup's military leaders. The human barricade the nation's Catholics mounted and the national outcry they engendered among the nation's majority Catholic population were enough pressure to force Marcos into exile.

Around the same time frame, the Catholic Church was also busy promoting nuclear non-proliferation. In 1983, a committee of Roman Catholic bishops took the unusual step of issuing a pastoral letter opposing nuclear arms. Titled 'The Challenge of Peace', it stated the Church's opposition to nuclear war, its support for large arms reductions by the United States and the Soviet Union, and its promotion of a curb on the development of new nuclear weapons systems. It would be wonderful if the Catholic Church was able to endorse civilian nuclear power as a reliable and safe means to get electricity for the Indian population, linking nuclear power to the reduction of poverty.

South African churches played an influential role in ending apartheid in the 1980s. In the vanguard was the Anglican Church of Cape Town and its archbishop, Desmond Tutu. Archbishop Tutu took his anti-apartheid message global and earned a Nobel Peace Prize in 1984 for his efforts. Secretary of State George Shultz lauded the positive difference he and other South African clergy leaders were making: 'South Africa's churches, many of them affiliated with U.S. counterparts, represent a major asset to help all those who wish to build rather than destroy their country. They represent voices of conciliation, decency, dialogue, and community service in the interest of the common humanity of all South Africans.'[3]

Other Christian institutions, including the World Council of Churches and the Roman Catholic Church, followed the lead and soon denounced apartheid as unjustifiable on Christian ethical grounds. President Ronald Reagan took action in 1985 and imposed trade sanctions on South Africa as a tangible sign of protest. In the fall of 1989, South Africa's new President, F.W. de Klerk, formally asked his nation's churches for their input, and their response was instrumental in his landmark decision in early 1990 to repeal all apartheid laws. Couldn't India's Hindu, Muslim, Sikh, Christian Buddhist and Jain leaders get behind the goals of the US–India nuclear agreement—that of getting electricity to the poor? Their pious followers would find their arguments more persuasive than those of the government's.

Many of the examples cited above illustrate some of the churches' more liberal advocacy roles in domestic and foreign policy. However, the Catholic Church has also taken some 'conservative' positions, most notably in support of the Contras in Nicaragua in the 1980s. The Contras were generally opposed by the left-wing, or communist, Sandinistas. At the time, the US Senate Foreign Relations Committee held numerous hearings in which I participated on the Contra matter. President Reagan wanted to support the Contras but could not get a congressional appropriation. Some of his staff secretly diverted some funds to help the Contras, in what came to be known in the United States as the 'Iran–Contra Affair', because secret arms sales were made to Iran—in violation of an arms embargo on Iran—to fund the Contras.

During this time I met with Cardinal Pio Laghi, the Apostolic Nuncio (the Vatican's ambassador) to the United States, who served as a diplomatic emissary for Pope John Paul II. He strongly supported using US military intervention against the Sandinistas. He told me and the Senate Foreign Relations Committee that Pope John Paul II intensely disliked the Sandinistas. Once, while on a visit to Central America, the Pope visibly jerked his hand away from one of the Sandinista leaders (a former priest) who tried to kiss his ring, saying that the 'Sandinistas were not worthy to call themselves Catholics'. In the United States (and especially in India), the Vatican usually plays a pacifist role. But not during the Iran–Contra affair; on the contrary, the Pope was in favour of military action in Central America against the communist Sandinistas.

While I will not weigh in on the political stands these institutions have taken, I do find it strange that none of these churches have spoken up about the need to get cheaper electricity for the population of India. After all, India is the second most populous country in the world, with more than 1.2 billion people. The fact remains that for many individuals and organizations—especially liberal ones in the United States—'nuclear' is a dirty word.

It is clear that religious institutions can play a pivotal role in foreign policy by educating a faithful populace; mobilizing a local, national or international community about an issue or policy; and effecting seismic changes *peacefully*. Academic communities, especially universities, can also serve as a place to incubate and socialize policies— including foreign policies.

State legislatures could also lend their support. For example, the state legislature has played a pivotal role in improving international trade for India. Not a single provincial parliament in India or the US was called upon to endorse the US–India nuclear agreement. Without this effort, I fear the Indian people will not understand the potential consumer benefits of cleaner and more reliable electric power.

A fourth group that has been conspicuously absent from the Indian nuclear debate is the charitable organizations. These philanthropic organizations should be touting the advent of nuclear power as a tool to reduce poverty. In point of fact, groups like OXFAM, Save the Children, Children International and Catholic Charities should be advocating for the US–India nuclear agreement, as it could help alleviate poverty in India. But, because of the controversy that surrounds nuclear energy and the charities' desire to be politically correct, they are silent on this important issue.

Because all these groups have not been involved from the beginning in shaping the terms of the deal and because these institutions have not been engaged in its advocacy and implementation, the Indian citizens who are living in hopeless poverty and who read about all the expensive payoffs will probably feel they are getting nothing out of the nuclear deal. The Indian public, the American public and the public of the world need to be engaged in the concept that the greatest help we might give to relieve pollution and poverty is to implement the US–India nuclear agreement.

Prime Minister Modi's meeting with President Obama in the US in June 2016 included a historic speech before the US Congress and an announcement that India is now a 'Major Defense Partner' with the US. The meeting also produced a stated intent for six nuclear reactors to be built in India by Westinghouse—with a deal to be completed by June 2017. Although I am told that Westinghouse is in the final phases of preparing to build six reactors, I predict construction will not begin if the liability issue is not resolved.

At the time of this writing, it appears that this deadline will not be met. This is bad news for India's masses, but good news for the defence industry in both countries. As our nations' diplomats continue to dicker over the details of the nuclear deal, the improved relationship between our two countries will result only in an increasing flow of conventional weapons to India. Boeing, Lockheed Martin and all the big defence companies are having a field day while India's poor population is once again forgotten.

Developed in total secrecy at the very highest levels of government and passed in Congress through the efforts of a host of lobbyists, US and Indian leaders failed to engage our nations' respective populations to secure their widespread support for this landmark deal. For that reason, I believe it will never be implemented. The Octopus will be the only winner in this deal and it only reinforces how much it dominates the formulation of public policy in the United States.

Money has always been a corruptive influence in Washington. Lawmakers and regulators have tried to make the flow of money more transparent. But the Octopus just finds new and more insidious ways to hide it. I think I have always been a bit too naïve for the harsh reality of Washington.

At my present age of seventy-five, I am one of the few Americans who can remember living without electricity. I can still vividly recall the moment I first turned on a light switch in my house. It was after World War II and this electricity made it possible for my family to have a water pump. No longer would my mother and three sisters have to haul water in buckets to the house. This changed our lives. Many Indians have not had that experience. I want them to.

9

The Roots of My Independence

'You can only look forward to a South Dakota winter if, as with childbirth, remodeling a house, or writing a novel, you're able to forget how bad it was the last time.'

—Dan O'Brien, author of *Buffalo for the Broken Heart: Restoring Life to a Black Hills Ranch*[1]

If the circumstances of one's birth and DNA were the only things that determined human destiny—a proposition I don't subscribe to for a minute—I would have followed in my father's footsteps and become a farmer. Farming is an honourable occupation and a self-fulfilling way of life, but farming was not to be my fate. Instead, through a series of twists and turns, luck, my own innate abilities, and what I believe was the intervention of God, I became, in Theodore Roosevelt's famous phrase, 'a man in the arena', one that I believe he used to describe men who get 'bloodied' by public service.

When I was born, on 29 March 1942, and christened Lawrence (or 'Larry') after my uncle, Lawrence Douvier, there was nothing in the stars that marked me for 'the arena'. My family scratched out a bare existence on a rented quarter section, 65 hardscrabble hectares, in the small town of Humboldt, South Dakota, which is 22 miles south-west of Sioux Falls, the state's largest city. With a population of 150,000, the city of Sioux Falls is named after the picturesque Big Sioux River rapids that run through the town. But we might as well have lived on the edge of the American frontier in a previous century.

Located in the midwestern region of the United States, South Dakota is a 'plains' state, one of the ten states in the region called the Great Plains, known for its vast expanse of flat prairie and grassland. The majestic beauty of this land has always reinforced my faith. I can always feel God's great spirit rushing right through me when I'm home walking on the plains of South Dakota.

The state has always been home to a large population of Native American residents and its economy was historically reliant on its natural resources. South Dakota has less than a million people in a state of only 77,000 square miles—about the same size as the Gujarat state. Those of us born and raised in South Dakota are used to vast, wide, open spaces and clean air. We are naturally independent people, self-reliant and hearty.

Providing for a large family on a rented quarter section—a standard-sized small farm—is an exceedingly hazardous existence. Forty per cent of everything we earned went to the landlord. In addition to the vagaries of the weather, a year-to-year renter never knows when the landlord might take it into his head to throw him off the property. It gave my family a constant feeling of instability. For the first several years of my life, I lived in a home with no electricity, no running water and no plumbing. Seven of us—my father, my mother, my four siblings and I—shared a wooden outhouse known as a 'two-holer' because it allowed two people to use the facility at the same time!

I remember the cattle in our barnyard with ice crystals on their eyelashes, standing through the South Dakota winter knee-deep in snowdrifts taller than myself. In the spring we placed salt blocks on a wooden trough. The cattle licked it until it was gone, and then continued licking the empty boards for days afterward—so like our own rough-grained life. I know many Indians also come from hardscrabble backgrounds. But from my experience visiting Indians, I have come to learn that not many of them are aware of how many Americans also struggle financially.

My family was devoutly Catholic, attending church every week in our neatest clothes and praying the rosary most nights together. The pads on the church's kneelers ran thin from the wear of regular prayer.

Despite not being very warm and always very reserved in front of us, my parents instilled in us a strong work ethic, sense of frugality, honesty and spirituality. They were Danish, an ethnic group that is not traditionally very expressive or emotional. In fact, they can be quite stoic. From Mother and Father, I learnt right from wrong. In those days, many farmers got away with turning in less corn from their federally subsidized storage bins than for which they had been paid. The practice was called 'grain skimming'. A farmer could pocket a few hundred dollars by skimming a couple of hundred bushels of corn. He could use that money to feed his family, get ahead on the next crop or pay down debts. It could have been used for any noble thing, but Father was scrupulous about turning in the exact amount. As he said to me at the time, 'I expect the government to be honest with me, as it always has been. I think the money we pay them goes for good purposes, so I'm careful to be honest with the government.'

My mother set a good example as well. Once, after shopping, Mother stopped to look at her hand, just outside the shop. She raised her finger and whispered something to herself and marched right back into the store. Mother realized that she'd been given too much change, so she handed over the extra dollars to the clerk, who seemed more annoyed than grateful. But Mother didn't mind. She didn't expect to be patted on the back for doing the right thing. Her example was instilled in us. She always naturally made the ethical choice.

As a result of my family's poverty, and the terrible insecurity that goes with being poor, I know what it feels like to be afflicted with a sense of self-doubt and low self-esteem. My speech impediment was this notion manifest. I first became aware of my stammer when I was three or four years old. Sometimes when I stumbled over a word, my father would say, 'Larry, just spit it out!' Father didn't mean to be cruel, but I don't think he ever identified with me the way he did with my younger brother, Dan. Maybe it was because I was a cerebral kid and that made my father uncomfortable. In any case, no one in the family ever made fun of me because of the stammer. However, I was teased by classmates in school. My speech impediment aggravated my natural shyness and, for many years, it made me reluctant to speak in public—definitely not an attribute normally associated with a future politician.

I also know what it feels like to desperately want to overcome your low status in life and better yourself. These are feelings that you never completely overcome. All of this may help explain two apparently contradictory sides of my personality: a bashfulness that makes me acutely self-conscious and reluctant to draw attention to myself; and—at the same time—a burning desire to be of service to others and to achieve great things.

It would be many years until I saw the world as more than just a flat place like South Dakota. When I discovered 4-H, I found a way to go out into the world and it was like God had said: 'Let there be light!' It was like somebody had suddenly turned on a light switch.

10

A Portrait of the Senator as a Young Man

'Larry has the brains to be something big.'

—A.L. Stoddard, Senator Larry Pressler's high school principal,
Humboldt High School, Humboldt, South Dakota, circa 1959

At the age of ten or eleven, a neighbour, Elmer Anderson, took me under his wing. He led the local chapter of '4-H', and invited me to join it. '4-H' stands for 'Head, Heart, Hands, and Health for Better Living' and these clubs were created more than a century ago to introduce young farmers to new agricultural technology. The 4-H programme teaches children new farming, livestock, science, citizenship, and public-speaking skills, and gets them involved in their local communities. I was taught that family-farm life was the best life in America, and that farming was a noble profession because we fed the world.

As the first Catholic invited to join the local 4-H chapter, called the 'Humboldt Hustlers', I felt very self-conscious. Mr Anderson, our chapter leader, disdained the religious divisions that then existed in our community. Many Americans forget that discrimination against

Catholics used to be quite common in the United States. While our isolation was not nearly as stifling as the caste system in India, I did experience prejudice because of my religion. In my little community, the 'state' religion was the Protestant denomination of Lutheranism— as it was in most states with large populations of Scandinavian immigrants. The Protestants' and the Catholics' doctrines are not that different. We are all Christians. But there is a long history of conflict between these denominations in Europe. This is probably analogous to the religious differences between Muslim Shi'ites and Sunnis. They have the same basic faith, but will kill each other over minor differences. I can only imagine if my community had been as divided as Jews and Muslims are, or as Muslims and Hindus were in India— leading to the creation of Pakistan. (I am pleased to see that Muslims enjoy a degree of religious tolerance in India—much more so than African Americans do here in the United States.)

Though the Protestants and Catholics coexisted peacefully in our town of Humboldt, we were socially segregated. Catholics shopped at the Catholic grocery store, Protestants at the Protestant grocery store. Catholics attended parochial schools and Protestants attended public schools. Catholics were also a bit given to self-segregation during this time. We were forbidden from marrying Protestants and, if we did, we insisted the Protestant spouse convert to Catholicism. Protestants were prohibited from attending Catholic weddings. By including me in the 4-H club, Mr Anderson made a courageous statement in our tiny community. He took a chance on me and I have always remembered it.

Getting involved in 4-H was a turning point in my life. No longer defined by the circumstances of my birth, economic status or religion, I was instead judged by what I could accomplish in my own right. I raised five or six livestock that I showed at county and state fairs. I became an expert in a breed of hogs known as 'spotted Poland-China hogs'. Interestingly, later in life I had several conversations with Britain's Prince Charles whose hobby it is to conserve the 'Old Spot' breed of hog. Old Spots are the purebred ancestor to the American spotted hogs. Little did I realize that my activities in a remote farm in South Dakota would be of conversational interest to the future king of England!

My father co-signed a note for me at the Community Bank of Humboldt for $125, which was a lot of money in 1954, to help me purchase a small pig house called a 'farrowing crate'. My first sow, Sally, a purebred spotted hog, gave birth to eight piglets—five boars and three gilts. Sadly, Sally accidentally lay on one of them and killed him—so I only weaned seven live piglets from her. Subsequently, one of the boars won first prize at the Sioux Empire Fair, and later at the South Dakota State Fair in Huron. My 4-H career was launched!

Life in 4-H taught me how to conduct and present original research on beef, swine, dairy, citizenship, electricity and entomology. After I entered Humboldt High School, I tentatively tried some 4-H public speaking. My first public demonstration was titled 'How to Make a Rope Halter', which I managed to deliver without too much stammering. I received an enthusiastic round of applause from my fellow 4-Hers, which further encouraged me.

At school, I was also starting to excel. I was getting straight As. My teachers and my high school principal were taking notice of my achievements and started to groom me for college. But my growing knowledge and self-confidence was starting to make waves at home. Father's withdrawn and introverted personality was reflected in his approach to farming. As I grew older, his old-fashioned ideas grated on me. I began arguing with Father at the dinner table, which caused a lot of tension. I wanted him to follow the example of several of our neighbours who had milking machines and raised purebred livestock instead of grade livestock. But Father stuck with his convictions and his inexpensive tractor, a sturdy Case brand tractor without a cab, which meant that when he worked in the field, he was exposed to the elements. He did not even have an umbrella to protect himself from the sun in the hot South Dakota summers.

Father had a basic farming strategy and he stuck to it, just like his father had. He focused on low-capital (and low-risk) investments and old-fashioned farming. He wasn't interested in the newest techniques or technology or expanding his farm. He knew what worked for him. He fed his family, paid all his bills, eventually bought his farm, and left enough money to care for his widow after he died, so I can't fault him for his resistance. Call it a generational divide or just my own form of rebellion.

Years later, I became friends with my fellow Rhodes Scholar and Harvard Business School professor, Clayton Christensen, who coined the term 'disruptive innovation'. By his definition, a disruptive innovation is one that helps create a new market and eventually disrupts an existing market, displacing an earlier technology. In part, 4-H was created to do just this type of disruption. The Department of Agriculture wanted to educate America's future farmers about new farming technology and products, in the hope that the younger generation would introduce them to their families. Without knowing it, I was trying to be a positive disrupter of sorts—but my father saw it as interference. That contributed to our discomfort with each other.

I never particularly thought of myself as a bright student. But I worked very hard, both in school and after school. I hired myself out to neighbouring farmers for the then standard $1 per hour. In the winter months, I pitched manure and cleaned out silos. On weekends, I tended to my 4-H livestock. I don't want to leave the impression that all was doom and drudgery in my South Dakota high school in the 1950s. Despite my family's poverty and my stammer, I had a pretty positive outlook on life.

I used to dream about travelling to exotic places like India, and becoming somebody important who would help others. I would get books from the state library, which had a free-mailing system throughout the state, and I read as much as I could about foreign countries. Having access to more books than any small-town library could house opened up my mind to the vast world beyond Humboldt.

It was during this time that I first read about the Hindu religion, *The Book of Mormon*, the Koran and, of course, the Bible. We did not emphasize reading the Bible very much in the Roman Catholic

Church in those days. Consequently, the nuns and our local priest became rather nervous at how many other faiths' religious texts I was reading. Studying other religions gave me a chance to develop my own sense of spirituality—a passion of mine that continues to this day. During this period, I also read about Confucianism and decided that this philosophy—based on kindness, mutual respect and an appreciation of character—might be the best way to serve mankind. I also read about Buddhism's beginnings in India and was fascinated with its history of having been a hotbed for new religions that started there.

Despite the challenges I faced growing up poor, and my severe stuttering, I was fortunate to have some great mentors, and I was determined to go to college. I still remember the strange mix of joy, wonderment, spiritual movement and apprehension that I felt when I set foot on the University of South Dakota's sprawling 216-acre park-like campus in Vermillion, a picturesque town nestled along the bluffs above the Missouri River. I arrived with all my farm-boy idealism and naïveté intact. It was the September of 1960, a watershed moment in American history and a watershed moment in my life.

The University of South Dakota (USD) is one of the best small public universities in the nation, and it boasts many distinguished alumni. Some of its famous graduates include historians, artists, businessmen, several United States senators and congressmen, *USA Today* and Gannett founder Al Neuharth, and a National Broadcasting Corporation (NBC) anchor, Tom Brokaw, who was a contemporary of mine while I was there. As one of the first in my family to attend college, I felt blessed by God. Like other poor farm boys attending college at the time, I earned my board washing dishes and serving food. I also had a work/study job in the Government Research Bureau, where I clipped newspapers from around the state and created folders on various subjects for professors. This little job further increased my knowledge and interest in public affairs and current events.

College opened up a whole new world for me, introducing me to a more diverse group of people and many professional mentors. One of those mentors was USD's legendary political science professor, Dr William O. Farber. He inspired in me a love of public service and shepherded the careers of a number of male students over several decades, including mine. I took several of Doc Farber's classes. He recognized and fuelled my ambitions and encouraged me to aim high. He boosted my self-confidence and offered me many new opportunities to excel and prove myself. His mantra was, 'Work hard!'

In my freshman year, I became a waiter in the university's faculty dining room. On John F. Kennedy's Inauguration Day, as I was serving lunch, I glanced at the television set up on the wall and saw the elderly poet Robert Frost with his papers blowing in the cold January wind as he tried to read a verse he had written. In contrast, the youthful new President approached the podium and began delivering the most riveting speech I had ever heard. He issued a call to all Americans that resonated with me: '... Let every nation know, whether it wishes us well or ill, that we shall pay any price, bear any burden, meet any hardship, support any friend, oppose any foe to assure the survival and the success of liberty ...' I was frozen on the spot. One of the dining room supervisors reprimanded me and demanded that I keep moving and clear my tables. I could not have imagined that, two years later, I would get the chance to meet the President in person.

At USD, I found my way to the school's speech clinic to attend a stammer/stutter workshop. The speech therapists there did the best they could with limited resources, but even they couldn't tell me exactly what caused my problem or how to fix it. I forced myself to join the debate team because I simply refused to let my affliction get the better of me. But I still have a stammer to this day.

And then, a blessing from God was bestowed on me: I was invited to spend the second half of my freshman year in Egypt, where I attended the International Agricultural Exhibition in Cairo as an American representative of 4-H and was able to shake hands with President Gamal Abdel Nasser at my livestock booth. (There I learnt to describe 4-H in French, as it was easier than learning it in

Egyptian!) What a thrill for a farmer's son from the sticks of South Dakota to travel overseas. I was the first in my family to get a passport!

When I returned to the university, I had to take a heavy dose of summer school courses to make up for the lost credits, but the trip was worth it. My independence had ignited my spirit and a desire for international travel.

In my junior year, I ran for president of the student body and won the election. In March 1963, I received another blessing from God: I was thrilled to be named one of four 'All-American 4-Hers' selected to present the '4-H Report to the Nation' to President Kennedy in the Oval Office. Standing next to President Kennedy was the most awe-inducing experience of my young life, although he paid much more attention to Fay Craig, my counterpart from Mississippi. She was really pretty with a deep Southern accent that charmed both the President and me. Kennedy, of course, was tragically assassinated a few months later.

By the first semester of my senior year, I had a girlfriend. Both of us were looking forward to graduation, but we had very different futures in mind. She wanted to get married and have children; I wanted to be a Rhodes Scholar and see the world. Doc Farber had told me about this prestigious scholarship and encouraged me to submit an application. In those days, Rhodes Scholars couldn't be engaged or married, so I broke off our relationship. I think I broke her heart. And I know I broke my own.

The Rhodes Scholarship is the oldest and most celebrated international fellowship award in the United States. Rhodes Scholars are chosen not only for their noteworthy scholarship achievements, but also for their character, commitment to others and to the common good, and for their potential for civic-minded leadership. The Rhodes Trust accepted very few candidates with my rural background and from my alma mater. The odds of my winning a coveted spot in the 1964 class of scholars seemed long indeed. Professor Farber urged me not to be discouraged. He pointed out that my farm background and my 4-H skills in judging purebred animals were just the kind of 'manly experiences' that Cecil Rhodes required when he founded the scholarships. In the Midwest, interviews for the Rhodes Scholarship were held in Chicago, and the announcement of winners was made at a formal dinner. Because of my lack of experience with proper table manners, I was scared to death that I'd make some terrible faux pas and lose out.

Luckily, I was seated across the table from an elegant Episcopal bishop from Chicago who was on the selection committee. I watched him handling his eating utensils and imitated his selection from the confusing array of forks, knives, spoons and glasses. Oddly enough, this particular bishop was very interested in cross-breeding livestock. It was one of his hobbies. He was fascinated by my knowledge of hybrid breeds of hogs and cattle and plants. As I think back, my rural background may have set me apart. And then, in the middle of dinner, I heard my name being announced as one of that year's Rhodes Scholars. In the course of four years, I had travelled from a farmhouse in South Dakota to acceptance at Oxford University. It was an unlikely journey, but just the type of challenge I have pursued throughout my life.

11

Debut on the International Stage

'My desire being that the students who shall be elected to the
Scholarships shall not be merely bookworms . . . [but should
exhibit] . . . moral force of character and of instincts to lead and to
take an interest in his schoolmates for those latter attributes will be
likely in after-life to guide him to esteem the performance of public
duty as his highest aim.'

—Cecil Rhodes, in his will outlining the vision for the ideal
Rhodes Scholar recipient[1]

In September 1964, I was one of thirty-two American Rhodes
Scholars and about a hundred additional American graduate students
who boarded the S.S. *France* in New York Harbor and set sail for
Southampton, England. Despite several days of rough seas, the trip was
an exhilarating adventure. There I was, in the middle of the Atlantic
Ocean, engaging in intellectually stimulating debate sessions with a
bunch of brilliant young men and women from all over America.
Most of the conversations were about the Vietnam War draft. Before
leaving for England, all of us had been required to go to our local

draft boards and obtain a document called 'Permission to Leave the Country', which had to be renewed each year. If you had a fair amount of money and the brains to stay in graduate school, or if your parents hobnobbed with members of the establishment or had political clout with the local draft board, you could avoid conscription until the age of twenty-six, when you were no longer eligible to be drafted. Another popular way of avoiding the draft at that time was to find a doctor who was willing to sign a letter saying you had some physical or emotional disability that made you ineligible to serve in the military.

Along with the topic of the draft, there were fierce debates aboard the S.S. *France* about the 1964 presidential race, which pitted President Lyndon Johnson, an avowed liberal, against Senator Barry Goldwater, a diehard conservative. Many of the Rhodes Scholars came from liberal schools and had been sponsored by left-leaning professors. Most of them were vehemently against the Vietnam War. On the contrary, I was raised to believe the government was trustworthy, so I believed our leaders at the time. What I experienced during the war myself, and learnt of the government's deception of the American people about it, led me to change my mind.

When we landed at Southampton, E.T. Williams, the warden of Rhodes House (or the Rodent of Wards House, as he was humorously referred to behind his back), met us at the pier with a lorry, a vehicle designed to carry military troops. The bumpy hour-and-twenty-minute ride to Oxford, the oldest university in the English-speaking world, was a lot rougher than some of our days at sea. As we approached Oxford, I saw the medieval spires, which looked like something out of a fairy tale. I was assigned to St. Edmund Hall, a college distinguished for its rowing prowess and undistinguished for its comfort. I soon discovered that student housing hadn't improved much in the several centuries since Oxford's founding. The rooms were monkishly bare. There was no central heating; if you wanted to go to the bathroom or bathe, you had to brave frigid morning temperatures and carry your clothes to a different building, where there were some rudimentary stalls and showers and not much hot water. Funnily enough, there were more plumbing 'luxuries' back on my family farm than in St. Edmund Hall, all of which compounded my feelings of loneliness and homesickness.

While I was engaged with my studies at Oxford, I met two individuals who became lifelong friends and important acquaintances for me when I later served on the Senate Foreign Relations Committee. One was from India, Montek Singh Ahluwalia, and the other was from Pakistan, Wasim Sajjad. (In those days, the United States was allocated thirty-two Rhodes Scholars—out of about ninety worldwide. In contrast, only two or three Rhodes Scholarships were awarded to students from India and Pakistan.) Meeting these two young men at such a young age was providential: they instilled in me a lifelong interest in the affairs of India and Pakistan, and all three of us played a leadership role in foreign policy in the 1980s and '90s for our respective governments.

As a traditional Sikh who wore a beard, moustache and turban, Montek stood out from the rest of us clean-shaven young men attending Oxford at the time. In contrast, Wasim was always very Western in his dress and demeanour. A consummate politician who was chairman of the Pakistani Senate and later served as interim President of Pakistan twice, Wasim was always all business. While we were friendly at Oxford, he later had to be careful not to be too amicable towards me in public because of the unpopularity of the Pressler Amendment in Pakistan. In fact, I once said to him while I was on a diplomatic mission to Pakistan, 'I know you have to be careful about being friendly with the devil.' (Since we are both no longer serving in public office, we can now warmly socialize at Rhodes Scholar reunions without any political restraints.)

Whereas Wasim and I have had a strained relationship because of my infamy in Pakistan, Montek and I have always been friends openly. He ended up rising to the top of the Indian civil service and then was deputy chairman of the country's Planning Commission from 2004 to 2014. An illustration of how he dominates policy in India came when the economic changes were called the 'Singh–Singh reforms' after Montek Singh Ahluwalia and Prime Minister Manmohan Singh. What an uncanny coincidence it is that the three of us—collegial peers then and mere students—would each, in one way or another, hold positions of leadership in our respective countries that would send us crashing together again decades later. At the time, my studies were fun and intriguing. But while we were all engaged in our intellectual pursuits in an academic cocoon, the threat of Vietnam was looming over my head.

12

Stirrings of War: Discussions on the Vietnam Draft

'If you decide not to go to Vietnam, it will mean that someone poorer and less able than you will have to go in your place. And knowing you, that will trouble your conscience for the rest of your life. So you might as well just go and do it.'

—Antoine Pressler

At Oxford, the students were collectively against the American war in Vietnam. To be in support of the war, or even silent on the subject, put you in an endangered minority among my Oxford peers. These young men opposed President Johnson's escalation of the war in Vietnam, but they hated Senator Barry Goldwater, the man that ran against Johnson, even more than the war. As a result, almost all of them were reluctant supporters of the President. I felt that many of these students were just mouthing leftist platitudes and giving the anti-communist Goldwater a bum rap.

At the time, my feelings about the Vietnam War were mixed. On the one hand, I believed Presidents Kennedy and Johnson when they said that America had to stand and fight for democracy in Vietnam. On the other, I had some doubts about the Secretary of Defense Robert McNamara's reports of progress. Much later in my life, when evidence of the White House's deceit became public, I realized that the American people had been duped, especially by President Johnson.

But what bothered me the most was that almost all the young Americans I was studying with in Europe did not seem to have pure motives in their anti-war sentiment. They seemed to be scheming to avoid military service. In my view, whether you agreed with the war or not, you had a duty to answer your country's call to serve. So I often found myself the odd man out, defending Senator Goldwater and President Johnson, when I only partially agreed with both men.

By the time I arrived at Oxford, student demonstrations against the United States had begun, and the depth of hatred for America distressed me. I was even more upset by the behaviour of some of my fellow Americans (including the Rhodes Scholars), who wholeheartedly joined in the hate-America binge. In our conversations, I came to the conclusion that what they really wanted to avoid was anything that might interrupt the upward trajectory of their privileged careers—especially military service. Had they come to Oxford to further their education and prepare themselves for a life of public service—as the Rhodes Scholarship founder envisioned for the scholarship's recipients? Or were they at Oxford to escape the draft and feather their own nests? I found it impossible to have a rational discussion with anyone wrapped in a cloak of self-righteous indignation about America's 'immoral' and 'wicked' foreign policy. As a result, I came to question the stated aims of some of my fellow American students at Oxford.

Looking back, I believe the ferocious battles that raged during the Vietnam War over the draft—battles that seemed magnified in the setting of a foreign university—created a fracture in the American psyche that has never healed. At least it's never completely healed in my own psyche.

Those battles often pitted the well-heeled elite—who found a multitude of ways to dodge the draft—against those of us who fulfilled our civic duty and served. It is hard to explain to the Indian reader how much this fissure divided our country at the time. The division between those who served and those who did not during this contentious war was visceral—and it persists to this day. The number of men who avoided the draft also created a shortage of draft-eligible men for the war effort. Those who could avoid service did. As a result, the government started to draft groups of wholly unqualified recruits—those who scored poorly on the mental and physical readiness tests. Officially called 'Project 100,000' by the Department of Defense, the programme was nicknamed 'McNamara's Morons'. It was Secretary of Defense Robert McNamara's idea and it populated the military services with developmentally disabled adults. McNamara defended the programme at the time as a way to 'salvage' and 'rehabilitate' these men. With low aptitudes, however, these recruits turned out to be sitting ducks on the battlefield. Their death toll was three times that of other combat soldiers. My friend and author Hamilton Gregory wrote a book about this tragedy in our military's history called *McNamara's Folly: The Use of Low-IQ Troops in the Vietnam War*.[1]

The elite of my generation argued that because the Vietnam War was 'immoral', it was honourable of them to resist the draft. In other words, they justified their decision on idealistic grounds. It is what I would call a 'noble' lie. This was an unconscious rationalization at best, and a complete cop-out at worst.

While they pursued their accelerated careers and rose to become leaders in their professions, others who were less well connected and with fewer resources went to Vietnam in their place. In short, with a tragic flaw in their reasoning and a distorted sense of values, this dishonesty infected an entire generation. I had respect for the very small number who were candid enough to say, 'I just plain don't want to serve. I don't want my career interrupted.' At least they admitted their true motivation. History has proved my suspicions to be true.

As soon as the draft was eliminated and the all-volunteer service was instituted, most of the anti-war movement vanished. To add insult to injury, avoiding the draft did not hurt the careers of many people— witness Presidents Bill Clinton and Donald Trump.

From my safe perch as a Rhodes Scholar at Oxford, I watched the Vietnam War rage on. I knew that I could probably prolong my student deferment and even stretch it out to the age of twenty-six, when I'd no longer be liable for the draft. The question for me was: what was the right thing to do? I had to confront the very basis of my idealism. And to do that, I had to speak with the man who had sown the seeds of it: my very modest, agrarian father.

A usually quiet, reserved man who kept his opinions to himself, he was surprisingly vocal about Vietnam. 'If you decide not to go to Vietnam,' Father said, 'it will mean that someone poorer and less able than you will have to go in your place. And knowing you, that will trouble your conscience for the rest of your life. So you might as well just go and do it.'

My father thought it would be a glorious thing if I became an army officer. He was 'old school' about military service and felt it was a civic duty of all Americans to serve if they could. He had not served in World War II because farmers were compelled to stay home and farm to alleviate the food shortage. The country needed its farmers during World War II, but my father always regretted his lack of service. He did not feel guilty, as he knew his job of farming was contributing to the overall 'war effort'. But I think he had a bit of a nagging feeling at the back of his mind that perhaps he could have done more.

So, when I was offered the opportunity to serve, he did not understand my internal debate. 'You mean,' he said in an incredulous tone, 'that you have a chance to become an officer in the United States Army and that you're actually thinking of turning it down? My God, son, you'll be the first officer in our family!'

In my father's eyes, being an army officer was worth a lot more than being a Rhodes Scholar. And despite our dinner table debates over farming methods and the divergent paths our lives had taken, I was no different from most sons. I longed to win my father's approval.

And so I told the warden of Rhodes House, E.T. Williams, that I was going to give up my draft exemption and join the army. Williams, who had served in World War II in the British Army, was delighted. 'Wonderful!' he said. 'You are the first and only Rhodes Scholar who has been willing to volunteer for Vietnam. I see a steady stream of them with complex plans to avoid the draft. If you want to leave early, I'll support you. Go and do the Vietnam military thing, and if you want to, you can come back to Oxford and do the second year at some future time. Whatever you decide, you will always be a Rhodes Scholar in good standing.'

My decision to join the military meant that I had to prepare for my diploma in public administration after only one year at Oxford. And that, in turn, meant I had to spend every waking hour in the Radcliffe Camera, an eighteenth-century architectural wonder that holds some 600,000 books and is the largest reading room of Oxford's main library, the Bodleian. There, I burnt the midnight oil to complete all the course work and exams in that first year and I subsequently submitted my thesis remotely from Vietnam. Unfortunately, I missed out on a lot of the social activities at Oxford.

Because of a childhood farm accident, when a heavy grain auger had fallen on me, I suffered from chronic back problems and almost did not pass the army's physical exam. You might say that this stammerer had to talk his way into uniform! That uniform was a big hit when I returned home to Humboldt after four months of basic training. My mother was so proud that she insisted I go around and visit all my relatives in uniform. I stood six-foot-three and weighed 165 pounds, and I must have looked like a scarecrow in my freshly pressed second lieutenant's uniform. I made the rounds to all my family and friends to say goodbye. I touched down in Vietnam in December 1965. When I stepped off the air-conditioned plane, I was immediately enveloped by the country's hot, dewy air. This was the rainy season, after all. It's a place where many Indians would feel right at home.

13

My Invisible Wounds from Vietnam

'One visit was to an extremely dangerous area . . . I afforded those officers who did not wish to continue [the chance] to drop out and about 40 percent did. Larry Pressler chose to continue the mission, for which he had volunteered . . . Larry was eligible for an award for that mission, but his modesty precluded his accepting any.'

—Senator Pressler's unit commander in Vietnam describing how the senator turned down a Purple Heart medal

As a newly minted second lieutenant on my first deployment to Vietnam, I was posted on the outskirts of Cần Thơ, the capital of Định Tường province and the largest city in the Mekong Delta, the rice basket of Vietnam. My unit's job was to provide military security along Highway 4 for the vital food supplies moving from the rice paddies and vegetable farms in the delta to the capital city of Saigon. Our encampment at Cần Thơ was surrounded by a deep defensive trench, which had been cleared of all trees by Agent Orange, the code name for the herbicides and defoliants used by the US military. It was later discovered that Agent Orange contained an extremely toxic dioxin compound that causes birth defects, mental disabilities, skin and respiratory disorders, and cancers. Years later, I tried unsuccessfully to get legislation passed that would have funded more Agent Orange research.

The Viet Cong (or 'VC'), the communist-led guerrilla force supported by North Vietnam, controlled the countryside at night, so we had to run our food convoys during the daytime. Many Vietnamese were reluctant to drive for us because we came under sniper fire from the VC. American troops ended up doing most of the driving. The snipers liked shooting at truck drivers, but they liked targeting American officers even more. I was always armed, but I still felt like a sitting duck. It was dangerous duty.

My work in Vietnam was in part agricultural and economic development in the provinces, coordinated with the United States Agency for International Development (USAID). President Lyndon Johnson said, 'We must win the hearts and minds of the Vietnamese people.' Doing this in a military uniform was very awkward. Even though I think that the United States' goals in Vietnam were honourable, development work of this type was somewhat resented because it was conducted by the military. Many of the locals did not trust our intentions and the VC viewed us as occupiers. I often wonder if some of the Indian population might similarly view foreigners coming in to build nuclear power plants as interlopers. Many parts of India are just as dangerous now as Vietnam was then. India is certainly not a war zone, but it does have indigenous insurgent groups that might cause problems in the implementation of the US–India nuclear agreement—just as the distrustful Vietnamese sometimes sympathized more with the VC than they did with us. It severely hampered our efforts.

On the way back to the delta region from Saigon, we transported agricultural supplies, farm equipment and small irrigation motor pumps. We distributed the pumps to farmers who were loyal to our cause. They were used for many things, including running small boats through the canals to transport goods and to irrigate the fields.

Farmers had to 'prove' they were not VC sympathizers in order to get this equipment.

Drawing from the economics expertise I had acquired at Oxford, I wrote a four-page report called 'The Distribution of Motor Pumps in Định Tường Province'. It was sent up the chain of command and was influential enough to get me transferred to the Military Assistance Command Vietnam (MACV) pacification programme at the army headquarters in Saigon to produce more of these types of reports. I soon realized that I had stumbled into the midst of a bitter debate between members of the State Department—who argued that the war was going badly—and the Pentagon, who argued just as vociferously that we were making progress.

One of the chief items in dispute was the amount of rice and produce that was getting through the roadblocks set up by the VC. On my own initiative, I went out and counted the number of vegetable trucks that were making it from Da Lat, a city in the Central Highlands north of Saigon. In my subsequent report, I noted that Vietnamese farmers had learnt how to bribe their way through the VC roadblocks, and that as a result, there was as much food reaching Saigon as there had been the year before. As a reward, I was sent to Da Lat, where I did a series of interviews with vegetable truckers. In my subsequent memo, titled 'Ruckus in a Radish Patch', I reported that, contrary to what the doomsayers in the State Department were saying, essential foodstuffs were in fact getting through to Saigon—a conclusion that added to my unpopularity among the foreign service types.

In late 1967, I contracted hepatitis and was sent to a military convalescent centre in South Vietnam. There, I experienced frightening nightmares. The events that triggered these nightmares had taken place earlier that year. At the time, the American news media was up in arms about the US military's accounting of enemy 'body counts'—or the number of enemy killed. Journalists charged that these counts were flagrantly inflated. To counter their negative stories, the South Vietnamese government instituted a body count verification programme to confirm the statistics. Teams of Vietnamese soldiers and some American advisers were dispatched into the field to provide eyewitness accounts. I accompanied one of these teams. What I saw during that mission was seared forever in my mind's eye: dozens of dead Vietnamese (it was impossible to tell whether they were VCs or civilians), their brains spilled out of their broken skulls, their teeth scattered on the blood-soaked ground. And worse—much, much worse.

The sights that met me at the convalescent centre were just as horrific as those on the battlefield. I saw soldiers and marines with empty eye sockets and half their faces blown away. Some of the men were in such horrible condition that they were kept strapped down and in induced comas until they could be evacuated to better-equipped military hospitals in Japan and the Philippines.

All of these encounters resulted in my having frequent flashbacks, which plague me to this day. I always thought that I must have been somewhat squeamish to feel such horror. But I have come to learn and accept that these feelings are a natural human reaction in men and women who go to war.

Spurred by producer Ken Burns's Public Broadcasting Service (PBS) documentary series on the American Civil War, I read an editorial in the *New York Times* called 'The Dead of Antietam'. The article, written in 1862, described the impact of a photography exhibit on the aftermath of the Battle of Antietam, which was on display in New York City at the time. The photographs of dead bodies and the battle scene, taken and assembled by the famous Civil War photographer Mathew Brady, were some of the most graphic war images ever displayed to the public—and they in part triggered anti-draft riots against President Lincoln in New York City. Visitors were shocked. This story justified my own horrific feelings.

Although I did not know it then, I was suffering from post-traumatic stress disorder (PTSD), an anxiety condition that used to be called 'battle fatigue' or 'shell shock'. While I was in Vietnam, the army awarded me a total of fifteen medals, including the Bronze Star and the Army Commendation Medal. Once, as we were making a helicopter landing with Vietnamese forces in the delta, several mortars detonated and my left hand was slightly injured. We were also under sniper fire. The commander, an army colonel, wanted to submit me for a Purple Heart medal.

Suffering a wound under enemy fire is the requirement for a Purple Heart. The colonel said I had qualified. But I declined because I had seen severely wounded soldiers who really deserved a Purple Heart and never received one. Wearing the Purple Heart for the rest of my life would have felt disingenuous. I saw the awarding of medals as haphazard; it depended entirely on who wrote you up and how much you pushed to be recognized. Also, I had seen men injured by friendly fire who did not receive the Purple Heart. I was turned off by the whole awards system.

More fundamentally, I was fast becoming disenchanted by the entire war. My rejection of the Purple Heart was a turning point in my feelings about the war and my feelings about life. From that point on, I never totally trusted government authority again.

14

A Lonely Vietnam Veteran at Harvard Law School

"'[There is] a very general discontent and unease in the student body and in the whole community." The war in Vietnam, he stated, is "a basic source of unhappiness and concern", and "a lot of the general unrest on campuses springs from valid concerns".'

—Harvard president Nathan M. Pusey, speaking in May 1969 about
the draft-related civil unrest on university campuses across the
United States and, specifically, in response to the student takeover
of the Harvard Administration building on 9 April 1969[1]

Until the Tet Offensive in early 1968, I thought we were winning the 'hearts and minds' of the Vietnamese people. I was young and idealistic enough to actually believe President Johnson's and Secretary of Defense McNamara's proclamations that we were going to be successful in Vietnam. I thought we were making a difference—trying our best to help the South Vietnamese build a democracy. Obviously, we were not. The Tet Offensive, which was North Vietnam's massive military campaign against the South Vietnamese and American forces and their allies over the nation's Tet holiday in January 1968, proved that our government's leaders had been lying to us all. Contrary to what they said, the North Vietnamese were not in retreat. Though we eventually regained the ground we lost during these surprise attacks, American morale suffered a devastating blow as a consequence. American public support for the war subsequently deteriorated.

The VC had control of the entire countryside and the loyalty of the common Vietnamese. We and our allies were only in control of a few cities. It became increasingly apparent that our economic development activities, which I strongly supported, were not making an iota of difference. The people just viewed us as occupiers. I came to the conclusion that many others have reached: that we cannot use ground forces or 'boots on the ground' for nation-building efforts. America's wars in Iraq and Afghanistan have proven that point again and again.

I also became convinced during that time that we cannot successfully influence civic development efforts unless we have a groundswell of deep and moral domestic support. During my work at MACV with USAID in Vietnam, the US government paid David Lilienthal, the former head of the Tennessee Valley Authority (TVA), to work with the South Vietnamese government on a project to build hydroelectric dams in the Mekong Delta—in an attempt to bring electricity to the region's population. I met Lilienthal during one of his visits to the region. My unit provided security for his team of advisers and I provided some assistance in some of his team's research. It was always my feeling, even though I was a lowly peon in the US Army, that no one was getting the support of the locals for this massive infrastructure project. None of the religious leaders, nor the local community elders, nor the farmers, nor the fishermen were involved in the deal. Millions of dollars were spent on consultants, studies, reports and plans to build these dams, but no effort was made to garner the support of the local population. In my opinion, the Vietnamese most likely saw the dams as a destruction of a revered natural resource. Later, the plans were abandoned by the United States and the dams were never built by the communists after the Vietnam War was over. Sounds familiar?

War protesters during that time assigned their anger over the war to the military members who served in Vietnam. It was not uncommon to hear stories of civilians jeering soldiers and sailors in public places in the US. I distinctly recall being advised not to wear my uniform in San Francisco, a hotbed for war protests. I was told I would perhaps be accosted or spit on—in fact, I was spit on in Madison, Wisconsin. Military service during that time frame became shameful. It took years for the rancour and acrimony in the United States over the Vietnam War to recede in memory.

Later, when I became one of the first Vietnam veterans to be elected to Congress, my combat experience actually bestowed on me a certain aura. Some of the very people who had heaped scorn on those who served in Vietnam began referring to us as valiant, even heroic. It seemed to me like an expiation of the guilt for those in Congress who had not served in Vietnam. But after seeing the horrors of war—and the amazing bravery of so many ordinary Americans—I felt that I was an improbable hero, and I looked for an opportunity to say so. The chance came one day when my fellow senator and Vietnam veteran John Kerry announced in a meeting, 'I am joined by a genuine hero of the Vietnam War, Larry Pressler.' I jumped out of my chair and, in a stammer-free voice, proclaimed: 'No, not a hero, not a hero. I just did my job.' I considered it part of my civic duty.

While still in Vietnam, I took the LSAT, the law school admission test, and received word that my scores were good enough to earn me a place at Harvard Law School. In the summer of 1968, I returned to the States, where I separated from the military at the old Oakland Army Base in the San Francisco Bay area. Once again a civilian, I set off in a used Volkswagen Beetle and drove across the country to Boston.

During my years at Harvard Law School, from 1968 to 1971, Harvard was a breeding ground for resistance to the Vietnam War. Students published dozens of leaflets on how to avoid the draft; they burnt their draft cards, held sit-ins, boycotted classes, and organized non-stop demonstrations. There was a drinking and marijuana culture associated with student life there that I did not like. I was working part-time, and was intensely busy with my studies, as we had classes six days a week.

As one of the very few Vietnam veterans in my class of 550 law students, I was lonely. My service in Vietnam was a black mark against me, and some of the more radical students viewed me as an accomplice to a crime. Even the faculty exhibited some hostility, as some joined their students in anti-war protests. They all assumed that I was pro-war because I had served, while in reality I had come to believe that Vietnam was a lost cause. In short, my service in Vietnam had seared my soul and instilled in me a feeling of responsibility to ensure that our nation never again engages in needless foreign wars.

The quality of the education I was receiving at Harvard Law School was top-notch. Upon graduation, I was offered a job at Cravath, Swaine & Moore, the second-oldest law firm in America and one of the most prestigious in the world. Although tempted to accept it—a career with a top law firm like Cravath could be financially very lucrative, and I was in debt—I turned it down.

Instead, I opted for a much lower-paying public service job as a foreign service officer with the State Department. Once again the Catholic school nuns' influence, the advice from my University of South Dakota professors, and my father's encouragement to volunteer in the military all led me to pursue a career in public service. And although I had left Vietnam disillusioned, convinced that it was foolhardy for the United States to intervene militarily in unfamiliar far-off lands, I still believed that America had a moral duty to help developing countries provide a decent life for their people.

Soon after I was mustered into the State Department, I was sent to Switzerland to work on negotiations regarding the General Agreement on Tariffs and Trade (GATT). For the next three years, I shuttled between Geneva and Washington, playing a small part in deciphering the intricacies of global trade. The work was demanding and interesting, but I did not feel that I was fulfilling a larger public service role.

So, in the spring of 1974, I made an audacious decision that was fraught with risk, but one I felt a calling to do. Against the advice of friends and family—and with no experience in electoral politics, no organization, no support from the state Republican Party, and practically no money—I resigned from my stable job in the foreign service, cashed in my retirement fund and my small savings account, purchased a 1969 Oldsmobile sedan for $760, and drove back home to South Dakota to launch a nascent campaign for the US House of Representatives from my mother's kitchen.

15

Getting Elected to the House and Senate

'Larry Pressler is predictably unpredictable.'

—Former Wyoming Republican senator Alan Simpson[1]

When I arrived home in the farming community of Humboldt in 1974 to begin the race for South Dakota's first congressional district, I was thirty-two years old. People asked me, 'Why don't you run for the state legislature?' or 'Why don't you wait a few years?' What they really meant to say was, 'Have you completely lost your mind?'

So, what made me do it?

In the United States, as in India, running for elected office is a brutal experience. My observation is that those who stand for Parliament in India suffer even greater slings than those who run for the House of Representatives in the United States. And today, the Internet has opened up a whole new way of discrediting political candidates. I subjected myself to much abuse when I decided to run for Congress in 1974 and, later, when I ran for the US Senate five different times, winning three six-year terms. I had to build a tough exterior to withstand all the verbal abuse, which was hard for someone as naturally sensitive as I am. But it was nothing compared to the online slander political candidates receive today.

On the other hand, constitutionally in both India and the United States, those who hold elected public office are given the opportunity to make some of the basic decisions for society. Appointed officials may come from more polished backgrounds and seem to get the most credit, but the individual who has gone through the electoral process holds the most power and the most hope for carrying out reform in the future.

Around the time I made my decision to run for the House in 1974, a grand jury had named President Richard Nixon as an unindicted co-conspirator in the Watergate scandal. Watergate refers to a major political scandal in the early 1970s that involved the Nixon administration and his personal involvement in a cover-up of a burglary at the Democratic National Party's National Committee headquarters in 1972. Investigations into this burglary slowly revealed a multitude of illegal activities personally ordered by President Nixon and a conspiracy to hide them.

Watching the scandal unfold from my comfortable State Department post, I was disgusted by the whole sordid Watergate mess. I had met President Nixon on a social basis on a number of occasions because his daughter Tricia had married my close friend and Harvard Law School classmate, Edward Cox. I had attended the White House engagement party and served as a groomsman at their wedding in 1971. I admired Nixon for his brilliant foreign policy decisions, especially his opening up to China and his historic meeting with Mrs Gandhi. But now, in the wake of Nixon's national scandal, I thought it would be best for the country and his family if the seriously compromised President resigned. It was time for people of strong will and good conscience to band together and help clean up Washington.

Although I gave myself only a slim chance of winning a seat in the House, I thought it would be worth the effort if I could inject new ideas into the campaign and do something to heal my country after the wounds of Watergate, which had taken a devastating toll on the nation's morale.

In 1974 my platform was based on five reform principles. I also typed up on my old portable typewriter simple, one-page issue statements on everything from small business and education, to helping family farmers and senior citizens. I made clear that I was strongly supportive of free trade legislation, as I believed in lowering tariffs and removing restrictions on imports and exports. This was controversial with the powerful unions in my congressional district. Pledging to serve a limited period of time, not to accept any special-interest money, and not to take honoraria, I vowed to try to be a more honest kind of congressman. A desire to serve God and my fellow men drove me.

This first race was an uphill climb. I would wake up before sunrise every day and head to the factory gates, the coffee shops and the hospitals to greet workers as they arrived at work. It was a really good way to meet lots of voters and get to know them and their needs. I would try to shake at least 500 hands every day, which means one hand per minute for eight hours straight. I estimate that I shook at least 300 hands daily for about eighty days during the campaign.

Although I was born and bred in South Dakota, Republican leaders saw me as an interloper. In the far-flung precincts of South Dakota, my credentials as a Rhodes Scholar, Harvard Law School graduate and foreign service officer made me look like an elitist outsider.

Yet, I made a strong impression on the voters during a primary debate. I declared that if elected to the House of Representatives, I would vote to give President Nixon a trial in the Senate. 'It is the only way to get at the truth about Watergate,' I said. This was a bit awkward, because many people knew I was a personal friend of Nixon's daughter. I emphasized that I liked President Nixon personally, but I was afraid that he had gotten into a situation that could only be resolved by a trial in the Senate. When the votes in the Republican primary were counted, I managed to win the whirlwind three-way race by a narrow margin. Voters said they liked my refreshing openness, my farm boy-to-Rhodes Scholar story, and my positive campaign.

God clearly had plans for me. As the General Election approached, I started to wonder if I had bitten off more than I could chew. 'I don't have any organization or money,' I complained to Dr Farber, my old political science professor and mentor at the University of South Dakota. 'Well,' Doc Farber replied, 'did you have any of these things in the primary?' I didn't.

My father thought I was in over my head and that I was setting myself up for a big disappointment. My mother volunteered to help out and soon became an indispensable contributor to my effort and my de facto campaign manager. She wrote thank-you letters to people who contributed money. She answered my phone calls. Gradually, this quiet, shy farm woman who hadn't graduated from high school, came out of her shell and began to enjoy the whirl of political life.

The campaign was not without its humorous moments. At one point, people complained they had received thank-you letters from my mother in someone else's handwriting. I immediately 'investigated' my mother, and discovered that she had fallen so far behind in her letter writing that she had indeed asked neighbouring women to help her out by signing her letters. I 'fessed up to this mini-scandal and it quickly went away. But most of the time, I was running scared. This campaign was a fearless and bold move, but the decision was just a continuation of a trend throughout my life: I have always opted for public service. And like previous bold moves in my life, it paid off. My bootstrap campaign and unorthodox methods of reaching out to voters was proving to be the perfect formula for electoral success.

On 8 August 1974, as I was sweating around the state going from one campaign event to another in my old jalopy, I heard on the car radio near Freeman, South Dakota, that President Nixon had resigned. The Watergate scandal had finally taken its full toll and it was stunning news for the entire country. Issuing a campaign statement later that day, I stated that the move was a good thing for the country and that our nation should move forward with the then vice president, Gerald Ford. In my heart, I really didn't know what was going to happen—for my campaign or for the country.

In the end, I scored a stunning upset victory and won the election by 14,927 votes, one of very few Republicans in America who unseated an incumbent Democrat in the House that year. This followed President Ford's very unpopular September pardon of former President Nixon. On the last day of the campaign, before the vote, I spent the balance of my modest funds on the following ad in South Dakota newspapers:

THANKS. I want to thank you, the people of South Dakota, for responding so well to my grassroots campaign. Together, we have done something unique in our time. We have successfully run a congressional campaign without any special-interest money. We have emphasized the good in our system. We have not been negative. More important, we have proved that politics can be positive, fun, issue-oriented, and close to the people.

On 3 January 1975, when the day finally arrived for me to take my seat in the US House of Representatives, I put on my best suit—a loud, plaid, off-the-rack number that plainly marked me as someone from the sticks—and entered the ornate House chamber. My parents, my sisters, Beverly and Sandra, my brother, Dan, my brother-in-law, Roger, and my aunt, Annie, watched from the packed visitors' gallery as I was sworn in. It was an emotional moment for them and for me.

Despite the wise advice I received from many political 'grey beards', I managed to make some serious mistakes during my first forays in Congress. During the election campaign, *Time* magazine had referred to me as a 'McGovern Republican' because I was against the Vietnam War—even though I was a combat veteran. They were comparing me with the liberal Democrat and senior senator from my state, George McGovern. For my part, I defined myself as an

Independent (with a capital 'I'), and was proud of it. I was used to speaking my mind and forging my own path. As one of very few Republicans to defeat an incumbent Democrat that year, I had a bit of hubris entering office.

The ornery midwesterner in me believed that I could operate with impunity as an Independent within my party's caucus. I soon learnt otherwise. Whatever disagreements I had with my sweet-natured father did not prepare me for dealing with 434 other members of the House of Representatives—hardened politicians who were driven by power and ambition and who gave no quarter. If I was going to carve out a successful career in Congress, I knew I had to adapt. I was no longer in 4-H—I was on the national stage now!

In the wake of my surprising 1974 election victory against an entrenched incumbent, I was eager to settle down to business in Congress. But that proved harder than I expected. Everyone was distracted by the national upheaval that was taking place at the other end of Pennsylvania Avenue, in the White House.

By early 1975, the war in Vietnam was reaching its deathly climax. Though I was now an opponent of the Vietnam War, I could not help but feel sorry for my party's man in the White House. President Ford naturally wanted to avoid becoming the first President to preside over the defeat of the United States in a foreign war.

By the end of April, the die was cast: communist forces were at the gates of Saigon, and President Ford gave the order for Operation Frequent Wind—a helicopter evacuation from the roof of the United States Embassy. I was despondent over the heart-rending photos of the American flag being taken down from the embassy. The awful consequences of America's folly in Vietnam hit me personally like a ton of bricks, and I questioned even more the value of the two years I had spent in the military.

I was warned that, as a public figure now, I should be guarded and not reveal my true political feelings about the Vietnam War. Ironically, when I later served in the Senate, I found myself debating the efficacy of military intervention with a group of defence hawks who had never served in the military, like President Bill Clinton and Vice President Dick Cheney.

In an effort to move on, President Ford declared, 'The war in Vietnam is receding into history.' However, as a Vietnam combat veteran, I knew that Ford was indulging in wishful thinking. The war overseas might be over, but the havoc it had wrought in our nation would not go away for a long, long time, nor would it stop torturing me personally. I was then and still am permanently wounded by that war, as is my whole generation.

But at the time, I had to focus on my new job. And I had a steep learning curve. Many people think serving in Congress is just giving speeches in Washington, but servicing constituents is tough, tedious and grinding work. To help me handle the load, I had three service offices in South Dakota, in addition to my Washington operation. Typically, I'd fly home to South Dakota on Thursday night and attend a weekend full of parades (riding my John Deere tractor), 'listening meetings' with constituents, and Sunday church services at which I'd frequently be asked to speak. In between, I hosted TV and radio infomercials urging people to get in touch with me about their problems (social security, farm subsidies, visa problems, small business loans, military service academy nominations, and so on). I found the job of helping people satisfying. Day in and day out, I focused on the casework, which not only helped my constituents, but also helped me understand the need and demand for certain policy changes and legislation. I was reminded on a daily basis why I had been sent to Washington.

A lot of people in the media today like to talk about the good old days when courtesy, conviviality and bipartisanship reigned in the House. But speak to anyone who was actually there in the 1970s and they will tell you that those memories are a figment of the imagination. Congress then was nowhere near as partisan as Congress is today, but the Democrats ruled the roost in the 1970s. The Republicans were just as partisan—but they simply didn't have the power. I was a soft-edged, gentle guy from a rural state that was very far away from

Washington, both geographically and culturally. I was a bit like a fish
out of water—an outlier and independent even then.

Nonetheless, I managed to rack up some successes and learnt how
to become an effective legislator. Among other things, I sponsored
successful amendments to the Older Americans Act of 1977, including
Meals on Wheels for elderly shut-ins and matching funds for
congregate housing. This idea allowed the elderly to live in individual
apartments with common dining areas. It maintained a degree of
independence for the elderly, and cost the government significantly
less than full-time nursing care. I sponsored the Vocational Education
Act, and the establishment of junior colleges for Native American
reservations throughout the country. I also successfully negotiated
three federally funded, major water pipelines through my state: the
WEB Water pipeline, the Oglala-Sioux pipeline, and the Lewis and
Clark pipeline. Adequate drinking water has always been a serious
problem in my state, especially on the reservations, so these pipelines
were very important. But they were also controversial, because many
landowners did not want a pipeline running through their property. In
order to educate the population about the benefits of these pipelines, I
engaged in a statewide speaking campaign and distributed educational
newsletters to my constituents. I had learnt in Vietnam that popular
support is critical to the success of infrastructure programmes.

The dedicated and tireless casework required to bring these
projects to completion led to public opinion polls indicating that I
was the most popular politician in South Dakota. I started receiving
calls from around the state, encouraging me to make a run for the
Senate. I stepped up the pace of my listening meetings to determine if
there was adequate support across the state. During the August recess
of 1977, I held sixty of them—not only in my congressional district,
but also in the western part of the state. In effect, I was laying the
groundwork for a statewide campaign.

In early 1978, I held a press conference at my family farm in
Humboldt. My mother was in charge of greeting everyone, and
my father sat there in his overalls and listened to me announce my

candidacy for the Senate. He had been diagnosed with Alzheimer's and was slowly drifting into the depths of the disease. I wondered what he thought of this new step that I had taken.

Once again manna rained down from heaven: 1978 turned out to be a Republican year, and I won the race with 68 per cent of the vote, a state record for a Senate race. In January 1979, my colleague, Democratic senator George McGovern, escorted me down the aisle to the well of the Senate, where I was sworn in as the first Vietnam War veteran to be elected to the Senate and the twenty-second senator from South Dakota since it had achieved statehood. It is a tradition in the Senate that a senior senator walk a junior senator from his or her state to the swearing-in ceremony.

George was the hero of the Democratic Party's far-left wing. I was a moderate conservative with a streak of unpredictability. As senators, George and I represented very different faces of South Dakota. He was a decorated World War II combat aviator, a B-24 pilot who had risen to national prominence as the leader of his party's anti–Vietnam War wing. In contrast, I was a Vietnam veteran who had become disenchanted with our country's military adventures. George had lost the 1972 presidential election to my friend, Richard Nixon, in the second-biggest landslide in American history. I was a moderate conservative who had won a seat in the Senate without the wholehearted support of the hard-core conservatives who increasingly controlled the Republican Party.

Despite our political differences, George and I genuinely liked each other. At age fifty-six, George had been a senator for sixteen years. He knew his way around the Senate, and he was a decent guy who said what he believed and believed what he said. The country might have been at a conservative tipping point in 1979, but George McGovern remained true to his liberal principles. I respected him for that even if we did not always agree.

At the young age of thirty-six, I was now stepping on to an even bigger and more influential role as a United States senator. I relished the opportunity to serve my country and my South Dakota constituents. But I was still a bit naïve about how Washington worked and I had not yet come face-to-face with the full force of the Octopus. I had my first, up close and personal wrestle with it just a few months later.

16

The 'ABSCAM' Scandal

'. . . Sen. Larry Pressler tells the undercover agent, in effect, to take
their sting and stick it.'

—*Washington Post*, in its front-page story
about ABSCAM on 4 February 1980[1]

In 1979, a group of Vietnam veterans recruited me to become a
candidate for President of the United States. My platform was
based principally on how we could improve the treatment of this
beleaguered constituency—an issue that was near and dear to my
heart. My campaign generated much enthusiasm among fellow
Vietnam veterans and that energized me. But running a national
campaign for the presidency of the United States was exhausting. I
gave speeches in more than thirty states and I had to raise money—
lots of money—from people I did not know. It was very different
from politics in my home state of South Dakota, where I knew
everyone. I had few deep-pocketed supporters. Therefore, when one
of my young and enthusiastic volunteers informed me that three
political action committees were eager to meet me and talk about

contributing to my campaign, I agreed to visit them at their various locations. In retrospect, it was probably too good to be true.

I vividly recall the events of that day. For one of the meetings, we drove to a two-storey red-brick colonial home on the fashionable W Street in the tony Washington neighbourhood of Georgetown. Inside, the house was furnished with exquisite antiques, elegant chandeliers, and, as I would later learn, a battery of hidden television cameras and microphones. Unwittingly, my inexperienced volunteer had led me into a hornet's nest—the most elaborate undercover sting operation ever launched by the FBI.

It was code-named 'ABSCAM'—short for 'Arab scam'—and it involved months of hard work by more than one hundred FBI agents in an extensive series of hoaxes and disguises. One of the FBI imposters I met that day was a leathery-skinned man who appeared to be from the Middle East. He told me that he represented a prominent sheikh who was seeking entry to the United States for himself and a number of his associates. This sheikh needed special bills passed by Congress in order to avoid the usual immigration procedures.

Growing suspicious, I asked the 'sheikh's' representative about his PAC.

'What's a PAC?' he said with a straight face.

He had never heard of a PAC, but offered to give me $50,000 if I would play ball.

'We want to invest in your state, but we don't want to do it under our name,' he said. 'We want to do it in somebody else's name.'

At that moment, I responded very clearly (as I later saw my words verbatim on videotape), 'Wait a minute!' I said. 'What you are suggesting may be illegal. It would not be proper for me to do anything in return for a campaign contribution, so I would not make any promises.'

It was not until a couple of months later, when the ABSCAM story burst on to the front pages of American newspapers, that I learnt the full scope of the FBI sting.

Seven members of the House of Representatives, two dozen state and local officials and their corrupt cronies, and another US senator had also visited the 'sheikh's' representative, but they had agreed to perform special favours in return for bribes. Many were ultimately indicted and sent to jail. It turned out that I was the only public official who had flatly refused to take the bait.

The 1987 Congressional Quarterly's book *Politics in America— The 100th Congress* described the incident this way:

> But the presidential campaign did give Pressler a round of priceless national attention. Late in 1979, FBI agents posing as Arab sheikhs invited him to a Georgetown house to offer him a bribe, knowing that he badly needed money for his presidential effort. It was part of the ABSCAM corruption probe. Pressler refused to have anything to do with the offer, and stormed out of the meeting. It briefly made him a minor hero.[2]

The secretly recorded ABSCAM videotapes were played on national television, and for a time I was hailed as a hero. Veteran news anchor Walter Cronkite singled me out for praise on the *CBS Evening News*. Syndicated cartoonist Jim Berry drew a caricature of me being greeted by the Greek philosopher Diogenes, who famously carried a lantern throughout the ancient world searching for an honest man. 'SENATOR PRESSLER?' read the caption under Berry's cartoon. 'I AM DIOGENES. I'VE BEEN LOOKING FOR YOU.'

The tributes continued to pile up. My former professor Alan Dershowitz used me as an exemplar of civic virtue in his Harvard Law School class. Many law students have asked me, 'How did you say just the right thing? Where did that come from? You must have learnt that at Harvard Law School or when you were a Rhodes Scholar at Oxford.'

'No,' I always reply. 'My values came from my hardscrabble life on a midwestern farm and the moral and spiritual guidance of my parents.'

Judge George C. Pratt, who reviewed the ABSCAM cases when they came up for appeal, declared:

> Pressler, particularly, acted as citizens have a right to expect their elected representatives to act. He showed a clear awareness of the line between proper and improper conduct, and despite his confessed need for campaign money, and despite the additional attractiveness to him of the payment offered, he nevertheless refused to cross into impropriety.[3]

Later, when the bipartisan Senate Select Committee on Ethics reviewed my involvement in ABSCAM, it sent me a letter stating that my rejection of the ABSCAM scheme was 'immediate, forthright and unequivocal. . . . In this test of integrity, your action upheld the honor of the United States Senate.'

Let me say that both India and the United States have some very corrupt politicians. Money seems to drive politics in both countries. In the United States, we have had many campaign-finance reform initiatives since ABSCAM, so our campaign contributions are usually fulfilled by cheque, not cash. This enables the transactions to be traced and reported. Back in the 1970s, however, politics was still the Wild West. Suitcases of cash and bribes were rampant at the time, as they are in India today.

In spite of all the accolades I received during the ABSCAM scandal, I did not feel like a hero. On the contrary, I was deeply embarrassed by the attention I received. After all, where I come from, South Dakota, your neighbours expect you to do the right thing, and they don't pat you on the back just for being a decent guy.

Judge Pratt's ruling is still the prevalent law on all types of entrapment cases. Entrapment policy always cites the 'Pressler standard' that almost every law student in the world reads. It is very simple: you can turn down a bribe. You can just say 'no'. Sometimes in life, one event can define you—and that event was a defining moment of my career.

In the wake of ABSCAM, I could not help but wonder: what has America come to when turning down an illegal bribe is considered a heroic act? In 1979, the arms of the Octopus were longer than I knew. That truth would only become apparent to me as I began to travel farther into the international arena, when I became involved in drafting and promoting the Pressler Amendment.

17

The Making of the Pressler Amendment

'I've only heard one opinion on reducing nuclear weapons—everyone else wants limited increases. Why on earth don't we accept Senator Pressler's view?'

—President Ronald Reagan in 1982[1]

For the first two years of my first Senate term, the Democrats controlled the Senate. Our Republican leader, Howard Baker, a moderate senator from Tennessee who had gained national attention for his integrity during the Senate Watergate hearings, skilfully juggled the moderate and conservative wings of our party and made sure that plump committee assignments were distributed fairly.

I was placed on the Commerce, Science and Transportation Committee, as well as the Foreign Relations, Small Business, and Budget Committees, which made for a heavy workload. I would sometimes have three or four committee meetings simultaneously, which meant that on most mornings I scrambled from one Senate building to another. Politicians who serve on the national level must have the mental tenacity to become experts on many subjects. An early-morning committee meeting might entail discussing budget deficits, only to be followed by another recommending a bill to improve the nation's ports and harbours. After lunch, another meeting might be held to discuss small business taxes, only to be followed by another before dinner to debate nuclear non-proliferation. I usually would have done a fair amount of homework the night before. A professional staffer would meet me as I left one committee hearing and would brief me on the next meeting as I walked through the underground tunnels that connect all the Senate and House office buildings with the US Capitol. It was both exhilarating and exhausting work.

As the first Vietnam veteran elected to the US Senate, and for several years the only one, I frequently questioned the size and influence of the Octopus. I also doubted the wisdom of spending hundreds of billions of dollars to keep huge phalanxes of fighting forces overseas. I believed we had to reduce the number of foreign military bases, including those in Europe. I opposed committing American ground troops to Asia and the Middle East. My stand on these issues put me at odds with members of both parties who were trying to prove their military mettle by advancing an aggressive foreign policy that included many, many military engagements overseas.

I was never very active on the social issues. I was more of a fiscal Republican, interested in economic growth, stimulating investment and new jobs through wise taxation policies. This sense of priorities boils down to the key question of what makes America the great nation it is. In my opinion, it is great because it has a strong economy and provides opportunities for its citizens to work hard and earn a good living. Its greatness does not hinge on the social issues that have become so divisive, such as whether or not abortion or prayer in public schools should be legal or illegal. While these vexing questions have their place in public debates, they are not the sine qua non for world leadership or historical greatness. For the Republican Party, an overemphasis on these issues tends to turn away moderates and independents.

However, I did not hesitate to vote against conservatives when I felt strongly about an issue. I co-sponsored the Equal Rights Amendment Bill for women, and I voted with moderates and liberals on arms control. I felt strongly that we needed to do more to slow the pace of the nuclear arms race. I questioned many of the agricultural subsidies that were intended for small farmers, but somehow ended up in the pockets of the larger, more corporate farmers. I feel my political philosophy was really much more like parts of the Libertarian Party. This political party's platform promotes civil liberties, laissez-faire capitalism, the abolition of the welfare state and the free use of drugs. I agree with Libertarians on the issues of economic and foreign policy, who advocate limited military intervention and offers a wide latitude for free trade.

Riding on Reagan's coat-tails during the 1980 election, the Republicans gained a majority in the Senate for the first time since the 1950s. Democrats reacted adversely to losing control of the chamber, while Republicans were eager to flex their new political muscle and carry out their ideas. The once genteel and collegial Senate began to descend into bitter partisan rancour. Leading Democratic senators such as Robert Byrd of West Virginia reacted particularly bitterly as they had to give up leadership positions and committee chairmanships that they thought they held almost by birthright. What created even greater tension were the ideological battles that broke out within both political parties.

There was a fight on the Foreign Relations Committee between Senator Charles Percy, a moderate Republican from the midwestern state of Illinois, and Senator Jesse Helms, a conservative Republican from the southern state of North Carolina, over who should be the head of the Arms Control Subcommittee. As often happens in the Senate when two powerful senators with substantial seniority spar over a choice chairmanship, the job fell to someone who was newer and not as well known—in this case, me. It was a neutral compromise.

When I was named the chairman of this powerful committee after Senators Percy and Helms had locked horns over it, I had to quickly make myself an expert on the subject. The truth was that either Percy or Helms would have taken it, but they had such disdain for each other that they would rather let me have it than either one of them. I always tried to maintain a pleasant friendship with all senators, at least as much as I could, and I was not the confrontational type. This sometimes led to the assessment that I was a pushover and forced me to toughen up in the end, but I did have a reputation as a 'nice guy'—sometimes too nice for my own good. The other Republicans on the Foreign Relations Committee already had chairmanships of subcommittees and were not interested in the Arms Control Subcommittee. So, it was mine to run.

Later, Republican senator Sam Hayakawa from California, one of my best personal friends in the Senate, saw me on the Senate floor and asked, 'Larry, how did you pull that off and become the chairman of the Arms Control Subcommittee as a freshman senator?' I replied, 'It took real talent, Sam—I just stood there and smiled!'

For the Indian reader to understand how the US Senate works, it is important to know that jealousy plays a large role. In fact, I would argue that it is one of the most powerful factors in American politics today (aside from money!). The jealousy that exists among members of Congress results in constant jockeying for power. I got my major committee assignment because two senior senators were jealous of each other. Indeed, jealousy is the reason many of the elected leadership positions in the Senate are held by legislators from smaller states. (Look at the examples of Democratic senator Tom Daschle from South Dakota, Republican senator Trent Lott from Mississippi, Republican senator Bob Dole from Kansas, and Democratic senator Harry Reid from Nevada. All represented small states and served as Senate Majority or Minority Leaders.)

The Senate rarely elects a senator for a leadership position from a larger state like Texas or California or Florida because its representatives have larger constituencies and are considered to be potential candidates for President. The small-state senators are jealous of the big-state senators. It seems childish for politicians to behave this way. The most qualified person should hold the job. But this jealousy is not unique to American politics. Indeed, I think the personal jealousy between Jawaharlal Nehru and Muhammad Ali Jinnah played a role in the formation of Pakistan.

My case back home for being on the Senate Foreign Relations Committee was that most South Dakota products (wheat, especially) were sold overseas, and our state needed a voice in international trade. But, for my constituents, arms control and nuclear non-proliferation were only of interest in South Dakota's university towns, where the student population was studying international relations and foreign policy as a topic of academic debate. Most of the population in my state did not really see how my leadership role on arms control benefited them. One sarcastic jokester from South Dakota commented on my becoming chairman of the Arms Control Subcommittee: 'Out here we consider arms control a good, steady aim!!!'

Everybody says they want a safer world with fewer nuclear weapons. However, my friends warned me that it was hard to convert anything on the Foreign Relations Committee into votes back home. At the time, the Foreign Relations Committee was known as a 'political graveyard' because so many of its members had later been defeated at the polls. The last two chairmen, Arkansas Democratic senator J. William Fulbright and Idaho Democratic Senator Frank Church, had been defeated in earlier elections, with Church's illustrious twenty-four-year career ending in a 1980 election loss. New York senator Jacob Javits, a ranking Republican on the committee who had served four terms, lost a 1980 Republican primary. Senator Percy, who chaired the committee starting in 1981, lost his 1984 re-election bid after three terms in the Senate.

Constituents from any state want to know what 'bacon' a senator brings home. By serving on the Commerce, Science and Transportation Committee, I could get some highway, rail, aviation and small business projects funded for my state. But the Foreign Relations Committee really has no bacon to bring home directly—it is a national interest committee. Had I instead chosen the Agriculture

Committee, my constituents would have appreciated it more as I could have advocated for more agricultural subsidies.

This attitude represents an ethical problem for the general public about how they view their representatives in Congress. I feel strongly that we must return to a time when congressmen and senators were rewarded for acting in the general public good and national interest and not just for the federal dollars they could bring back to their state. Upon being elected, a US senator is supposed to be a senator for all the states, not just his or her home state. The same is also true for a congressman. The public should not expect their elected representatives to just grab every single dollar for their home district. That is unethical thinking.

I took on the job because I thought it was the right thing to do and it gave me a chance to serve in a whole new and much bigger arena. But I realized that I was probably causing myself some political problems back home in South Dakota—especially when it would be time for re-election a few years later.

In any event, I had my own subcommittee to chair and was off and running in the arms control world. I began to attend all sorts of disarmament and arms control treaty talks in Russia and in Washington. I travelled to Moscow for a high-level and much-publicized meeting with Ambassador Victor Karpov, the deputy Soviet foreign minister at the time. I was frequently interviewed on TV about upcoming arms talks and whether or not the Senate might ratify an arms control treaty with the Russians.

How did I become engaged with India and Pakistan and nuclear non-proliferation? I was always interested in the issue of non-proliferation and my application to the Rhodes Scholarship programme in 1964 stated that I wanted to be a foreign service officer specializing on this issue.

In addition, my relationships with Wasim Sajjad and Montek Singh Ahluwalia allowed me to cultivate close contacts in the Pakistani and Indian governments. Over time, I also became a friend of Benazir Bhutto, who had also studied at Oxford University. I was in regular

touch with her until her assassination in 2007. I also saw her in her
various stints as prime minister of Pakistan.

Back in 1977, while still a congressman, I supported legislation
to apply pressure on Pakistan to stop it from building a nuclear
bomb. Several members of Congress, including Missouri Democratic
senator Stuart Symington, had become increasingly concerned about
Pakistan's quest for nuclear capability and the country's denial of
the critical role the scientist Dr Abdul Qadeer Khan was playing
in developing its nuclear programme. In an attempt to prevent the
transfer of nuclear materials and technology, Senators Glenn and
Symington had sponsored and passed the Symington Amendment
just a year before, in 1976. This amendment to the 1961 Foreign
Assistance Act banned all US economic and military assistance to any
country that was delivering or receiving, acquiring or transferring
nuclear enrichment technology when the country was not complying
with IAEA regulations and inspections. A year later, the Glenn
Amendment added more language to the Symington Amendment,
imposing sanctions on any country that acquires or transfers nuclear
reprocessing technology or explodes or transfers a nuclear device.
These amendments were clearly directed at Pakistan and were
intended to close any loophole that Pakistan, the ISI or the Octopus
tried to find.

The Glenn–Symington Amendment was tested two years later
when President Jimmy Carter received solid intelligence reports that
Pakistan was continuing its nuclear weapons development programme
at a facility in Kahuta, outside Islamabad. In April 1979, he enforced
the amendment and cut off all military aid, bringing the issue to a
head. But that did not stop Pakistan from continuing its furtive efforts
to develop a nuclear bomb. Then the Carter administration decided
to provide F-16 jet fighter aircraft to Pakistan. President Carter
was somehow convinced that providing the Pakistani government
conventional arms would deter it from pursuing a nuclear weapons
programme. In other words, the United States justified renewed military
aid to Pakistan as an instrument of the nuclear non-proliferation

Courtesy White House

Fay Craig (centre) and I (right) were two 4-H members—selected from
2.3 million 4-Hers from around the country—to present the '1963 4-H Report
to the Nation' to President Kennedy in the White House Oval Office. Tragically,
Kennedy was assassinated just a few months later.

Courtesy Larry Pressler

As a lieutenant in the US Army in Vietnam in 1967–68,
I found wearing a helmet in the Vietnam heat and humidity miserable!

I continued to meet with Richard Nixon throughout his life.
I thought he had an amazing grasp of international affairs.

President Ronald Reagan and I became personal friends over our discussions
of my father's Alzheimer's disease.

I met President Reagan several times in the Oval Office with his Cabinet foreign policy team, including this meeting in September 1982. From left to right: Secretary of State James Baker, President Ronald Reagan, Vice President George Bush, Senator Larry Pressler, Deputy Secretary of State Ken Dam and National Security Advisor William Clark.

I was honoured to meet Queen Elizabeth on several occasions. I admire the United Kingdom's parliamentary tradition, a tradition that India holds close. Both India and the United States are 'children' of the United Kingdom.

I demonstrated my independent streak when I first visited Cuban President Fidel Castro in Havana in 1991, a time when few other politicians and businesses dared.

I had the chance to meet with Indian Prime Minister Rajiv Gandhi on several occasions. Tragically, he, like President Kennedy, was assassinated shortly after.

This negative cartoon depicted me as a pirate about to steal Pakistan's aid away under the provisions of the Pressler Amendment. It appeared in a Pakistani newspaper during my congressional delegation visit to India and Pakistan in January 1992, while the Pressler Amendment was being enforced.

Playing Holi with Indian Prime Minister Atal Bihari Vajpayee (second from left) in 1999.

I accompanied President Bill Clinton on his visit to India in 2000. Here I am seen shaking hands with Prime Minister Vajpayee, with President Clinton on the left.

President Clinton and I had been on friendly terms even before our days in public office because of our Rhodes Scholar connection.

My wife, Harriet, and I in Chennai in 1998 at an economics conference.

During my days as an Infosys Technology director, I would find time for side trips to learn more about India. Here I am in 2001 at a national park in the south of India.

I served on the board of directors for six years at Infosys, an international company. In 2013 I participated in the opening ceremony as honorary chairman for a day when the company became listed on the New York Stock Exchange.

CNN's Dana Bash conducted a live interview with me after my poetry reading in Sioux Falls during my 2014 Senate campaign. I love reading Western cowboy poetry.

policy. It seems absurd now, but that is truly what our government's diplomats believed at the time.

Relations between our two countries became even more tense when a group of Pakistani students burnt the US embassy in Islamabad to the ground in November 1979. Intelligence sources reported at the time that Pakistan was continuing its defiant pursuit of nuclear weapons.

Then, on 24 December 1979, the Soviet Union invaded Afghanistan and everything changed. President Carter, and later President Reagan, put their concerns about Pakistan's development of a nuclear weapon on the back-burner. They now needed Pakistan to bolster the resistance fighters trying to oust the Soviets in Afghanistan. These resistance fighters were Islamic fundamentalists—the same fundamentalists we are fighting all over the world today in the War on Terror. But at the time, because they were fighting communists, the Islamic fundamentalists were our allies. Presidents Carter and Reagan effectively ignored Pakistan's nuclear programme and began to turn the spigot back on for military aid to flow to Pakistan.

Pakistan had an odd assortment of supporters in the United States at the time—most notably the CIA, a Democratic congressman from Texas named Charlie Wilson and a Texas socialite named Joanne Herring. Their story was chronicled in a bestselling book and Hollywood movie, *Charlie Wilson's War.*[2] Charlie Wilson was known around Washington as a hard-drinking playboy who happened to have a coveted seat on the House Defense Appropriations Subcommittee, the subcommittee that holds the purse strings for the Pentagon. According to the movie, he cavorted with many women. One of them was Joanne Herring, whose late husband, Robert Herring, had been a Texas oil tycoon.

During the Herrings' business and international travel to the Middle East and South Asia, they were offered a position of honorary consul representing Pakistani interests in America because Bob Herring was going to build a pipeline in Pakistan. Bob didn't want the position, but Joanne did. She relished her new role, educating herself on Pakistani culture and trade. She soon became a confidante of the then President, Zia-ul-Haq. When the Soviet Union invaded Afghanistan, Joanne—vehemently anti-communist and an avowed Christian—was worried about the domino effect of its invasion. First Afghanistan, then the warm-water ports of Pakistan, and what next? The Straits of Hormuz, between the Gulf of Oman and the Persian Gulf, where American international trade could be disrupted? Joanne, along with her son and a film-maker, smuggled themselves into Afghanistan a few months after the Soviet invasion to document Soviet atrocities on the ground and make the case for support of Afghani resistance fighters, the mujahideen.

The world condemned the Russian invasion in Afghanistan, but both Presidents Carter and Reagan did not want an open confrontation with the Soviet Union. The secret film footage Joanne brought back was instrumental in securing covert aid to the mujahideen. The CIA and Pakistan's ISI began what has been cited as the largest covert operation in American history: Operation Cyclone. Pakistan was secretly given billions of dollars to funnel to the resistance fighters in Afghanistan. In the movie, Joanne uses her relationship with Charlie Wilson to advocate for this gargantuan aid deal.

She convinced him to accompany her on one of her many clandestine adventures to Afghanistan and secured his help on Capitol Hill. I doubt that she was ever registered as a lobbyist, but many in Washington were convinced at the time that she was somehow being paid by the Pakistanis. Just one more tangled Octopus tentacle, as far as I can make out.

Of course, while those resistance fighters in Pakistan and Afghanistan were fighting a proxy war against the Soviets on our behalf, they certainly did not share our values of freedom and democracy. Pakistan was one of the primary beneficiaries of this war. They controlled the purse strings. Anyone in Afghanistan who wanted American aid money had to request it from President Zia and the ISI. There were many religious and nationalist factions in Afghanistan fighting the Soviets. The most radical of these Islamic groups was

Hezb-e-Islami and it was the one most favoured and well financed by President Zia. This group later emerged as an aggressive militant, anti-Western group who claimed responsibility for many attacks on coalition forces and the administration of the then President, Hamid Karzai, in Afghanistan after 9/11.

Among those fighters were also some foreign volunteers, radical Muslims from all over the world, who came to Afghanistan to defend their Muslim 'brothers'. One such volunteer was Osama bin Laden. Indeed, the mujahideen in Afghanistan were the precursor to al-Qaeda. The seeds of today's War on Terror were being sown during this time and the United States probably fuelled their growth.

When Ronald Reagan ousted President Carter from office, I was hoping that the Reagan White House would act differently towards Pakistan. Despite my moderate views on many issues, I found an unlikely ally in the conservative Reagan White House. I was one of the few people in the entire Congress who became close personal friends with Ronald Reagan during his presidency. Usually, Nevada Republican senator Paul Laxalt was listed as his best friend, and I once heard him remark that Reagan had only a few personal friends. And I actually became one of them!

My original friendship with Reagan was based on two things. The first was that he had read a 1980 *People* magazine article about my relationship with my father as he declined into Alzheimer's fog. At a White House Christmas party, he startled me by asking how my father was doing. He invited me to a special meeting in the Oval Office on Alzheimer's disease, which Princess Yasmin Aga Khan, whose mother, actress Rita Hayworth, had too. (Princess Yasmin chaired a foundation to fight Alzheimer's.) His thoughtfulness to remember, inquire and include me was both surprising and touching. But his concern became steadfast; in fact, Reagan usually asked me about my father every few months.

In our private conversations, I shared with Reagan the arguments I used to have with my father about his old-fashioned farming techniques. After my father died, I told Reagan I would stand at my father's grave and tell him how sorry I was for putting so much pressure on him at the dinner table and belittling his farming operations. Reagan told me his children gave him the same trouble at the dinner table. Two of his children did not share his political philosophy and would criticize his work and political activity. I thought it strange that my life on a simple South Dakota farm had such a stark resemblance to the glamorous life of a Hollywood actor. I suppose conflict between children and their parents is universal.

When Reagan was in office, I believed that he and I saw eye to eye on arms control. In addition to group meetings, he invited me to the Oval Office on a number of occasions, and encouraged me to speak my mind, which I was glad to do. Many of the people at those meetings, including the Pentagon brass, assumed that a staunch conservative like Reagan could not possibly favour dealing with the Russians on reducing arms or limiting arms sales to developing countries. They were wrong.

Reagan was particularly interested in my views on South Asia's balance of power. He also told me that he admired me for not reflexively supporting the 'mutually assured destruction' (MAD) concept, which he opposed, often remarking that the idea was called MAD 'for a reason'. In those days a whole priesthood of arms control experts made a career out of each new treaty, which usually allowed each side to build more nuclear weapons. The limitation of such treaties was to allow for an increase of weapons on each side, but never to propose a real reduction. I was considered a rogue newcomer to the arms control debate. Once, a dozen experts were sitting on the sofas and chairs in Reagan's Oval Office and the President went around the room listening to them, with Vice President George H.W. Bush also present. I was the only one to speak for the US to start pursuing a total reduction or elimination of nuclear weapons worldwide. In the end, Reagan asked, 'I've only heard one opinion on reducing nuclear weapons—everyone else wants limited increases. Why on earth don't we accept Senator Pressler's view?' Defense Secretary Caspar Weinberger, the leading hawk present, growled, 'Because Senator Pressler does not know arms control very well.'

Like most presidents when they assume office, Ronald Reagan had little experience in diplomacy, coming into the foreign policy world from the role of governor of the state of California. He was not steeped in the traditional clichés and protocols of the arms control community. He seemed to support the Pentagon generally, but he liked that I was willing to say controversial things that his staff was probably afraid to utter. During one Oval Office meeting, I was sitting silently when President Reagan suddenly asked, 'And what does Senator Pressler think of the situation in Pakistan?'

'Mr President,' I replied, 'we're helping Pakistan get nuclear weapons—and in fact our Pentagon is helping Pakistan pay for its nuclear weapons!'

A puzzled expression came over Reagan's face. 'Why on earth would we do that?' he asked.

'Mr President,' I repeated, 'our Pentagon is actually supporting Pakistan in getting nuclear weapons. We are not doing anything to stop them from importing the materials they need to make nuclear bombs, and secretly in the background the boys in the Pentagon are doing everything they can to help Pakistan get a bomb.'

Secretary Weinberger grumbled, 'That's not true.'

'But it *is* true,' replied one of the undersecretaries of the State Department, who supported my argument.

And it *was* true.

Furthermore, the Defense Department, the CIA, the National Security Council and all the other Octopus forces looked on me as a congressional nuisance who did not have the proper background to deal with these complex nuclear issues. They saw me as an interloper from the plains. But President Reagan seemed to like that I spoke in plain English and did not resort to arcane arms control terminology.

'I want you to keep meeting with my foreign policy team,' the President told me. National Security Advisor William Clark visibly cringed and gritted his teeth when he heard President Reagan say that.

How did I get included in so many meetings with Reagan? As chairman of the Arms Control Subcommittee, I was naturally invited to them. When the Octopus, particularly the Pentagon, saw that I was able to pass amendments and had some influence with Reagan, they asked presidential assistant Michael Deaver to limit my access to the President. Luckily, though, Deaver liked me and even agreed with me. He coached and advised me that a way to see the President personally without getting on his official schedule was to attend more of the signing ceremonies for various unrelated bills. After those bill signings, Deaver would arrange for me to walk back to the Oval Office with the President. Then I would have a meeting that would not show up on the President's schedule, and the generals and the admirals in the Pentagon would not get jealous or wary of me. Mike Deaver continued to be a close friend of mine even after I left the Senate. I was asked to speak at one memorial for him when he died. I told the story of how Mike Deaver seemed to have a sense for trying to help people who were struggling to communicate their message. He was a wonderful man.

At one of these private meetings, President Reagan said, 'Larry, some of our good friends over at the Pentagon tell me that you are anti-Pakistan and pro-India because you have so many Indian constituents and you raise a lot of your campaign money from Indian Americans.'

I replied, 'Well, Mr President, I do have a lot of Indian constituents, but they are all Native Americans.' (Indeed, I had plenty of Native Americans in my state, but only a handful of voters of Indian descent, and I had not received a single penny for any of my low-budget campaigns from any Indian Americans. It was just a play on words.)

Despite what President Reagan said publicly and in those meetings with me, containing communism was far more important to him than Pakistan's efforts to get a nuclear weapon. The Soviet occupation of neighbouring Afghanistan was a much bigger foreign policy concern for the Reagan administration. He needed Pakistan: he needed their military's support; he needed their supply routes; and he needed their intelligence. He also made his priorities clear when he sought an exemption to the Glenn–Symington Amendment restrictions. He wanted to provide a steady stream of aid money and weapons to Pakistan. Lots of it.

In December 1981, a new section was added to the 1961 Foreign Assistance Act. It allowed the President to exempt Pakistan from the original Symington Amendment 'if he determines that to do so is in the national interest of the United States'. (It is important to note that Pakistan was the only nation specifically exempted by name from these restrictions.) Almost immediately, Congress also authorized a six-year $3.2-billion package of military and economic assistance to Pakistan. I was opposed to this move, as I knew it would further encourage Pakistan to continue the development of their nuclear weapons programme.

Many of us in Congress knew that we could not trust President Zia to be honest with us about his nuclear ambitions. Everyone knew that Pakistan was continuing to acquire material and technology to develop a bomb. Despite this fact, the Reagan administration wanted a new law that would give him a permanent waiver from the Glenn–Symington Amendment. At the time, guaranteeing Pakistan's assistance in the fight against the Soviets in Afghanistan was more important than stopping Pakistan's acquisition of nuclear weapons technology. The only way the administration could get Congress to go along with this permanent waiver was to include language in a new law that would punish Pakistan if it was determined that Pakistan actually *possessed* a nuclear weapon. This made the Glenn–Symington waiver more politically feasible to those of us in Congress who were working hard on non-proliferation issues. I was tapped to carry the ball and the Pressler Amendment was born.

My goal was to give this new amendment as much 'teeth' as possible. On 24 March 1984, the Senate Committee on Foreign Relations introduced an amendment offered up by California Democratic senator Alan Cranston and Senator Glenn. This first amendment stipulated that 'no military equipment or technology shall be sold or transferred to Pakistan' unless the President could *first* certify that Pakistan did not possess nor was developing a nuclear explosive device, and that it was not acquiring products to make a nuclear explosive device. On 18 April 1984, the committee instead introduced a substitute offered by me, Maryland Republican senator Charles Mathias and Senator Charles Percy.

My former staff member, the late Dr Doug Miller, recalled that Senator Cranston's face appeared 'crestfallen' when his amendment did not pass. In retrospect, while Cranston's amendment and my subsequent amendment were very similar, I feel his amendment would have cut off aid to Pakistan sooner. But the Republican Party was in control at the time. They wanted a Republican name on the amendment.

The revised amendment offered by Senators Mathias, Percy and me instead tightly tied the continuation of aid and military sales to two presidential certification conditions: (1) that Pakistan did not possess a nuclear explosive device; and (2) that new aid 'will reduce significantly the risk' that Pakistan would possess such a device. This text was further revised with a provision offered by me, Senator Mathias and Minnesota Republican senator Rudy Boschwitz that the 'proposed U.S. assistance [to Pakistan] will reduce significantly the risk of Pakistan possessing such a [nuclear] device'. It forced the President to affirm that increased aid was reducing the risk of Pakistan getting nuclear weapons. I thought at the time that this was going to be impossible for any President to certify—based on Pakistan's past behaviour and what President Reagan had assured me he would do.

The final text of Section 620E of the Foreign Assistance Act of 1961 read:

No assistance shall be furnished to Pakistan and no military equipment or technology shall be sold or transferred to Pakistan, pursuant to the authorities contained in this Act or any other Act, unless the President shall have certified in writing to the Speaker of the House of Representatives and the chairman of the Committee on Foreign Relations of the Senate, during the fiscal year in which assistance is to be furnished or military equipment or technology is to be sold or transferred, that Pakistan does not possess a nuclear explosive device and that the proposed United States assistance program will reduce significantly the risk that Pakistan will possess a nuclear explosive device.

This text, which was signed into law by President Reagan on 8 August 1985, soon became known as the 'Pressler Amendment', even though I was not the only sponsor. I never referred to it as the Pressler Amendment. But when President George H.W. Bush later enforced it, the Pentagon wrote a series of worldwide memos and briefings explaining that Bush had to act in such a way towards Pakistan because of 'Senator Pressler's amendment', mentioning me by name and making the amendment eponymous. It is important to understand that this legislation was passed at the request of and with the support of the Reagan administration. That is why I was so astounded when later Reagan never enforced it.

In summary, it made a law out of what had already been an official policy: our conventional arms assistance and financial aid to Pakistan would reduce the risk of nuclear proliferation. It used the power of the purse. It allowed us to pursue our communism-containment goals in the region, but it was also intended to force our leaders to proactively assert—on the record—that Pakistan was not making progress on its nuclear goals. Again, this policy seems counter-intuitive and, unfortunately, it had the opposite effect on Pakistan. And, with the help of the Octopus, Pakistan took our aid *and* flagrantly ignored the Pressler Amendment restrictions.

18

The Immediate Impact of the
Pressler Amendment

'In our view, no amount of U.S. security assistance or political
pressure will cause Islamabad to forsake its nuclear weapons option.'

—State Department intelligence assessment of
the Pakistan–United States relationship, September 1985[1]

As I later learnt, the Octopus started devising ways to circumvent
the Pressler Amendment the minute it was passed. One government
agency or another was trying to sabotage the law from the very
beginning. Consequently, Pakistan was not deterred.

Less than one month after the signing of the Pressler Amendment,
the *Los Angeles Times* published reports that Pakistan had recently
tested a nuclear triggering device. According to the article, the Reagan
administration sent two high-level officials from the State Department
and the National Security Council to South Asia to express ongoing
concern about Pakistan's possible development of a nuclear weapon.
Although the officials, Michael Armacost and Donald Fortier, publicly
told the questioning media that the meeting was 'mainly just a strong

follow-up on the [Prime Minister Rajiv Gandhi's] visit' (which had taken place the previous June in Washington), these September meetings in New Delhi and Islamabad were really intended to confront Pakistan about the reports of nuclear testing.[2]

Publicly, President Zia denied that Pakistan had a bomb or was making a bomb. 'Pakistan has neither the resources nor the means nor the desire' to develop a nuclear weapon, he told the *New York Times* on 21 October 1985.[3] But our intelligence sources told us otherwise. Zia was lying. A secret message dated 7 December cites Defense Intelligence Agency (DIA) sources that suggest Pakistan had 'produced an atomic weapon in early October' of 1985 with onsite Chinese technical assistance. This document was released by the State Department in 2011.[4] It was obtained and made publicly accessible by the National Security Archive at George Washington University in Washington, D.C. At the time, I felt confident that Pakistan was going to be sanctioned for this flagrant violation of the new Pressler Amendment. But I was naïve.

Rhode Island Democrat senator Claiborne Pell, the then chairman of the Senate Foreign Relations Committee, travelled to India and Nepal in late 1985 and prepared a report for his committee colleagues on the state of 'South Asia after Indira Gandhi'. In it, he raised the critical question facing many of us working in arms control at the time: why were we continuing to support Pakistan, given their continued record of lying about their nuclear ambitions? As Senator Pell wrote so eloquently at the time, 'Some American analysts have suggested that the United States, in its military supply relationship with Pakistan, is backing the wrong horse in South Asia. There is a certain irony in a situation where India, the world's largest democracy, has its military connection with the Soviet Union while the United States, the second largest democracy, is backing an undemocratic Pakistan.'

He went on to predict that Prime Minister Rajiv Gandhi's 'orientation would likely be more pro-Western than his mother's. This, combined with an Indian desire to develop scientific and technological links with the U.S., provides an opportunity for a considerable improvement in the U.S.–India relationship.'[5]

Senator Pell also predicted that the new prime minister would, however, maintain his mother's foreign policy priorities and continue the arms supply relationship with the Soviet Union. That type of foreign policy was sure to taint many in the Reagan administration and the Senate about our relationship with India. As I surmised at the time, if India was still publicly aligned with the Soviet Union, the United States would keep a bit of a distance in the diplomatic relationship—both publicly and privately. Every other objective seemed to be secondary. This was a continuation of the old Cold War mentality and was, in my opinion, short-sighted.

I had first met Prime Minister Rajiv Gandhi earlier that year on a trip to India, Nepal, Bhutan and Bangladesh. While in India, I asked my friend, the parliamentarian Murli Deora, and his wife, Hema, to arrange a private meeting with Gandhi—without involving the State Department. I wanted to have a private and candid meeting without the foreign service officers present to witness and relay our conversation. Hema was a world-class bridge player, very socially active and seemed to know everybody, including Rajiv's wife.

Upon being introduced, I was immediately struck by how small in stature Rajiv was, as well as extremely quiet and bookish. His demeanour reminded me of a shy college student. As an accomplished airline pilot, he was a bit of a fish out of water in the world of international politics. I got the feeling that he never really wanted to be prime minister and it was apparent that he depended heavily on his staff. I cannot say that we became friends, as he was self-conscious and soft-spoken. He was hard to read. It was so tragic when he was assassinated just six years later. One report I read said that he was blown into more than one hundred pieces by the powerful explosives carried by the smiling suicide bomber. I felt terrible for his beautiful wife and family.

But when he became prime minister in 1984, it gave India the appearance of being led by a young, forward-looking, high-tech leader.

And with the last name of Gandhi, he was guaranteed a lot of votes, regardless of his background. Rajiv Gandhi was not well versed in the intricacies of US politics and he still held views that were somewhat pro-Russian and anti-American. He questioned the motivations of the US government and told me in our meeting that day that he would consider the situation 'irretrievable' should he become aware that Pakistan possessed a nuclear weapon. He believed that small and developing countries could handle nuclear weapons just as well as developed countries—but just not Pakistan. He also shared his hopes that the US would reassess its policy of providing high-technology military assistance to Pakistan.[6]

Later on that trip, I told a reporter with the Voice of America network that the new Indian prime minister and his recent landslide victory in elections 'represents a new beginning for relations between the United States and India', but that the 'American aid to Pakistan [was] the number one stumbling block'.[7]

In Senator Pell's report about Rajiv Gandhi, he also categorically stated: 'India and Pakistan are approaching a state of "near nuclear" détente in the subcontinent, in which the nuclear status quo is maintained with both countries able to make nuclear weapons but neither actually doing so.' Senator Pell, because of his modest nature and gentle demeanour, was well respected and his word was always good. He was one of my best friends in the Senate and I agreed with him on Pakistan, but his assessments always seemed to be underestimated.

The Reagan administration ignored this report and Senator Pell's advice. We were in the middle of the Cold War. Repelling the Soviets in Afghanistan trumped all concerns about nuclear proliferation, even though all kinds of evidence that Pakistan had already acquired all the elements to build a bomb were popping up in public and classified sources. Kenneth Adelman, the then director of the Arms Control and Disarmament Agency, wrote a comprehensive memo to John Poindexter, the President's national security adviser, in June 1986: 'It is clear now that Pakistan has overcome the last major obstacle to nuclear weapons by producing enough highly enriched uranium for one or more nuclear devices.'[8] Adelman said that President Zia had lied to the United States on more than one occasion. Indeed, it is my judgement that Zia told us a stream of lies throughout the course of his tenure as President.

With September 1986 approaching, when the time came for the first certification required under the Pressler Amendment (for the fiscal year 1987), the Reagan administration *should* have triggered the Pressler Amendment restrictions.

Furthermore, a State Department briefing book prepared for a July 1986 visit of Pakistan's prime minister, Mohammed Khan Junejo, also recently declassified, said that the Pressler Amendment certification for fiscal year 1987 would prove 'very problematic' and that Pakistan would need to show 'absolute criticality of actions, not pious words' about the state and future of Pakistan's nuclear programme in order for the US aid to continue. Nevertheless, the briefing concluded that it was 'our assessment . . . that Pakistan does not possess a device'.[9]

It was pure lunacy. Like the classic fable of the 'Emperor's New Clothes', where everyone knew the emperor was naked but no one would say so for fear of embarrassing the emperor, everyone knew that Pakistan was flagrantly violating our laws and developing nuclear weapons capability, but no one would say so.

Pakistan was confident that the Octopus and its minions in the Reagan administration would outflank any of us who wanted to stop the unfettered aid the country was receiving. Indeed, many diplomats serving in Pakistan at the time boastfully and privately told me that the administration would never pull the trigger on the Pressler Amendment. I was exasperated.

During his visit that July, Prime Minister Junejo repeated President Zia's bold-faced lie that Pakistan was committed to only peaceful uses of its nuclear programme and pledged not to enrich uranium above the 5 per cent threshold required for a nuclear weapon. In the fall of 1986, President Reagan once again provided the required Pressler

Amendment certification, keeping the aid spigot—an enormous amount of money—flowing to Pakistan. Not surprisingly, Reagan cherry-picked the intelligence on which he justified his decision. A full $4.02 billion was promised over a six-year period (this followed a $3.2-billion aid package delivered between 1981 and 1987).

In November, the *Washington Post* reporter Bob Woodward alleged that Pakistan had 'detonated a high explosive test device between September 18 and 21 as part of its continuing efforts to build an implosion-type nuclear weapon' and that they had successfully enriched uranium to a 93.5 per cent level.[10] The article went on to say that this intelligence made no difference to the Reagan administration. 'Said one official directly involved in monitoring the program, "This administration wouldn't come down on Pakistan if we found a bomb in Zia's basement."' It seemed that the Reagan administration's tough talk on nuclear non-proliferation was just lip service. The Octopus was in control and Pakistan's nuclear programme appeared to be untouchable.

What was called in the *Los Angeles Times* 'one of the worst-kept secrets in South Asia'[11] became more of an open secret in February 1987 when two stunning admissions became public. First, the US ambassador to Pakistan, Dean Hinton, said in a speech, 'There are developments in Pakistan's nuclear program which we see as inconsistent with a purely peaceful program.'[12] Secondly, on 1 March 1987, the British newspaper *Observer* published an interview with Dr A.Q. Khan. In this article, he told Indian journalist Kuldip Nayar that Pakistan did possess nuclear weapons and that they had been developed to defend Pakistan against an Indian attack.

I was not surprised by Dr Khan's admission in this media interview. Over the previous few years, many former and disgruntled CIA and military intelligence officers would contact my office with classified intelligence information about the progress of Pakistan's nuclear weapons programme. These veteran intelligence officials would reach out to me because they were frustrated that the Reagan administration was doing nothing about it, and I had a reputation

as a willing ear. But without verification, there was little I could do
to help them in their whistle-blowing efforts. Dr Khan's admission
was a bombshell, as it proved once and for all that Pakistan had been
blatantly lying all along.

In response to these two admissions, Assistant Secretary of State
Richard Murphy prepared an 'action plan' memo for Secretary of
State George Shultz.[13] He said that, given all the recent publicity
about Pakistan's aggressive pursuit of and bragging about their nuclear
programme, Congress was going to really put the pressure on the
State Department to limit or halt aid. The memo clearly states that

> [Zia] has reached a threshold which he cannot cross without
> blatantly violating his pledge not to embarrass the President....
> to keep Congress on board, and to secure our non-proliferation
> interests over the long term, we need not only to obtain specific
> actions demonstrating restraint, but in a systematic way to convince
> Pakistan to 'rest on its oars' and avoid further elaboration of its
> nuclear capabilities. This will require Indian restraint as well.

Murphy and the ambassador-at-large for non-proliferation issues,
Richard Kennedy, recommended that Ambassador Hinton present to
Zia a list of four actions he must take to continue to receive aid: (1) no
assembling of a nuclear device; (2) no uranium enrichment above 5
per cent; (3) no more nuclear-weapons-related high-explosives testing;
and (4) no more illegal procurements of products and technology in
the US. It does not appear that this memo had any traction, as no
major pressure was exerted on Zia that year.

It did not help that Murphy was saying something different in
public. This is a classic example of how the Octopus can talk out of
both sides of its mouth. Murphy testified before the Senate on 18
March 1987, saying:

> Our assistance relationship is designed to advance *both* our non-
> proliferation and our strategic objectives relating to Afghanistan.
> Development of a close and reliable security partnership with

Pakistan gives Pakistan an alternative to nuclear weapons to meet its legitimate security needs and strengthens our influence on Pakistan's nuclear decision-making. Shifting to a policy of threats and public ultimata would in our view decrease, not increase our ability to continue to make a contribution to preventing a nuclear arms race in South Asia. Undermining the credibility of the security partnership with the U.S. would itself create incentives for Pakistan to ignore our concerns and push forward in the direction of nuclear weapons acquisition.[14]

Once again, the emperor was wearing no clothes, but everyone was pretending he was.

Senator Glenn was extremely confounded by the continued obfuscation by the Reagan administration. He made a statement on the floor of the Senate Foreign Relations Committee on 23 March 1987 condemning the administration's policy towards Pakistan.[15] He and I both knew that the massive amounts of conventional aid we were providing Pakistan was not the nuclear deterrent the administration believed it would be. Senator Glenn admonished the Reagan administration and the Octopus that day, saying: 'Six years and $3 billion later, we see Pakistan poised at the nuclear threshold.... It is amply clear that Pakistan gained the status of "nuclear threshold state" during the period when the U.S. assistance was at its highest level. The American taxpayer has a right to ask how much "nuclear restraint" his previous tax dollars have purchased in Pakistan, before another four billion are provided.'

Senator Glenn also wrote a strongly worded letter to President Reagan that same month. He said, in his expert opinion—and he was generally considered to be one of the foremost experts on this subject in the US at the time—that 'all the components and means for assembling a working nuclear device are in Pakistan's possession'.[16] His prescription was that the administration should undertake a comprehensive review of the intelligence that the United States possessed about Pakistan's nuclear programme at the time *and that all aid should be suspended during this review*. Clearly, Senator Glenn was ignored. Despite my personal fondness for President Reagan, I was extremely disappointed with his administration's lack of commitment to nuclear non-proliferation in South Asia.

It wasn't until we had hard evidence of Pakistan's furtive and aggressive actions to develop their nuclear weapons programme that the Reagan administration's hand was forced. In July 1987, a Pakistani native named Arshad Pervez, who lived and worked in Canada, was arrested in Philadelphia for attempting to illegally purchase and export 'maraging steel', a key material used in gas centrifuge enrichment technology to make nuclear weapons. Pervez and his 'client' in Pakistan, a retired Pakistani brigadier general named Inam-ul-Haq, bribed an undercover US Customs Service agent to get an export licence.

The arrest made national news in the United States. It would now be embarrassing for the Reagan administration to deny that Pakistan was in violation of the Solarz Amendment, which required that aid be cut off to any country trying to illegally import material from the United States that could be used for a nuclear weapon. My friend, the late congressman Steve Solarz, a Democrat from New York, was Senator Glenn's and my counterpart in the House of Representatives on the issue of non-proliferation. He was just as dedicated to it as we were.

The Pervez case also showed that Pakistan was in violation of the Glenn–Symington Amendment. And, of course, this would make it impossible for the President to certify—as required by the Pressler Amendment—that Pakistan *was not pursuing a nuclear weapon*. At least I thought it would.

The State Department immediately dispatched Undersecretary of State Michael Armacost to meet with President Zia, where the latter once again lied through his teeth. He denied that Pervez and Inam were agents of his government. He went further, claiming he and his country were insulted by the national condemnation in the US. A classified message from the State Department to the US embassy in Islamabad summarized the meeting. It quoted Zia as saying, '. . . it seems the entire effort was to get one Pakistani in order to hang the entire government'.[17]

He went on to allege, incredulously, that the illegal procurement activities must be some sort of a 'conspiracy' instigated by those who wanted to destroy the US–Pakistan security relationship. Looking now at these historical documents, I must say that Zia had a clever way of putting our diplomats on the defensive. He then promised that, if it was proven that his government was involved in the Pervez case, he would resign and apologize to President Reagan.

Ken Adelman shot off a memo to President Reagan on 23 July, recommending that he enforce both the Solarz and Pressler amendments and cut off aid to Pakistan. He warned that the United States would lose all credibility on the issue if the administration did not act forcefully. 'If we now "lawyer our way around" the Solarz Amendment,' Adelman wrote, 'Zia will conclude once again that he need do nothing about his bomb program.' He sent another memo to Reagan on 21 November that emphatically said,

> I recommend against any certification now. It would be seen as 'business-as-usual' and take the pressure off Pakistan—at the very time we should be trying to increase pressure on them to stop enriching uranium above 5 percent (as they earlier promised they would do) and to stop illegal procurement activities in the US.[18]

Ken Adelman's courageous stand against the Octopus probably cost him the chance of advancing to the highest levels in the government. He stood up for what was right and he paid a price for it. And I am somewhat in the same category. What I am saying is that Ken Adelman, who is a friend of mine, could have been a secretary of state or secretary of defense if he had played the Octopus's game. But, in my opinion, he sacrificed himself for his principles. Ken Adelman is one of my heroes in the bureaucracy.

Adelman's voice seemed to be a lonely one in the Reagan administration. That fall, Secretary Shultz, incredibly, sent a memo to President Reagan, recommending that the President issue the certification required under the Pressler Amendment—that *Pakistan did not possess a nuclear weapon and was not pursuing one*. President

Reagan agreed and, in December, he sent his third annual certification to Congress, stating:

> I have made my best judgment based on the information available
> to the United States Government, taken as a whole. I have also taken
> into account the fact that the statutory standard as legislated by
> Congress is whether Pakistan possesses a nuclear explosive device,
> not whether Pakistan is attempting to develop or has developed
> various relevant capacities.' In essence, he admitted that he was
> 'lawyering around' the laws.[19]

Incidentally, as of 2017, this memo is still classified, despite a 2014 request to release it to the public. It would be very illuminating to learn *exactly* what Secretary Shultz's rationale was at the time.

The Reagan administration finally *did* invoke the Solarz and Glenn–Symington Amendments in January 1988. These two amendments cut off aid to any country that tries to illegally import nuclear weapons-related materials from the US, or acquires or transfers nuclear reprocessing technology or explodes or transfers a nuclear device. The administration then promptly issued a waiver and so the aid to Pakistan continued to flow. Apparently, the public pressure as a result of the Pervez case was too strong to ignore.

In my opinion, the overwhelming public evidence that Pakistan was pursuing a nuclear weapons programme forced the Reagan administration to respond in some tangible way. But it was really only a warning. The indefatigable and invincible Octopus won the battle that day. A White House statement issued on 15 January 1988 said, 'This waiver action was based on the recognition that disrupting one of the pillars of the U.S. relationship with Pakistan would be counterproductive for the strategic interests of the United States, destabilizing for South Asia, and unlikely to achieve the non-proliferation objectives sought by the sponsors.'[20] President Zia was cleared to continue 'business as usual'.

Reagan had always claimed to me that he was steadfast on the issue of nuclear arms control and keeping them out of the hands of Pakistan. But his actions proved otherwise time and again. It was very disappointing to me that he never invoked the Pressler Amendment sanctions. Why not? In Washington, D.C., it is he who last talks to the decision maker who can have the most impact. With less access to Reagan during his second term because Mike Deaver was sidelined, I was not able to personally reinforce the importance of my amendment. I knew that Secretary Shultz, his top foreign policy adviser, was recommending against the enforcement of the Pressler Amendment, and I knew that he was getting selective intelligence from the Octopus. He became more and more reliant on his staff to make decisions for him. In retrospect, I wonder if this increased delegation of duties was due to early symptoms of Alzheimer's. We will never know.

When Reagan's successor, President George H.W. Bush, took office, those of us in Congress who were concerned about nuclear proliferation in South Asia hoped to have a more receptive leader in the White House. And then the Soviet Union began to withdraw from Afghanistan, in May 1988. By February 1989, the Soviet troops were gone. We now had no foreign policy rationale for ignoring Pakistan's aggressive pursuit of nuclear weapons.

19

The Enforcement of the Pressler Amendment

'It was the most dangerous nuclear situation we have ever faced since I've been in the U.S. government. It may be as close as we've come to a nuclear exchange. It was far more frightening than the Cuban missile crisis.'

—Richard J. Kerr, former deputy director of the CIA,
in an interview with reporter Seymour Hersh, describing
the 1990 nuclear standoff between India and Pakistan[1]

In June 1989, Pakistan's new prime minister, Benazir Bhutto, addressed a joint session of Congress in the US, where she said, 'Speaking for Pakistan, I can declare that we do not possess, nor do we intend to make, a nuclear device.'[2] I was present when she made that public testimony. It was an outright lie to Congress. But she just did not know it. When she was accused of lying, I came to her defence. She did not know about the nuclear weapons because the ISI never told her. They had developed a bomb without the approval or the knowledge of the prime minister and Parliament. Incredible!

The incident testifies to the power that the ISI wields in the Pakistani political system. When I spoke privately with her at a prayer breakfast during that same visit, she told me how hopeless she felt trying to govern when the ISI, with American generals coaxing them on, controlled everything in Pakistan.

Consequently, I was disappointed when President Bush followed Reagan's lead and, once again, issued a certification that Pakistan did not possess a nuclear weapon, in October 1989. An exasperated Senator Glenn took to the floor of the Senate in November of that year to protest this certification, asserting that

> I must conclude that the President had to make the most narrow possible interpretation of law to conclude that Pakistan does not possess the bomb—a statement I find very difficult to accept and really believe. To me, the President's action represents both bad policy and a disservice to a good law.[3]

Almost a year after the Soviet Army had withdrawn from Afghanistan, why did we feel the need to continue to funnel aid to Pakistan? I could not understand it. In October 1990, *five years after the Pressler Amendment became law*, President Bush finally invoked it. Why did President Bush enforce the law when President Reagan did not? Maybe it had something to do with the nuclear face-off between India and Pakistan in May 1990, a nuclear catastrophe narrowly avoided but kept largely under wraps by the US government until journalist Seymour Hersh revealed the details in an article in the *New Yorker* magazine on 29 March 1993. Hersh was a controversial journalist, but on matters of Pakistan and the South Asia region, he was dead on.

In this article, Hersh described how the American intelligence community witnessed in horror the fast-rising tensions between India and Pakistan in the spring of 1990, originating where it always seemed to, in Kashmir. Protests, rioting and an Indian police crackdown resulted in hundreds of Kashmiri civilian deaths. The Pakistanis' reaction was frightening: intelligence analysts believed that Pakistan was training Muslim Kashmiri 'freedom fighters' on the border *and* outfitting a nuclear bomb that could be placed under the wing of an F-16. The National Security Agency (NSA) had intercepted an order from the Pakistan Army's chief of staff, General Mirza Aslam Baig, to actually assemble a nuclear weapon.

The situation quickly escalated as India prepared an offensive ground strike into Pakistan and Pakistan planned to preempt this ground invasion with a nuclear hit on New Delhi. A quick intervention by American diplomats, including Robert Gates (who later served as President George W. Bush's and President Obama's secretary of defense), was planned. Gates and his team were dispatched to the region to meet with the leaders of both India and Pakistan. They convinced both countries to stand down and move their troops away from the border. India agreed to improve the human rights conditions in Kashmir, and Pakistan agreed to shut down insurgent training camps in Kashmir. All sides agreed and war was averted, but many involved in the event consider it to be the closest the world has come to a nuclear exchange since the Cuban Missile Crisis in 1962.[4]

Everyone in Washington who was involved in non-proliferation knew about this crisis before Hersh's article was published a few years later, but no one talked about it publicly. After this crisis, making the certification required under the Pressler Amendment was going to be very difficult and the State Department knew it. In August 1990, the department sent a 'Top Secret' memorandum to Brent Scowcroft, the President's national security adviser. In it were recommendations that President Bush send letters to both Pakistan's Prime Minister Bhutto and President Ghulam Ishaque Khan. The memo and draft letters, recently declassified and released, outlined a proposed diplomatic strategy that would allow President Bush to rationalize the Pressler Amendment annual certification. 'We believe that non-certification would spark an accelerated Indo-Pak nuclear race, putting the pro-nuclear elements in both governments under highly public and emotional pressure to move ahead full tilt.'[5] Weren't they *already* moving ahead 'full tilt'—with American taxpayers' support?

The memo went on to recommend asking Pakistan

> to demonstrate tangibly that it is complying with the three steps
> we had earlier told them are essential for certification (cease
> production of highly enriched uranium, refrain from production
> of highly enriched uranium metal, ensure that Pakistan does not
> possess any highly enriched uranium metal in the form of nuclear
> device components).

The State Department made it clear they believed that Pakistan would
never allow US officials to inspect its nuclear facilities:

> Demanding inspection of all Pakistan's HEU [highly enriched
> uranium] has almost no chance of acceptance. In these circumstances,
> if we believe the Pressler standard can be met with less than [an]
> inspection of HEU, we should not limit the President's ability to
> certify by setting our standards at an unrealistically high level.

Essentially, the State Department was arguing that President Bush
should be satisfied with Pakistan's stated intentions. I could not
understand how we could *ever* be satisfied by Pakistan's promises.
They were empty.

President Bush obviously agreed. Two months later, he finally
invoked the Pressler Amendment and refused to certify to Congress
that Pakistan did not have a nuclear weapon. He bucked the State
Department. *How could he ever have made any other choice?* Bush's action
stunned the world—and particularly the Octopus.

I was so happy and proud that Bush took this bold action. It was
risky, because he might have incurred the wrath of all those who stood
to gain from arms sales to Pakistan, including the delivery of numerous
fighter jets with a nuclear delivery capability. I recalled Bush's careful
participation in some of my meetings with Reagan when I clashed
with Defense Department officials over the issue of Pakistan. And,
of course, Bush had been working with the Pakistani military for

decades—since he became director of the CIA. I personally believe he made this decision because he knew that the Pakistani generals had lied to his face during his numerous meetings with them in Pakistan and Washington, and he was fed up. Indeed, George told me as much.

For the first time in history, real sanctions were used to halt nuclear proliferation, and it worked in the sense that Pakistan promised to stop their building projects. But that did not satisfy Bush—he demanded verification. This enforcement of the Pressler Amendment was the first time that the US did more than just issue empty threats.

This singular episode of Congress asserting its power in foreign affairs and challenging the Octopus had an enormous impact. When President Bush enforced the Pressler Amendment, it meant that all military and economic aid to Pakistan ended, and our major businesses had to cease all operations in Pakistan. As a result, Pakistan lost $200 million in aid in 1991. The delivery of military equipment to Pakistan came abruptly to a halt. The sale of more than thirty-eight F-16 fighter jets was halted. Joint military exercises between the US and Pakistan, and mid-career training in the US for Pakistani military officers were also cancelled. Pakistani officials were in disbelief. They claimed publicly that the enforcement caught them off guard. Their friends in the Pentagon tried to blame it on this 'rogue' South Dakota senator who they claimed was micromanaging foreign policy!

Meanwhile, the Indian government and the Indian people were delighted with the enforcement. The term 'Pressler Amendment' soon became a part of everyday vocabulary in both India and Pakistan. In India, I became a revered hero, while in Pakistan I became something of a demon. Ironically, I became much more famous in South Asia than I ever was in the United States.

20

The Fallout from the Enforcement of the Pressler Amendment

'When the war in Afghanistan was going on, the United States Government looked the other way ... Now the United States Government is suddenly turning moralistic on the issue.'

—Syeda Abida Hussain, Pakistani ambassador to
the United States, in an interview with
the *New York Times* in 1991

When President George H.W. Bush enforced the Pressler Amendment in 1990, the Pakistanis claimed that it hurt their country's most poor and vulnerable. According to their government, primary school construction and teacher training projects were halted, a public health population planning campaign to distribute condoms was ended, and agricultural programmes designed to increase farm incomes and food supplies in rural areas were affected.[1] As I mentioned at the time, I found it 'paradoxical' that Islamabad was blaming the US for its inability to feed and support its poverty-stricken people when our financial assistance was being spent primarily on weapons.

Around this time, a new organization started to form in the United States called the Pakistani American Congress. It was conceived as a federation of several organizations and its mission statement claimed that it was primarily concerned with the civil rights of Pakistani Americans. However, promoting the foreign policy goals of Pakistan was foremost in its members' minds. The Government of Pakistan did have some registered lobbyists then, but their efforts seemed to be more focused on the issue of Kashmir. The Pakistani American Congress felt that their members' efforts had been piecemeal to date, fragmented with no national agenda. So, they incorporated their organization and set their sights on improving Capitol Hill's perceptions about Pakistan. They wanted to educate US legislators about the atrocities committed against the Kashmiri population. But they also sought to influence the American news media and think tanks by lobbying for removal of US sanctions against Pakistan.

Syeda Abida Hussain was appointed as the new ambassador of Pakistan to the United States in late 1991. I began to see her in the Senate dining room, often as a guest of conservative Republican senators who were pro-Pakistan. One senator she seemed to spend a lot of time with was Colorado Republican senator Hank Brown. It wasn't until later that I learnt why.

At a time when Pakistan–US relations had seemed to reach their lowest point in decades, Ambassador Hussain was dispatched to try to patch things up. She insisted that Pakistan was ruled by a moderate government and she repeated her country's official denial of their nuclear weapons programme. She also said that Pakistan was suffering in the aftermath of the Soviet retreat from Afghanistan with a gun culture, rampant heroin addiction and three million Afghan refugees.

The best advocate Pakistan had during this era, however, was the Octopus, especially its friends in the Pentagon (the heart of the Octopus). Despite the Bush administration's public punishment of Pakistan, the Pentagon continued to try to funnel aid and arms to Pakistan, using every back door and grammatical twist it could to squirm its way around the Pressler Amendment's restrictions. In some cases, it just manipulated and downgraded intelligence reports about Pakistan's covert efforts to acquire nuclear weapons. Sometimes, Pentagon officials outright lied to Congress about their knowledge of this intelligence. They were, essentially, covering for Pakistan.

At no instance was this more evident than the story of Richard Barlow, an expert on weapons of mass destruction (WMD) who exposed a tome of evidence in the late 1980s and early 1990s showing that Pakistan was illegally procuring 'dual use' components from all over the world *and in the US*. He discovered that they were doing it with the help of US officials. At best, these government employees feigned ignorance of Pakistan's illegal activities. At worst, they offered assistance.

Barlow's story is a cautionary one, as he was publicly disgraced and had his reputation ruined by the Octopus—all because he dared to speak the truth. He was convinced that certain officials in the Pentagon, those responsible for the lucrative F-16 sales to Pakistan, were ignoring his intelligence reports and even manipulating them so that the White House could avoid enforcing the Pressler Amendment. Naïvely, he became a very loud 'whistle-blower' and it cost him dearly.

Barlow was the CIA operative who set up a sting and caught Arshad Pervez in 1987, the Pakistani businessman who was arrested at a hotel in Pennsylvania trying to illegally purchase metal which is only used in constructing centrifuges designed to enrich uranium. Barlow found evidence that a pair of high-ranking US officials had actually tipped off the Pakistanis to this sting.

In the 2007 book, *Deception: Pakistan, The United States, and the Global Nuclear Weapons Conspiracy*, authors Adrian Levy and Catherine Scott-Clark describe a closed-door hearing in the House of Representatives where congressman Solarz asked a White House representative, General David Einsel, if Pervez was an agent of the Pakistani government. General Einsel said they were not certain. Barlow was astounded. It was illegal to lie to Congress. When Barlow was called to testify and was asked the same question, he said, 'I told the truth. I said it was clear Pervez was an agent for Pakistan's nuclear program.'[2] Everyone in the room started shouting and the White House representative discredited Barlow's testimony. Barlow was shaken up by the incident and left the CIA soon afterwards. But he was able to land on his feet at the Pentagon as its first intelligence analyst in the area of WMD.

At the request of and supported by his boss at the Pentagon, Barlow wrote a comprehensive intelligence assessment in 1989 for Secretary of Defense Dick Cheney. He revealed that, contrary to what the State Department was saying to the President, the Pakistanis were diligently working to adapt the F-16s to carry and deliver nuclear weapons. No one at the Pentagon wanted to admit this and potentially derail this lucrative revenue stream. Neither did the American F-16 manufacturer, General Dynamics. So, certain Department of Defense officials asked Barlow to change his conclusions.

Barlow claimed he was asked to remove whole sections of his report—especially those that outlined Pakistan's flagrant violation of the Pressler and Solarz Amendments. Barlow was furious because, as he said, 'The intelligence was rock solid.'[3] What the Pentagon and the State Department were advocating was unethical.

And then, strange things started to happen to Barlow. Pieces of his files started disappearing. A secretary tipped him off to the fact that one of the procurement officials was taking documents from his office, but it was hard to prove. Moreover, no one was paying heed to Barlow's alarm bells about Pakistan. His reports were falling on deaf ears.

Later that year, when a deal to sell even more F-16s to Pakistan was unveiled, several State Department and Pentagon officials were hauled before the House of Representatives to testify and assure legislators that Pakistan did not have the capability to turn these conventional fighter jets into nuclear weapon delivery vehicles. According to Levy and Scott-Clark's book, the officials lied through their teeth.

Barlow complained to his boss that the corruption was ubiquitous: 'The whole place stank. Given what I had written for Secretary Cheney, I felt there was a deliberate and widespread conspiracy at work to lie to Congress so that a billion–dollar fighter deal could go through.'[4]

On 4 August 1989, Barlow was fired from the Pentagon. When he asked why, he found out that a case was building to paint him as a 'security risk'. In other words, they were trying to label him as an unstable traitor. They accused him of infidelity, they accused him of being an alcoholic, and they accused him of being psychologically unstable. They stripped him of his security clearance, thus making him unemployable in the intelligence or security field. The squeeze of the Octopus can be deadly.

While I was never threatened the way Barlow was, the 1990 enforcement of the Pressler Amendment did put me in the political crosshairs of the Octopus. I expected some personal fallout from the Pentagon, Pakistani Americans and some in the State Department. But what I did not expect was the fallout from some of my constituents in South Dakota. They were fed false information about me. The soybean, sunflower, wheat and credit card industries all began receiving materials suggesting that I was hurting my state economically. With all imports and exports now banned under the Pressler Amendment, the export of agricultural products to Pakistan also became prohibited. Pakistan at the time represented about 50 per cent of US soybean oil exports. This prohibition caused a severe erosion of soybean oil prices. Sunflower seed prices are based on soybean oil prices, so these eroded as well. However, the fact was that the fluctuation in soybean prices was mostly due to massive production increases in Brazil and Argentina. Despite this fact, the blame was placed squarely on me.

The credit card industry also became very critical of the Pressler Amendment because the law's requirements forced it to suspend banking operations in Pakistan. Global banks like Citibank provided financing for the defence industry. The Pressler Amendment enforcements created a dent in its defence revenue, and Citibank's leadership was not happy about it. The fallout bit me politically because South Dakota has a large Citibank credit card operation at

Sioux Falls. In fact, Citibank was the second single largest employer in South Dakota.

I received numerous complaints from the American Soybean Association, the National Sunflower Association, and Citibank about the Pressler Amendment. The Bush administration was obviously receiving complaints as well—probably from the Octopus tentacles in the Pentagon, the CIA and the State Department. I knew there were many in the administration who did not want Congress to meddle in affairs they deemed to be solely under their purview, that of foreign aid and foreign military sales. They accused me and the Pressler Amendment of meddling. It did not take long for the Octopus to mount another assault.

On 12 April 1991, the Bush administration attempted to eliminate the Pressler Amendment, indicating that they wanted to remove any country-specific language from the Foreign Aid Bill and to address what they called 'urgently needed reforms' of the Foreign Assistance Act. The administration's letter to Congress talked about wanting more 'flexibility' and 'coherence' in this law. On the Pressler Amendment, President Bush stated, 'While the proposed elimination of the Pakistan-specific certification requirement is intended to uphold the general principle of Presidential Authority, I will continue to insist on unambiguous specific steps by Pakistan in meeting non-proliferation standards, including those specifically reflected in the omitted language known as the Pressler Amendment.' What kind of doublespeak was this?

On 9 May 1991, I went to the floor of the Senate to complain. On the record, I said: '. . . the President of the United States is saying that the administration is still going to adhere to the Pressler standard even if the Pressler Amendment is repealed, although it is recommending that the Pressler Amendment be repealed.'[5] If the President agreed with the intent of the amendment, I felt strongly that the amendment should remain intact in the Foreign Assistance Act. Even though the Octopus was breathing down my neck, I pledged to vote against this repeal.

One of the issues I knew the Bush administration was weighing was Pakistan's most recent assistance to us during Operation Desert Storm, the United States' offensive against Iraq's annexation of Kuwait. I knew they wanted to reward Pakistan and continue to exert influence on its powerful military. They were in a quandary. But, as I said in an editorial that was published in July of that year in the *Christian Science Monitor*:

> Eliminating the Pressler Amendment won't solve the problem. The events of the past year show that Congress must be more vigilant than ever on matters of weapons proliferation. While President Bush has pledged to hold Pakistan to the 'Pressler standard,' I believe that it is important for Congress to express an unequivocal view on this issue. As Congress considers the administration's new foreign-aid proposals, I will oppose any effort to eliminate the nuclear non-proliferation provision.[6]

The Octopus did not have enough support in Congress to overturn the Pressler Amendment that year. It survived. President Bush's proposed revisions were defeated in the House on 12 June 1991, by a significant margin of 151 to 252. The Pressler Amendment would remain the law, at least for a while.

While I felt badly for the impoverished people of Pakistan who were clearly suffering from the economic fallout of the enforcement of the Pressler Amendment, I continued to be frustrated that many countries like Pakistan willingly took our economic aid and spent most of it on their military in general, and on a destabilizing pursuit of nuclear weapons. Wanting to see first-hand the effects of the Pressler Amendment, I began to plan an official visit—what's called a congressional delegation, or a CODEL—to South Asia in January 1992. I wanted to look the leaders of Pakistan and India in the eye and see what they would say to me.

21

Stepping into the Line of Fire

'It would be difficult to exaggerate Senator Pressler's notoriety in Pakistan.'

—State Department message, January 1992[1]

I had not visited the South Asia region since 1985, so a trip there was long overdue. My staff, headed by Tom Hohenthaner (who later became a leader of the Millennium Challenge Corporation), accompanied me. We planned a two-week trip to India, Pakistan and Sri Lanka for mid-January, and my staff began outreach to our diplomats in those countries to arrange private meetings and public appearances. A politician's official visit to any foreign country is bound to make some headlines. But I had no idea how notorious I had become in Pakistan, how popular I had become in India, and what a firestorm my comments would create. I will never again take for granted the power of my words. In retrospect, I probably would have prepared my talking points even more carefully than I did.

CODELs are sometimes characterized in the US media as 'boondoggles'—or taxpayer-funded overseas vacations, of sorts—that

congressmen and senators take when Congress is out of session. What
most of the general public does not realize is that they are purely
work trips, packed with meetings from sunrise to sunset and flights to
multiple cities and countries over a short period of time. The tours,
the dinners and the receptions are all laid on the schedule with a
policy objective in mind. There is very little downtime on these trips
for sleep and relaxation. We were lucky to get four or five hours of
sleep every night. The hour I went jogging every day on these trips
was one of the few times I had to myself. However, sometimes a staff
member from the embassy would accompany me, so we would end
up talking about work on our jogs. Occasionally, I would jog with
Indian officials. It provided a wonderful opportunity for speaking
candidly—and off the record.

In any event, my staff worked hard to organize the trip so as to
maximize the number of officials I met with in each country. In India, my
schedule included meetings with Prime Minister P.V. Narasimha Rao;
the minister of defence, Sharad Pawar; the chief economic adviser to
the minister of defence, my old friend from Oxford, Montek Singh
Ahluwalia; the foreign secretary, J.N. Dixit; the high commissioner
to London, Krishna Rasgotra; members of Parliament; members of
the business community—including Ratan Tata; the chairman of the
Atomic Energy Commission, Dr P.K. Iyengar; representatives of the
Indian Space Research Organization (ISRO); the US ambassador to
India, William Clark; the ministers for agriculture, communication,
petroleum and natural gas, defence; and many, many journalists.

In Pakistan, my schedule included meetings with President
Ghulam Ishaque Khan; Prime Minister Nawaz Sharif; Minister of
State for Foreign Affairs Mohammed Siddique Khan Kanju; Air
Chief Marshal Farooq Feroze Khan; US Ambassador Nicholas Platt;
Minister of Finance Sartaj Aziz; the ministers of food and agriculture,
economic affairs and finance; some owners of Pakistani and American
businesses in Pakistan; the chairman of their joint chiefs of staff
committee; the chief of air staff and the chief of naval staff; Speaker
of their National Assembly; and my old friend from Oxford, the

Pakistani Senate chairman, Wasim Sajjad. Our itinerary also included visits to Bangladesh and Sri Lanka, where I was the first US senator to visit in almost two decades.

On the eve of my departure, the State Department distributed what they call a 'scene-setter' for my trip. It was intended to give me a snapshot of the political and economic environment of the region, to help prepare me for the mood of the people I was about to meet. The memo opened its summary of Pakistan's perceptions of me and my amendment by saying,

> It would be difficult to exaggerate Senator Pressler's notoriety in Pakistan. While very few Pakistanis understand much about the Pressler Amendment, much less the Pak nuclear program, and little is known about the senator, every Pakistani who reads newspapers identifies Senator Pressler as the man who halted U.S. economic and military assistance to Pakistan. Most Pakistanis are unwilling to acknowledge that it was their government's own actions which led to the cutoff in aid, and even if they do, they will argue that the Pressler Amendment is nonetheless biased, unfair, and discriminatory.

It turns out I would need to brace myself for impact!

The message went on: 'Senator Pressler will almost certainly hear these charges from his hosts, who will say that similar U.S. sanctions have never been applied to Israel or India, which also have nuclear weapons programs.' However, that was not entirely true. At that time, Brazil and South Africa were very near to developing nuclear weapons. Pressure from the US and threat of sanctions caused them to back down.

The scene-setter brief continued:

> Recently, improving relations between India and the U.S. have given new force to this view. Many Pakistanis believe that, after forty-eight years of friendship, during which Pakistan stood alongside the U.S. in opposition to the Soviet Union and, more recently, the Soviet invasion of Afghanistan, the U.S. now no longer needs Pakistan, and has used the Pressler Amendment as an excuse to

abandon its former friend. Pakistanis are particularly concerned by a perceived U.S. military tilt towards India, the formerly close friend of the Soviet Union and Pakistan's principal enemy.

It concluded with what turned out to be a grand understatement:

> Inevitably, therefore, the senator's visit will evoke great interest. The Pakistani press has noted the 'significant' coincidence that the senator will arrive in Islamabad on the heels of the official visit to the U.S. of the Pak Chief of Army Staff Asif Nawaz. There is speculation that some kind of deal on the nuclear issue might be in the works. Pakistani officials, however, are simply looking forward to the opportunity to present their arguments for Pakistan personally to the senator. We believe they will do so politely but perhaps on occasion with passion.[2]

Little did I know that the Pakistanis would react with outright hostility to me on this trip. The State Department was obviously trying to soften the blow I was about to receive.

The next day, 9 January 1992, Tom and I headed to New Delhi. We landed at the New Delhi airport and we were greeted like movie stars. It was a visceral experience. We were immediately barraged by a throng of well-wishers at an arrival ceremony. They literally pelted us with garlands of flowers. I was weighed down with so many flowers draped around my head that I had a hard time holding up my neck. I just could not tell the well-wishers that I suffered from allergies! When we headed south to Mysore and Bangalore, the crowds greeting us got bigger and more boisterous. They carried posters that said, 'Welcome, U.S. Senator Larry Pressler!', and they cheered in the streets as our car travelled through the main boulevard. It was surreal and it contrasted quite starkly with our arrival in Pakistan a few days later where we were greeted solely by the US ambassador.

The morning after we arrived in New Delhi, we dove into a marathon of meetings. I first met Sharad Pawar, a heavyset, imposing man—someone who personified the look of a minister of defence. Next

I paid a call on my old friend from Oxford, Montek Singh Ahluwalia. Lunch with him was followed by a meeting with Foreign Secretary J.N. Dixit, who also was a former Indian ambassador to Pakistan. Ending the day was a meeting with Prime Minister Narasimha Rao, one of the most thoroughly competent technocrats I have ever met. He was quite humourless and kept a very straight face during our whole meeting. He certainly wasn't as enthusiastic about me as the rest of his constituents were. Later that night, US Ambassador William Clark treated us to a lavish dinner at the Roosevelt House. The famous Indian sitar player, Ravi Shankar (who once played with the Beatles), was one of the guests.

I also held a press briefing where I reiterated to the attending media what I had said publicly before and what I believed at the time. That is, I was convinced that, while India had clearly tested a nuclear weapon in the past, they were now not pursuing one. I also confirmed what was common knowledge: Pakistan was still pursuing nuclear weapons. When asked about rumoured terrorist activity in the Indian Punjab and in Kashmir, I said that I thought the Government of Pakistan was supporting this activity. And finally, I raised one of my growing concerns, that of nuclear weapons in the former Soviet republics. My fear was these weapons would not be returned to Russia and that these nations would ally themselves with the other Muslim-dominated countries in the region, forming a type of Islamic nuclear 'confederation'. I feared then, as I do now, that tactical nuclear weapons in the hands of Islamic fundamentalist groups could lead to a worldwide nuclear disaster—not to mention the threat it posed to neighbouring India.

I wasn't the only public official warning about a so-called 'Islamic bomb'. The BBC aired a major television documentary at the time on the possibility of a Muslim bomb and how much this would increase the power of radical Islamists. There has always been a concerted effort to prevent Muslim-dominated governments from obtaining nuclear weapons, but the Pentagon seemed to exempt Pakistan from this reasoning. Saudi Arabia is rich enough and could buy a bomb from somewhere, but they have always refrained from doing so. (They probably fear Israel's response if they overtly pursue their own nuclear weapons programme. Instead, they financed Pakistan's programme.[3] Also, most Muslim states are so afraid of a massive nuclear retaliation from Israel that they would rather not have a bomb around in the first place.)

The Pakistani media reports blasted me and attempted to discredit me. The editorials clearly painted me as a puppet of India. An editorial that appeared in *The Muslim* newspaper on 13 January was dripping with icy sarcasm:

> Senator Larry Pressler says Pakistan has the nuclear bomb. If that is news, what would his second statement be? He also says in the same breath, India has none. . . . Pressler conjures up the vision of the entire caboodle of Muslim nations of Asia and the Arab Middle East rising, armed to the teeth with nuclear weaponry, all targeted against meekly non-violent India . . . who could ever have thought this character can be all muck and malice and absolutely nothing else? It is not permitted to us to ask a visitor to make himself scarce. For once we feel our culture is rather ill-equipped for eventualities like a Pressler call.[4]

Other media echoed the clarion call that I sounded on that CODEL— the very real threat of an Islamic bomb and an Islamic nuclear 'confederation' of sorts. The Middle East News Network published an article on 13 January, saying that

> [Pressler's] fears of an Islamic federation had been dismissed as baseless on Sunday by Pakistan's minister of state for foreign affairs, Mohammed Siddique Khan Kanju, but many leading Pakistanis have talked about such a dream, an Economic Cooperation Organization (ECO) has already been established, linking Pakistan to Iran to Turkey, with several former Soviet Islamic republics currently expressing an interest in joining.[5]

Two days later, the Middle East News Network commented again, 'The "civilized world" has now woken up to find that the Islamic genie is out of the bottle in which the West has kept it, and that the Islamic peoples are looking for an acceptable role in this world that knows nothing but the logic of power.'[6] All this foreshadowed the rise of global terror groups like the al-Qaeda, and more recently, the Islamic State of Iraq and Syria (ISIS).

Ironically, a think tank called the Cato Institute published a study later that year dismissing Islamic fundamentalism as a significant threat to the security of the United States. The author of the study, Leon T. Hadar, asserted that the end of the Cold War necessitated the creation of a new enemy by the American foreign policy establishment. In the absence of a communist peril, Hadar accused this establishment of hyping the Muslim threat. He called it the 'Green Peril': 'That peril is symbolized by the Middle Eastern Muslim fundamentalist— the "Fundie," to use a term coined by *The Economist*—a Khomeini-like creature, armed with a radical ideology, equipped with nuclear weapons, and intent on launching violent jihad against Western civilization.'[7] That is *exactly* what I feared.

We left New Delhi the next day for a quick visit (twenty-four hours, really) to Pakistan. We arrived in Islamabad on a Sunday morning and were met by our ambassador to Pakistan at the time, Nicholas Platt. Once Tom and I settled in his Lincoln Town Car, Ambassador Platt turned to me and said quite forcefully, but with a friendly smile, 'Do you really want to do this trip?' He was there on the ground, and he had seen the media coverage resulting from my visit and press conference in India. He knew how unpopular I was in Pakistan. I assured him that I was looking forward to talking to Pakistan's leaders myself, face-to-face. He then told me that *all* my appointments had been cancelled. Prime Minister Nawaz Sharif said publicly that he didn't have time 'to meet with every Tom, Dick and Larry'. The press was informed of this very public 'snub' and it was widely reported, with relish, that I had arrived in Pakistan and no one would meet with me. Of course, many of these appointments were quietly restored over the next couple of days, but the press wasn't alerted to this fact. Pakistan wanted to publicly humiliate and humble me.

While we were waiting to see if our appointments in Islamabad were going to be rescheduled, Tom and I headed to the local market.

Ever since I served in Vietnam, I had made a point of visiting local outdoor markets. They are one of the best barometers of the health of a local or regional economy. With a yawn, Tom and I told our State Department 'handlers' that we needed to rest in our hotel rooms, and dismissed them for the afternoon. Within a few minutes, he and I reconvened in our hotel lobby and headed out of the door to explore the prices and availability of seafood, vegetables and fresh fruit.

Compared to the rich colours of India, Islamabad's scenery disappointed me. The architecture was bland and harsh. Tom and I walked around the markets, introducing ourselves and asking questions. Tom was surprised that I used my real name: 'Hi, I'm Larry Pressler. How are you? What are you selling?' Given the amount of hostile media coverage about me during that time, Tom was prudent to be a bit concerned. I was probably a bit too naïve and dismissive. Tom finally said, 'Senator, do you think this is a good idea?' Clearly, I had not thought it through.

I was scheduled to have a quick briefing given by the American diplomatic staff and then lunch with my old friend from Oxford, Wasim Sajjad. He was rumoured at the time to be a potential candidate for President of Pakistan (he was later appointed to the position twice). Given my unpopularity in his country and his future political ambitions, it was risky for him to meet with me. He hosted me for lunch and invited Minister of State Mohammed Siddique Khan Kanju, Foreign Secretary Shaharyar Khan and Secretary General Akram Zaki. The attendees were polite, but a bit reserved and cool towards me. When I asked them about their nuclear ambitions, they all denied having nuclear weapons. They all complained to me about how much the sanctions were harming the poor people of Pakistan.

Wasim was especially cold to me, at least in front of his colleagues. I did not take it personally, as I know he had a lot of political goodwill with his constituents at stake. When we did get a few minutes alone without his entourage around, his demeanour and attitude changed totally and he became much more friendly, warm and open.

While my cancelled appointments with President Ghulam Ishaque Khan and Prime Minister Nawaz Sharif were not rescheduled, I did meet privately with Mohammed Siddique Khan Kanju and the then air chief marshal, Farooq Feroze Khan, later that afternoon.

Kanju clearly wanted to make an impression in a dramatic way. Tom and I met with him and one or two of his aides in a small office with the curtains drawn. We exchanged pleasantries and then, suddenly, all the lights went out and we were left sitting in complete darkness. Within seconds, the doors flew open and a small group of military aides stormed into the room, blinded us with flashlights, and ordered us on to our feet. It was a bit unnerving. It felt like we were being marched to an interrogation—or worse. In Pakistan, the military is never more than half a step away from any civilian government official.

The anonymous military henchmen with the glaring flashlights guided us along a hallway, down a dark stairwell and outside the building. They made a point of telling us that they did not have enough money in their government's budget to keep the lights on continually and that they were forced to have rolling blackouts as part of a nationwide load-sharing programme.

The whole episode was suspicious. Most countries I have visited would exempt a critical government office from participating in a rolling blackout, especially on a business day. In my opinion, it was pure theatre planned and intended to give me a signal.

I had dinner that evening with numerous Pakistani officials, military leaders and businessmen, and the next morning, I met with the minister of finance, Sartaj Aziz. This was followed by another press conference. Held in a hotel ballroom, I stood on a stage behind a podium in front of forty or fifty reporters. The lights came on, the cameras started rolling and the reporters commenced their barrage of questions. It quickly became clear that they had an agenda. Their questions never veered too far from the approved script: that the cut-off of aid was hurting the Pakistani people, that America was abandoning its old friend Pakistan because the United States did not need their help any more, and that the nuclear nuisance was just a convenient excuse. Once again, I fed the controversy.

When asked by an Associated Press reporter if I thought Pakistan was rolling back its nuclear programme, I answered truthfully:

... there was nothing said to me that would indicate that Pakistan is willing to roll back its nuclear weapons programme ... I think there is great concern on the part of our taxpayers in terms of giving foreign aid to a country that is developing and has developed a nuclear capability because our taxpayers are increasingly saying that we cannot give aid that is indirectly used to develop a nuclear weapon or to develop arms.

When probed by the same reporter to give some verification that the United States was in fear of an 'Islamic bomb', I defended my earlier statements:

Now insofar as fear in the United States of an Islamic bomb or a bomb anywhere, there is that fear. There is great concern that some of the republics in the Soviet Union will keep nuclear weapons. There is a fear that some independent military commander somewhere who is able to launch or utilize some group, who is able to move a bomb, will do it ... There is also growing concern about Islamic fundamentalism because of the Iranian experience, the experience our country has had with Iran ... But we do have here a belt of countries, so to speak, connected, that would appear in the late 1990s or some point in the future that that is a possibility, that Islamic fundamentalism would go from Pakistan to Iran, to Afghanistan, to parts of Turkey, to the five or six Islamic republics in the Soviet Union to sort of form a new strategic group in the world. Perhaps they would have a warm water port in Karachi or elsewhere and that is something that, strategically, we would have to deal with differently than we have in the past. If that bloc were a confederation of some sort, and if two or three of the countries in it had nuclear weapons, that would be of great concern to my countrymen, and many others.[8]

This press briefing and the briefing in India generated a tome of national and international media coverage in the US, Europe, India, Pakistan, and in Arabic publications across the Middle East.

Indian media expressed their satisfaction that my visit and my comments reinforced their feelings that our two countries' relationship was continuing to improve. They agreed with me that the Pressler Amendment need not be extended to India, as there was no evidence that India was using US aid money to pay for military operations. In contrast, Pakistan had clearly been using US aid to give relief to its domestic budget, freeing up money to spend on conventional and nuclear weapons. In my opinion, the Pakistanis would make almost direct transfers of US aid money to their military programmes.

On this visit and on subsequent visits, I was frequently hosted by high-level Pakistani military officers for social functions. They live in compounds that are secluded from the rest of the population and are absolutely luxurious, not unlike the country clubs and gated residential communities you find in warm–weather cities in the United States. Driving into one of these compounds, you are suddenly in the presence of palaces, lush golf clubs and swimming pools. That is the way the Pakistani military and their families live while the rest of their country lives in poverty. I was convinced the Pakistanis were using US taxpayer money to support that lifestyle. In India, there was no such use of US tax dollars.

The Pakistani media did not seem to know this, or feigned ignorance. All they knew was that this rogue senator from a small, rural state in the United States was hurting Pakistan and it was patently unfair. They said incendiary things like: 'The hatred and animosity towards Pakistan which Senator Pressler has demonstrated, and the manner in which he has projected Pakistan, Iran, Turkey, and Central Asian republics as a threat to peace, are fully in accord with the American line' (the independent Urdu daily *Nawa-i-Waqt*); 'America in collusion with India has begun to tighten the noose on Pakistan' (independent Urdu daily *Jang*); and 'The suggestion made by Pressler of dealing with the possibility of nine or ten Muslim states forming into a "new strategic group" with Karachi as their warm water port must awaken the entire Muslim world to a more reckless hostility from Americans in the near future' (the government–controlled *Pakistan Times*).

My experiences on this CODEL convinced me more than ever that the Pressler Amendment should continue to be enforced. Visiting these countries and meeting the leaders in India and Pakistan only reinforced my view. While the Indian leaders were frank and open in their discussions with me, the Pakistani leaders were hostile, did not answer my questions, and all gave me the same spin. These trips are an important part of a US senator's job. If our elected officials spent more time travelling overseas, I'm convinced they would better understand the policies they need to legislate and would make more informed foreign policy and oversight judgements instead of relying on the guidance of the Octopus. They would see that, while arms sales are profitable for both countries, they do little to help the average citizens of countries like India and the United States.

The budgets for official congressional delegations, the 'CODELs', have been significantly curtailed in recent years, which has contributed to the decrease in the number of these trips overseas.[9] I think a bigger factor in the reduction in the number of CODELs, however, is one of perception. The media coverage about the costs of these taxpayer-funded 'junkets' during congressional recesses can deeply hurt a legislator's re-election efforts. Consequently, congressional members just do not take them as much any more. They fear that their constituents will question the cost and the return on that taxpayer investment. In this increasingly global economy, however, it is important for our elected leaders to have a broad understanding of the world outside our borders.

A few weeks after I returned from my trip, Pakistan finally came clean and admitted what the rest of the world already knew. Addressing a United Nations audience and in a subsequent interview with the *Washington Post* in February 1992, Pakistani Foreign Secretary Shaharyar Khan said that his government indeed possessed the elements of a nuclear device. He claimed that Pakistan had this capability as early as 1989.[10] This was the same foreign secretary who had shared lunch with me in Pakistan a few weeks earlier and lied to my face, saying his country did not have nuclear weapons. It was patently obvious to me that we needed the Pressler Amendment enforced now more than ever.

22

The Octopus Strikes Back

'...the decision to allow commercial military sales to Pakistan
was first made on October 1, 1990, when the President refused to
certify that Pakistan was not trying to develop an atomic bomb.'

—*Los Angeles Times*, 6 March 1992[1]

It was not long after my controversial CODEL that I began to learn
of a new assault on the Pressler Amendment. My fears about the
Octopus's intent on dismantling it were well founded. The Octopus
considered Pakistan and its military a 'pet state'. The Octopus worked
in the shadows to get what it wanted, using various 'fronts' like
law firms and consulting firms that reach into every aspect of the
administration, Congress and the media.

In early February 1992, it came to my attention that the US
government was continuing to allow the licensing of commercial sales
of military parts and technology to Pakistan. When Secretary of State
James Baker testified before the Senate Foreign Relations Committee
on a different issue, I asked him about his department's interpretation of
the Pressler Amendment. He was prepared and his staff had obviously

given him a carefully worded statement. In response to my questions, he stated that 'we reviewed the legislative history, and as a legal matter we do not believe it applies to commercial sales or exports controlled by the Department of Commerce'.[2] The Department of Commerce? I should have known that the Octopus would find a way to make an end run around the Pressler Amendment. We should have asked the secretary of commerce these questions.

According to a *Los Angeles Times* article that was published on 6 March of that year, I was not the only member of Congress to be kept in the dark about these quiet arms sales to Pakistan.[3] Even more infuriating, the article included an admission by a Bush administration official that commercial military sales to Pakistan had begun on the same day that President Bush had invoked the Pressler Amendment sanctions. So, for the entire duration of the Pressler Amendment enforcement, the Commerce Department had been secretly permitting commercial sales. Baker was probably in a tight spot. He might have agreed with me personally, but he could not control the Commerce Department's activities. It is also my belief that if President Bush knew about these sales, he would not have allowed them.

Having worked at the State Department, I knew they needed to have a formal legal opinion prepared to support this position. When I asked for a copy of the memorandum of law the State Department used to reach this policy decision, I was provided an unsigned summary of the reasons why a suspension of such licensing was not legally required by the Pressler Amendment. It was annoying. Clearly, the Octopus was at work. In retrospect, perhaps I should have been making my request to the Commerce Department. The US government is so vast that it is difficult to figure out where the legal loopholes are. The Octopus has enough resources to find them. I did not—congressional staffs are much smaller than Cabinet-level bureaucracies.

I wrote a formal letter to Secretary Baker, arguing that his paper had failed to answer how the State Department, as a matter of law, could permit the licensing of private sales to Pakistan in light of the statutory ban (the Pressler Amendment) on the sale or transfer of military equipment or technology to Pakistan. I also complained about the fact that the memorandum of law was unsigned.

About a month later, I received a formal response from the State Department with their explanation: 'The paper was drafted by the staff of the Legal Adviser's Office and personally approved by the Legal Adviser as the legal opinion of that office on the interpretation of the amendment. You may treat it as such.'[4] I found this statement rather strange and unresponsive. I had never seen such a blatant case of lying by a public official. It was more doublespeak. It was a cloud of Octopus ink—a classic case of government obfuscation. Without a signature, nobody is accountable!

In June of that year, I contacted Secretary Baker again, asking for—once again—a copy of the memorandum of law that he referenced in his testimony in February. On 30 July, on the morning the Senate Foreign Relations Committee was scheduled to hold a hearing to specifically discuss the 'interpretation of the Pressler Amendment', I received a response from Secretary Baker with their official position: 'No formal memorandum of law was prepared on this issue at the time of the application of the Pressler Amendment, in part because the matter was not considered to be so unusual, in light of past practice, as to require elaborate written explanation.'[5] The State Department diplomats justified the commercial sales exclusion without any formal legal opinion. They were flouting the law. It was infuriating.

The State Department submitted a formal statement for this congressional hearing and made their intent clear:

> While it was decided that funds should not be obligated nor [Foreign Military Sales] be made during such a period [the period of the Pressler Amendment enforcement], there was never any serious suggestion that the licensing of arms exports pursuant to private sales had to be suspended or modified. This reflected the Administration's confident belief that the Amendment had no application to these private transactions.[6]

Wow! The Octopus had found a loophole they really thought would stick. It was inconceivable to me that my government would feel somewhat justified in licensing private sales and munitions to maintain current military capabilities which the Pakistani foreign secretary now told us include nuclear weapons. It flew in the face of the *intent* of the Pressler Amendment.

During the course of that hearing, Senator Glenn and I made our positions clear. I said emphatically, 'By licensing the export of arms and military technology to the government of Pakistan, it seems to me that the Administration is in violation of both the letter and spirit of the Pressler Amendment. Nothing I have seen from the State Department convinces me otherwise.'[7]

Senator Glenn was even harsher:

Evidently, this is what we are now down to: elements of our bureaucracy are grasping at straws to perpetuate the myths that additional military transfers will buy us influence over Pakistan's bomb program and that such transfers are perfectly legal. The rationale that our Government is somehow justified in licensing sales and munitions to maintain current military capabilities which the Pakistani Foreign Secretary now tells us includes nuclear weapons, flies in the face of the black and white words of the Pressler Amendment.[8]

While the policy conflict between the US Congress and the Bush administration was yet to be resolved, the debate over the Pressler Amendment continued with a mincing and parsing of the amendment's words. It was testing the United States' resolve to develop a strong nuclear non-proliferation policy. And with the election of William J. Clinton as President of the United States in November 1992, the assault on the Pressler Amendment only got more intense.

23

The Battle for the Pressler
Amendment Continues

'It's a wonderful smokescreen,' said an aide to Mr. Pressler. 'The
State Department has always wanted to get rid of the Pressler
Amendment because it has no waiver.'

—Response to a question from the *New York Times*
about the Clinton administration's proposal to repeal
the Pressler Amendment, 27 November 1993[1]

It did not take long for the newly elected President Bill Clinton
to attempt to do what the State Department had been unable to:
repeal the Pressler Amendment. His deputy secretary of state at the
time, Strobe Talbott—who now heads the Brookings Institution—
alleges in his 2004 book, *Engaging India: Diplomacy, Democracy, and
The Bomb,*[2] that Clinton's lifelong fascination with India dates
back to their days as Rhodes Scholars at Oxford in the late 1960s.
(Though Clinton, Talbott and I did not attend Oxford at the same
time, I did get to know them both while attending Rhodes Scholar
reunions.)

President and Mrs Clinton both claimed they wanted to make the US–India relationship a hallmark of the Clinton administration's foreign policy. Talbott said that, when Clinton became President, he would often cite India as the United States' natural ally in South Asia because it was a well-established democracy, had a gigantic consumer market, and boasted a thriving high-technology sector.

This made his administration's attempt to repeal the Pressler Amendment all the more puzzling to me. He tried to sneak it past Congress by burying it in a sweeping set of revisions to the Foreign Assistance Act that was sent over to Capitol Hill without a public announcement, right around the Thanksgiving holiday of 1993. They called it a 'discussion draft'. Hidden in these revisions were edits to the Pressler Amendment—removing the Pakistan-specific language in the amendment and adding an executive waiver that would allow the President to provide assistance to any country 'if the furnishing of such assistance is important to the national interests of the United States' and 'will further U.S. non-proliferation objectives'.

President Clinton's press secretary, Michael McCurry, said to reporters that, 'as a matter of administration policy, we will continue to apply Pressler standards to Pakistan' and that President Clinton 'remains concerned about proliferation of weapons of mass destruction, especially in a volatile region such as South Asia'.[3] More doublespeak.

I was furious. I knew that the waiver was added because President Clinton intended to use it. The State Department had always wanted to get rid of the Pressler Amendment because *it did not have a waiver.* It forced the President's hand and the Octopus did not like it. As I said at the time, 'The President calls this foreign aid reform; I call it an anti-proliferation retreat.'

What was the Clinton–Gore administration thinking? President Clinton and Vice President Al Gore had campaigned hard as champions of nuclear non-proliferation. Was it all talk? I vowed not to let this legislation get passed without a fight. I fired off a formal letter of protest to President Clinton in which I stated:

Taking the current international climate into consideration,
especially the 'rogue' countries that continue to insist upon
developing technology to produce nuclear weapons, I find it
most surprising that your Administration would try to repeal such
an effective measure .... I will not allow my amendment to be
jettisoned under the guise of foreign aid reform.[4]

I also decided to make my case to the court of public opinion and
submitted an editorial to the *Washington Post*, which appeared on 14
December. In it, I wrote:

> The existence of the Pressler Amendment and its possible extension
> to other countries undoubtedly has been a key consideration in
> the decision-making of these countries' political leadership when
> the question of pursuing a nuclear weapons program has come up
> for discussion. The fact that these countries have not gone forward
> with a serious nuclear weapons program, or in one case dismantled
> an existing program, is probably not accidental.[5]

Indeed, many foreign policy experts at the time considered the
Pressler Amendment to be a key factor in deterring Egypt, Brazil
and South Africa, recipients of foreign assistance from the US, from
seeking nuclear weapons.

I set off for another two-week CODEL with the primary purpose
of studying and discussing non-proliferation issues in the region,
specifically in three critical areas: North Korea, India–Pakistan and
the Middle East. I visited South Korea, Burma, India, Pakistan, Kuwait
and Austria. In my trip summary, I was frustrated to have to report
that the Clinton administration's efforts were 'longer on pontification
and rhetoric than on performance'.[6]

While in New Delhi, I once again met with the prime minister,
the vice president, the minister of external affairs and the finance
minister—some of the same officials I had met with in January
1992. All of them expressed their deep concern over, and opposition

to, the Clinton administration's efforts to overturn the Pressler Amendment. In Pakistan, I was once again met with derision by all the officials I met—including the President, the prime minister, the defence minister, the minister of foreign affairs, and the president of the Senate. I also met with the Pakistan representative of Citibank (only later did I realize how important to my re-election this meeting probably was!). I made it clear during my meetings in Pakistan that, while I viewed the Pressler Amendment as a means to an end (non-proliferation) and not an end in itself, it served as an important barrier to a nuclear-armed South Asia. I also raised my fears once more of an 'Islamic bomb', this time at a formal dinner. Once again, it ruffled feathers among the politically correct diplomats who were present.

I did establish somewhat of a personal rapport with Prime Minister Benazir Bhutto over the course of a lengthy dinner meeting on this trip, as we discovered we had mutual friends at Oxford. She was smooth; she talked like a Westerner when she was in Western countries and reeled me in with her charm and poise. But our social connection was not enough to smooth ruffled feathers. She reiterated privately and publicly the tough line her government was taking on the Pressler Amendment.

When I returned from this extended overseas trip, the controversy did not abate. The Pakistani chargé d'affaires to the United States, Ali Sarwar Naqvi, secured an editorial in the *Washington Post* on 21 December with an incendiary headline: 'Discard The Pressler Amendment'. It purported:

> The proposal to delete the Pressler Amendment from a revised Foreign Assistance Act is not out of consideration for Pakistan but is motivated by a desire to revise U.S. foreign assistance legislation to render it more rational and effective. Further, the Clinton administration's strong position on nuclear non-proliferation is well known. The proposed legislation on non-proliferation merely seeks to cover what was woefully lacking in the 1961 act—i.e., a rational and effective approach toward this subject.[7]

I was beginning to doubt the Clinton administration's 'strong position' on nuclear non-proliferation. I sincerely thought that the Clinton–Gore administration would be more enthusiastic about the Pressler Amendment, given its vigorous campaign rhetoric in support of non-proliferation. As soon as Clinton became President, he seemed to embrace the Octopus. He had obviously made campaign promises to donors that he wanted to keep. He was politically savvy. I was naïve to think that a new administration would change the climate.

I received a formal response to my November letter to President Clinton on 27 December that was full of more obsequious doublespeak:

> I share your belief that non-proliferation belongs at the top of our policy agenda for South Asia. The draft Foreign Assistance Act in no way indicates that we intend to change our policy towards Pakistan's nuclear program. The Administration's draft bill retains strong proliferation sanctions. While we have sought to remove all country-specific provisions from this bill, including the Pressler Amendment, I can assure you that I will not waive nuclear proliferation sanctions unless Pakistan satisfies the Pressler certification conditions. Moreover, should we consider such a waiver in the future, we will consult fully with the Congress.'[8]

This was a total lie, clearly intended to placate me.

In March 1994, I sent another directed plea to President Clinton asking for a few minutes of his time to discuss the Pressler Amendment: 'Despite repeated assurances from members of your Administration, including Deputy Secretary of State Strobe Talbott and Secretary of State Warren Christopher, I have from several sources within the Administration heard about an attempt to grant an exception to the Pressler Amendment.'[9] My letter was ignored.

Thankfully, however, the Pressler Amendment in its original language was maintained that year. There was not enough support in Congress to offer concessions to Pakistan at this time. But I knew that if Pakistan's importance to some other foreign policy objective became a priority, then my country would overlook Pakistan's nuclear weapons programme and its ties to certain Islamic fundamentalist factions. For now, the Pressler Amendment did not have enough detractors in Congress to be overturned. But this reprieve did not last long.

I was asked many times during that time period why I seemed to be singling out Pakistan on this issue, while India was developing nuclear weapons but was not being punished by the United States in the same way. At the time a US policy response was being developed to address nuclear proliferation in South Asia, India's programme was already in place and was built without US taxpayer assistance. India was and is a democracy with a clear chain of command and civilian oversight of its military and nuclear programme. Pakistan, however, had not yet admitted to acquiring the technology. Pakistan was only in a position to do so when US aid was considerable. And Pakistan used US taxpayer money to develop a bomb. With Pakistan's power in the hands of just a few generals, the US had reason to worry. In addition, because of its smaller industrial base, Pakistan turned its attention to acquiring critical technology and components from abroad— sometimes in violation of the United States' and other countries' export laws. Furthermore, Pakistani violations of US domestic laws governing the export of sensitive materials and technology were particularly vexing, especially the Pervez case.

Many United States policymakers also believed Pakistan was susceptible to a 'carrot-and-stick' approach. As a major provider of economic and military aid to Pakistan, the US felt it had leverage over Pakistan's nuclear ambitions. That carrot-and-stick approach also proved to be compelling to other countries that contemplated the pursuit of nuclear weapons technology. In contrast, the level of US assistance to India was insufficient to serve as a bargaining tool in obtaining US non-proliferation objectives in India. Plus, we shared India's fear of China's bomb.

Finally, another basis for focusing US initiatives on Pakistan was US concern over potential Pakistani ties to Islamic fundamentalism. Anti-Western factions were taking hold in several Islamic countries at the time, including Iran, Libya and Syria. While it was certainly not governed by religious fanatics, Pakistan was viewed likelier than India to cooperate with these governments—given shared religious and cultural foundations. There was also the question of the stability of the Pakistani government and its ability to ensure that nuclear weapons technology did not end up in the wrong hands. In this regard, my view of US foreign policy was designed to slow the possible proliferation of nuclear weapons beyond South Asia to the Middle East.

Why did Pakistan even need a nuclear programme? Pakistani leaders claimed that they had to do whatever was necessary to protect themselves against potential aggression from India. Although India is known to have exploded a nuclear device in 1974, there was no evidence that India sought to develop a nuclear arsenal. Even if it did, it was certainly as a counterweight to China's nuclear ambitions. So, was it really protection that Pakistan was seeking, or was it something else?

In a book chapter I wrote in August 1994:

As already mentioned, anti-Western factions have taken hold in several Islamic countries in recent years. Such forces are on the verge of victory in Algeria and have enough power to threaten the stability of Pakistan's government. The direction the now independent Soviet Islamic republics will take is unclear. Should control of these nations shift to religious fanatics, these countries could find that they have much in common, both ideologically and geographically. This could well be enough incentive for these countries to form, at the very least, some kind of loose-knit alliance. It is true that several of these countries historically have had serious disputes. However, religious fundamentalism may very well be the tie that binds.[10]

This turned out to be incredibly predictive, as Islamic fundamentalists are now trying to form a caliphate in the Middle East and South Asia—with tacit support from within Pakistan.

24

On the Home Front: Domestic
Legislative Achievements

'I consider this to be the most important piece of legislation I have
ever signed.'

—President William J. Clinton, at the signing ceremony for
the Telecommunications Act of 1996 on 28 February 1996[1]

While the Octopus and the Clinton administration continued to try
to work around the Pressler Amendment, I found myself unable to
defend all the assaults against me and my reputation because I was
too bogged down in other pieces of legislation. I became consumed
by a domestic piece of legislation that was very important to me—
the Telecommunications Act of 1996. When I became chairman
of the Senate Commerce Committee in 1995, I was delighted with
the assignment because I was most interested in leading an effort to
rewrite the Communications Act of 1934.

Since 1992, I had worked unsuccessfully on a new
telecommunications Act. Two bills that had been passed in the Senate
had died in the House. Now I had a chance to take a leadership role,

and I went to work. I visited every single member of the Senate and more than 150 members of the House. After I found out what each one of them wanted in the bill and negotiated the bill's language with them, together we worked out a bipartisan bill that was passed at the end of a very tough fight. The Telecommunications Act of 1996 was a huge bill, the magnum opus of my time in the Senate, and one for which I am known nationally in the United States. It became the international standard for developing the Internet and modern communications.

Like every major piece of legislation that has become law, it took many years in the making. By the 1970s, the Communications Act of 1934 was clearly obsolete. If the United States was to be a world leader in telecommunications, as it must be, that old patchwork of laws had to be replaced. The new law had to be cogent, effective and comprehensive. At the same time, it had to cover a multitude of particulars. It had to understand the complexities of modern telecommunications, recognize the realities of an international environment, acknowledge marketplace forces, encourage research and development, and benefit the American people in the long run. This was clear to everyone in the telecommunications industry, to members of the relevant committees in Congress, and to everyone with any kind of stake in electronic communications. As a member of the Senate Commerce Committee, I decided to take up this cause, and to make it *my* cause, in part because the people of South Dakota could only keep up with the rest of the world if they were 'connected'. In the years to come, that meant being linked via the new electronic medium, or the Internet.

In the bill, we created a non-governmental fund that diverts a tiny fraction of a cent of every dollar collected by telecommunications companies to a 'universal service fund'. This fund provides a subsidy to inner-city and rural telecommunications providers. As a result, remote communities in sparsely populated states like South Dakota benefited enormously because this universal service fund subsidized the cost of building the network infrastructure everywhere in the

United States. It enabled even the most rural communities to have access to the Internet. Today, when I walk around and see the large number of cell phones and computers being used, I feel a great sense of satisfaction.

The cost today of a telephone call is less than it was when I was a young adult. Texting and emailing is less expensive now than in the 1990s. The term 'long-distance call' has been dropped from the American vocabulary. For the first time, all the companies in the telecommunications industry could openly compete, allowing rapid development of new, more reasonably priced technologies. We could not have the Internet as we know it today without the Telecommunications Act of 1996. Vice President Gore took a lot of the credit for this law when he intemperately claimed to have helped 'invent the Internet'. He and President Clinton presided over the signing ceremony, but I knew who had done the lion's share of the detailed legislative work in the trenches to get it passed.

The Telecommunications Act of 1996 had a tremendous impact on the modern world in terms of communications, but it was not the only work I did that had such influence. I also worked on the 'US–Germany Open Skies' agreement which became the standard for regulating the international aviation industry. It released the chokehold that London's Heathrow Airport held on the commercial aviation industry outside the United States.

Not long after that agreement was signed, the competitive pressure it unleashed encouraged France to sign an Open Skies agreement. A little over a decade later, the US and the European Union (EU) signed a landmark, more comprehensive Open Skies agreement. But without the historic US-Germany Open Skies agreement, it was unlikely those other Open Skies dominoes would have fallen. 'Open Skies' agreements allow free-market competition for all commercial carriers, and lift restrictions on air routes, capacity, frequencies, and types of aircraft. India greatly benefitted from these agreements, as it enabled anyone to fly from New York City to New Delhi non-stop, which was prohibited earlier. These two acts—Telecommunications and Open Skies—were paramount in establishing the interconnected world that so many of us take for granted today.

During this time, I also worked on a handful of other issues, authoring and securing the passage of several other pieces of domestic legislation, including the Federal Aviation Administration Reauthorization Act of 1996, the Interstate Commerce Commission Termination Act of 1995, and a major piece of pipeline legislation. I also created the independent UN Inspector General office and was the co-founding member of the Senate Internet Caucus and Tourism Caucus.

The Pressler Amendment was very important to me, and I put a great deal of time and effort into it, but it was not the only work that occupied my time then. I do not know if I could have afforded to focus more attention on the Pressler Amendment. If I had, perhaps it would have withstood the assault it continued to face from the Clinton administration, Secretary of Defense William J. Perry and, of course, the Octopus.

25

The Clinton Administration Weakens
the Pressler Amendment

'I don't think what happened was fair to Pakistan. I don't think it's
right for us to keep the money and the equipment. I'm going to try
to find a resolution.'

—President Bill Clinton in 1995 discussing the F-16s
that were sold to Pakistan in the 1980s but never delivered[1]

While I was concentrating on the massive new Telecommunications
Act, the Octopus continued to try to work around the restrictions
imposed by the Pressler Amendment in any way that it could.
Secretary of Defense William Perry made an announcement during
a January 1995 meeting with Pakistani legislators in Islamabad that
he was going to revive joint exercises and military educational
exchanges that had been cancelled since the Pressler Amendment's
enforcement took effect in 1990. The Pakistani legislators were
elated and provided encouragement: 'We are glad you are trying to
bypass [the Pressler Amendment],' one legislator told the Americans.
'It has become a household word ... translated into Urdu and

Sindhi.'[2] They urged Secretary Perry to repeal the ban, as 'we think this is all unfair'.

President Clinton said publicly in a meeting in Washington with Prime Minister Bhutto in April that he agreed. He thought the sanctions were unfair. He vowed to resolve the issue of the twenty-eight F-16s that Pakistan had purchased in the 1980s which were still gathering dust at a desert airfield in Arizona.

When asked about her country's nuclear weapons, Prime Minister Bhutto brazenly lied. 'We don't have nuclear weapons. We have enough knowledge and capability to make and assemble a nuclear weapon, but we have voluntarily chosen not to.'[3] I'm not sure how she could say this with a straight face. News had surfaced just four days earlier about a new nuclear reactor that, when completed, would give Pakistan access to substantial quantities of plutonium.[4] This would allow the country to build far more powerful and compact nuclear weapons than it previously possessed. On this visit she told reporters that she doubted such a reactor existed until she was shown evidence—at which point she immediately reversed herself and said it was only a 'small reactor for experimental purposes'.

I issued a blunt statement: 'I find it simply preposterous any proposal that would transfer even one F-16 to Pakistan. I am astounded that an administration that pays so much lip service to the cause of nuclear non-proliferation would consider providing Pakistan with aircraft capable of carrying a nuclear weapon.'[5]

It was infuriating to me that the Clinton administration, which continued to tout itself as a strong advocate of non-proliferation, would show such hostility towards the Pressler Amendment—the only nuclear non-proliferation law with teeth.

I knew that Pakistan had enough nuclear material at the time to assemble six bombs. It was rumoured that Pakistan was advising the treacherous state of Iran on how to start its own nuclear programme. The world knew that Pakistan was harbouring the 1993 World Trade Center bombing mastermind, Ramzi Yousef, and that the nation remained a safe haven for other terrorists. Why was President Clinton now offering to compensate Pakistan for the undelivered planes? It would deliver a blow to regional peace, and would generate renewed hostilities and a nuclear arms race in Asia. It could increase the likelihood of nuclear weapons falling into terrorist hands. Plus, it would also send a message to Pakistan and the world that there were no long-term penalties for going nuclear.

But the political tide was rising against me, and the Octopus was setting its sights on me. Relations between Pakistan and the United States were chilled, the State Department and the Pentagon were working behind the scenes to get around the Pressler Amendment restrictions, and President Clinton was publicly working to undermine the aid ban. I thought that we needed to get past this impasse in the interest of overall regional security. There was no way I would support the United States turning over nuclear delivery devices like the F-16s to Pakistan with US taxpayer dollars. So, I offered up a proposal that would 'resell' the F-16s to Taiwan and the Philippines, and give the proceeds from the sale to Pakistan. My rationale was that Taiwan and the Philippines were our allies and we had planned to sell them some F-16s anyway. At the time, it seemed like a good resolution to this issue and, at a minimum, I believed the proposal would end any talk of letting the jets go to Pakistan. I was not the only policymaker suggesting this idea. Secretary Perry and other officials had also talked publicly about a third-party sale—as a somewhat neutral compromise that would appease both Pakistan and India. None of these proposals received much traction.

In May that year, my colleagues on the Senate Foreign Relations Committee started to whittle away at the Pressler Amendment. They voted to free up aid to Pakistan for narcotics control, military-to-military contact, peacekeeping and antiterrorism. But the coup de grâce was the amendment submitted by Hank Brown, the senator I had seen dining occasionally with Syeda Abida Hussain, the Pakistani ambassador to the US from 1991 to 1993. Now I knew why.

Senator Brown introduced an amendment to the Foreign Assistance Act that provided for a one-year waiver of the Pressler Amendment certification. Backed strongly by the Clinton administration, it passed fifty-five to forty-five in the Senate on 21 September, freeing up $368 million worth of missiles and other military equipment. During the long debate on the amendment in the Senate the day before, Senator

Brown argued that it was an issue of fairness, a point the Pakistanis had made over and over and over again. I disagreed. The timing was especially egregious, given that intelligence sources were reporting that Pakistan possessed M-11 missiles from China capable of carrying nuclear warheads.

Many Democrats broke with the White House and voted against the Brown Amendment, which was a vote to keep the Pressler Amendment intact. In addition to me, one of the most vocal supporters of maintaining the Pressler Amendment was my old friend Senator Glenn. As he said on the floor of the Senate,

> Please note that the argument about the Pressler Amendment being unfair because it only applies to Pakistan is completely disingenuous because it ignores the fact that Pressler was created to shape further the unique special exemption from United States proliferation law given to Pakistan years earlier. If we had not had the waiver, we would not have needed the Pressler Amendment.

He went on:

> The issue is: Does the United States of America have a nuclear non-proliferation policy worthy of the name or not? That is basically what we are talking about. Do we have one and are we willing to abide by it? Or is it a sham? Is it only for press conferences? Is it only for campaign talk and little else? That is the question.

Later, Senator Glenn's words became even more biting:

> Let us not be blind to what we are proposing to do: after years of fighting for nuclear non-proliferation, the Congress under this proposal would put on the statute books America's first proliferation law. Rest assured, if this proposal passes, America will not be the only country with other nuclear proliferation laws on their own books. The race will be on to cash in on proliferation, rather than to prevent it. This is an extremely dangerous course and one which the Congress should summarily reject as contrary to the national

security interests of the United States. It is an embarrassment to this
legislature even to be debating this extremely ill-advised scheme.

Senator Glenn reserved some of his harshest criticism for the Pakistani
prime minister, Benazir Bhutto:

> Let me just quote—I am going to put some of this in the Record
> later on at the end of my remarks, but let us bring it up to date here
> with the present Prime Minister, Benazir Bhutto. Listen to some
> of her comments on this. Going back when she was opposition
> leader, Benazir Bhutto, shortly before she became Prime Minister,
> *The Washington Post* quotes her as saying: 'We don't want any
> controversy with the U.S. on the nuclear issue. We want it clear
> beyond doubt that we are interested only in energy, not nuclear
> weapons.'

Senator Glenn continued with several other examples of where
Pakistan or Bhutto had lied. He gave a most recent example:

> And the last one that I will read here out of a number of other
> examples I could give was in 1994, last November, on November
> 18, 1994, being interviewed by David Frost on PBS, Prime
> Minister Benazir Bhutto said, 'We have neither detonated one
> nor have we got nuclear weapons. Being a responsible state and a
> state committed to non-proliferation, we in Pakistan through five
> successive governments have taken a policy decision to follow a
> peaceful nuclear program.'

Senator Hank Brown appealed to his colleagues to support
President Clinton on this issue: 'If we turn down the President after he
has negotiated a settlement, after he has taken the lead and gotten an
agreeable settlement in this very sore situation, we not only discredit
the President but we undercut his ability to negotiate for us in the
future.' Note that Senator Brown said publicly that this amendment
did not necessarily reflect his own convictions about the Pressler
Amendment. He just wanted to support the President.

Senator Brown also countered Senator Glenn's arguments, insisting that the US needed to be fair to Pakistan. However, he did not address Pakistan's repeated lies. 'I must tell you,' he said, 'my own view is I do not want to get involved in arms sales to the subcontinent that will create an escalating arms race or that [sic] change in the balance in favor of one side or the other. I want the United States to be friends with both countries.'

Senator Brown continued with what is a basic fallacious argument, that India and Pakistan should be treated as equals:

> We have now gotten ourselves into a much greater mess of 'what do we do about Pakistan now'? We have said they are a rogue state, that they should not show any signs of launching, expanding, or moving their nuclear weapons. It seems to me, if we are going to be consistent, we ought to apply our concerns about nuclear technology to both India and Pakistan. If we are concerned about nuclear technology, we ought to be willing to apply the laws that restrict its development and spread to both India and Pakistan, not just to one of the two.[6]

During the time of the Brown Amendment debate, a classified intelligence briefing was hosted for the Senate. There were those within the CIA, the State Department and the Pentagon who supported the Pressler Amendment but were prohibited from publicly expressing their views because the Clinton administration was intent on repealing it. These officials within the national security apparatus were eager to demonstrate how damaging the Brown Amendment would be. They just had to be cautious in how they did it because they were contradicting their higher-ups in the Clinton administration. Senators were invited to listen to the raw and recent intelligence available about the state of Pakistan's nuclear weapons programme. While the briefing was not well attended or well advertised, it actually had the effect of reducing the number of Brown Amendment supporters. If the entire US Senate had attended that briefing, I believe the Brown Amendment would have been defeated.

Throughout the consideration of the Pressler Amendment, many veteran diplomats, career military officers and other authorities would say privately that they supported the Pressler Amendment as the best of US foreign policy. To my amazement, once President Clinton was in office, they were browbeaten into silence. I have never been able to understand this, except it is my judgement that President Clinton was playing 'footsie' with potential donors for the Clinton Foundation.

Most of the media's editorials lambasted the news, rightly stating that the Brown Amendment sent the wrong message to Pakistan. And the Government of India issued a sobering statement:

> ... We firmly believe the proposed U.S. action would not be conducive to promoting peace, security and stability in South Asia, was likely to trigger an arms race, and would be seen as legitimizing Pakistan's clandestine acquisition of nuclear weapons even while receiving massive U.S. military equipment and economic aid. . . . The Government of India is committed to taking all necessary measures to counter the adverse effect on our security caused by the proposed transfers. We hope the U.S. authorities will reconsider the issue and reflect on the consequences before taking any further steps.[7]

The clash between Senators Glenn and Brown on the Pressler Amendment illustrated the whole problem with the nuclear debate in South Asia. We, as a nation, must not look upon India and Pakistan as equals. They are not. India is our ally and has our values. Pakistan is not our ally except when it wants money and military weapons from us or when we want its help with a geopolitical goal. We do not share its values. Pakistan is dishonest and dangerous. To continue to equate the two as equals is one of the great mistakes of American foreign policy.

With the passage of the Brown Amendment, the South Asia arms race was about to accelerate and the Clinton administration had played right into Pakistan's hands. What I did not expect was the political fallout I was about to receive back in South Dakota—on the eve of my re-election campaign to the US Senate.

26

The Death of the Pressler Amendment and the Success of the Octopus

'Who will speak up for restraint in nuclear trade if the United States shows it cares more about bucks than bombs?'

—Senator John Glenn, in a letter to President Clinton,
12 February 1996[1]

One of the great mistakes in the United States' relationship with the South Asian subcontinent was President Clinton's efforts to weaken the Pressler Amendment and, as a result, US nuclear non-proliferation policy. Had he stood by the law rather than attacked it, Pakistan would not have resumed its development and testing of a nuclear weapon. But the Octopus, primarily the Pentagon, actually helped Pakistan get a nuclear bomb. It wanted to reward Pakistan for taking the Afghan refugees and helping drive the Russians out of Afghanistan—which, in turn, created the modern al-Qaeda.

The Octopus also wanted Pakistan to have a nuclear bomb to counterbalance China's power. Finally, enabling Pakistan to have a nuclear weapon would give the country leverage over India, which at the time was still more closely aligned with Russia. As I have said, Pakistan has always been a favourite client state of the Pentagon, since Pakistan's generals have been a compliant (and pliant) ally of the Pentagon. It was a classic example of the US being more comfortable dealing with a rogue-state dictatorship than with another democracy!

I argue that Pakistan was and is an inherently flawed state without a core set of ethical beliefs and no real central government. They always seemed much more of a tribal state and I had nightmares about a government as corrupt and dishonest as Pakistan's possessing a nuclear weapon. At the time, I warned about the prospect of 'the Islamic Bomb'—and the powder keg such a bomb could create in South Asia. Pakistan's nuclear bombs are built in such a way that they can be hauled in a pickup truck across any terrain and any border into a neighbouring country. Potentially, they could be put on a boat, transported to Mexico, and transported across the US border. When a government so inherently unstable as Pakistan has a nuclear weapon, it can have disastrous repercussions. I will never forgive the Octopus for allowing it to happen. It had enough control over Pakistan at that time to keep it from developing a weapon, but it did not exercise that control. Instead, it destroyed the Pressler Amendment.

Soon after the Brown Amendment was passed, it became clear that India's threat to accelerate the region's arms race was not a veiled one. Less than two months later, in December 1995, US intelligence sources reported that India was preparing to test a nuclear device, the first time since 1974. Publicly, India's leaders lied and denied the rumours. In fact, everyone on the subcontinent seemed to be dishonest with the US at the time. It was a swirling cyclone of deception all around.

President Clinton and his diplomats scrambled to discourage the planned underground test, fearing the worldwide reaction. In his 2004 book *Engaging India*, Deputy Secretary Strobe Talbott described a meeting between Frank Wisner, the US ambassador to India, and A.N. Varma, Indian Prime Minister Narasimha Rao's principal secretary. In that meeting, Wisner put Varma on the spot and showed him the satellite imagery that our intelligence sources had captured.

He threatened sanctions if the test proceeded. President Clinton personally called and appealed to Rao to reconsider, but President Clinton was not given much reassurance. He was only told that India would not act irresponsibly.[2] When the news of the planned test leaked to the *New York Times*, Pakistani Prime Minister Bhutto responded tersely: 'India must be restrained, if the [Indian] subcontinent is to be saved [from a nuclear tragedy] . . . As a non-proliferationist, I feel this will trigger a proliferation race [in South Asia].'[3] If only she had looked in the mirror when she made these statements!

With the eyes of the world now on India and its surprise foiled, the test was cancelled. I honestly don't think it was the pressure from the Clinton White House or the State Department that forced them to cancel the test. I believe it was the fact that they had lost the element of surprise. It was only a matter of time before they would try again and would try even harder to keep it under wraps. And now that the Pressler Amendment had been weakened, I knew Pakistan would quickly counter. There was nothing holding them back any more.

Four months later, the Clinton administration used the Brown Amendment waiver to approve a major arms deal with Pakistan. Clinton also resumed granting government-subsidized loans, and offered loan guarantees for US exports to China. In mid-April, the administration agreed to give $368 million in military equipment and $120 million in cash to Pakistan to repay them for weapons and spare parts they had paid for but never received. Part of the deal for these twenty-eight F-16s included $200 million in credits from the US government. What this means is that US taxpayers underwrote the sales cost of some of these planes. The claim that these equipment were due to Pakistan because they had 'paid' for it is not true. US taxpayers were footing most of the bill. The Octopus is very skilful in giving money to foreign governments, who then turn around and 'buy' arms from the US.

This surprising new arms deal came in the wake of news that China was secretly providing Pakistan with specialized magnets that could be used to enrich uranium for nuclear weapons. Deputy Secretary Strobe Talbott sent a letter to all of us in Congress justifying the action as providing 'the best opportunity to engage Islamabad in our [nuclear] non-proliferation strategy and to improve cooperation with Pakistan on such vital issues as counterterrorism and counternarcotics'.[4] I was dumbfounded that the Clinton administration would do this. What is worse, they knew about these clandestine technology transfers between China and Pakistan at the time they were trying to get the Brown Amendment passed.

Prime Minister Bhutto was visibly pleased. She, along with other civil and military officials, personally witnessed the arrival of the goods at an airbase and announced: 'It gives me considerable satisfaction to receive the second consignment of our embargoed military equipment.'[5] She claimed that the spare parts and test equipment for F-16s, tanks, guns, howitzers and armoured personnel carriers would bolster her country's defence posture and deter aggression.

The F-16 fighter jets, however, remained in escrow in the Arizona desert and were still a sore point for the Pakistanis. The fact that these planes had been sitting there for so long and were not sold to another country or used by the Pentagon was, in my opinion, ridiculous and wasteful. But, for the Octopus, I'm sure it was intentional. They wanted a 'photo opportunity', something tangible to show the negative impact of the Pressler Amendment. They knew that photos of those planes ageing in the desert would irk the Pakistanis.

And I knew President Clinton wanted to do something about those planes. He had said as much publicly back in 1995 when Prime Minister Bhutto pressed him on it. But the Brown Amendment was only a one-time waiver of the Pressler Amendment sanctions against Pakistan. President Clinton needed additional legislation to do it again. Senator Glenn and I wanted to prevent that. We vowed to continue the fight and repeal the Brown Amendment.

As it turned out, I didn't have much time to do it. As my third six-year term was expiring at the end of 1996, I was facing a re-election campaign to the Senate in November. The Octopus was determined to punish me for my foreign policy 'meddling' and to ensure I was run out of the Senate. One of their tools? Citibank!

During my 1996 campaign for re-election, the company's workers in South Dakota were told through a series of mailings that said something to this effect: 'Your Senator Pressler is working to reduce jobs in Citibank worldwide and that might eventually harm your job here in South Dakota.' Although the Pressler Amendment had no impact on the Citibank credit card operation in my home state, and unemployment rates in South Dakota were very low at the time, Citibank lobbyists proved to be a very discreet, dangerous and effective political force.[6] The company's efforts had a serious impact on my campaign to be re-elected for a fourth term to the US Senate.

The Pakistani lobby in the US had set its sights on disrupting my re-election campaign and it employed an interesting tactic. The lobby's hired guns asked every Pakistani doctor in the United States to send $1000 to my opponent, South Dakota Democratic representative Tim Johnson. Through the Association of Physicians of Pakistani Descent of North America (APPNA), a group of Pakistani doctors held a fundraiser for congressman Johnson near the White House and President Clinton attended and spoke to the attendees, promoting my opponent's Senate candidacy.

President Clinton had essentially promised me and a few other senators that if we voted for NAFTA (the North American Free Trade Act, which was passed in 1994), he would never campaign against us in any of our future elections. That is my recollection. President Clinton spoke at three fundraisers for Tim Johnson and then visited South Dakota. Indeed, his airplane was on the ground in South Dakota on the eve of election day in 1996 and he stayed there from about 5 p.m. until a little after midnight, when he flew back to Arkansas to vote in his home state.

The next day, I lost that last election by 1 per cent of the vote. Subsequently, I saw Bill Clinton at a Rhodes Scholar event and we shook hands. He grabbed me by the shoulder and said, 'Are you okay, Larry?' And I said, 'Yes, but I will always be disappointed that you campaigned against me after you promised not to if I voted for NAFTA.' He replied, 'I said I *probably* wouldn't, but that's just politics,

Larry. You know that.' And that was the last time I talked to Bill Clinton. (I still admire Bill Clinton for some of his accomplishments, including passing a balanced budget. I also publicly endorsed and campaigned for Hillary Clinton in 2016, so I don't hold grudges.)

Despite all this good work, I was kicked out of the Senate and subsequently became a professor, in January 1997. I was forced to watch the demise of the Pressler Amendment as an outsider. The South Asian subcontinent's arms race continued unabated. The Clinton administration clung to the belief that their efforts to ease sanctions against Pakistan were an effective nuclear deterrent for both India and Pakistan. This belief was quickly debunked when, on 11 May 1998, the world woke up to the news that India had successfully conducted five underground nuclear tests. The White House, the Pentagon, the Central Intelligence Agency and the State Department all learnt about it on CNN![7] Our intelligence had failed this time. The Indians had not been candid with us and they achieved their goal of complete surprise.

The test site was just a little more than ninety miles from the Pakistan border. I thought a response from Pakistan in the form of its own nuclear test was inevitable. But President Clinton still insisted publicly that he did not think a Pakistani nuclear test was imminent. I can only hope that he was a bit more realistic in his private deliberations over what to do. Deputy Secretary Strobe Talbott and Marine Corps General Anthony Zinni were dispatched to meet with the new prime minister, Nawaz Sharif, but they came away from their meeting empty-handed. The Pakistanis would promise nothing. I knew the Pakistanis would respond.

Meanwhile, with the tacit encouragement of the Clinton administration, two senators were introducing a new piece of legislation that would offer more waivers to the Pressler Amendment. Kansas Republican senator Sam Brownback and Iowa Democratic senator Tom Harkin justified their amendment as an incentive for Pakistan not to conduct their own underground nuclear test. The years before the Pressler Amendment's enforcement proved that more arms and more economic assistance to Pakistan had been anything but an incentive.

On 28 and 30 May 1998, while the world held its breath hoping
Pakistan would not do what we expected them to, Pakistan went ahead
and conducted six underground nuclear tests. The country's ministry
of foreign affairs described the events as 'Pakistan's finest hour'.[8] It
was a stunning reaffirmation of the existence of an Islamic bomb and
a dramatic demonstration of the disastrous effect of the failure of the
Clinton administration to enforce the Pressler Amendment.

President Clinton immediately announced he was invoking the
Glenn Amendment sanctions against both India and Pakistan. But his
words were really an empty threat, given the momentum that the
Brownback Amendment was gaining in Congress. Officially called
the India–Pakistan Relief Act of 1998, the Brownback Amendment
was adopted that year, giving the President the opportunity to issue
a one-year waiver of the sanctions under the Glenn, Symington and
Pressler Amendments. Another nail in the coffin.

But President Clinton still did not have the legislative loophole
he needed to fulfil his promise to Benazir Bhutto to repay Pakistan
for those pesky F-16s. So, he found money he could access without
bothering Congress in a federally managed fund within the Treasury
Department called the 'Judgment Fund'.

Announcing in December 1998 that he was going to repay
Pakistan $464 million for the planes they never received, the Clinton
White House characterized the move as a creative way to fulfil a
valid contract, not as an acceptance of Pakistan's nuclear weapons
programme. But this announcement proved that President Clinton
was accepting Pakistan's nuclear weapons. He was putting up a
smokescreen to justify even *more* aid to Pakistan. While this payout
was the better option than handing the Pakistanis nuclear delivery
vehicles, I continue to this day to be stunned at the Clinton–Gore
administration's total reversal of the stance on nuclear weapons while
in office. It was such a stark contrast to the way they had campaigned.

By taking money from this special fund, the Clinton administration
avoided having to ask Congress for appropriated funds. Money from the
Judgment Fund can be used to settle a lawsuit that the US government

has lost or expects to lose. Incredibly enough, the US government was facing a lawsuit from our so-called 'allies', the Pakistani government, over the issue of these planes. Who was representing Pakistan? Lanny Davis, President Clinton's former White House special counsel, who had gone through Washington's lucrative revolving door to the law and lobbying powerhouse Squire Patton Boggs.[9]

Later that year, a second Brownback Amendment was adopted, giving the President extended waiver authority over the Glenn, Symington and Pressler Amendments. With that move, these powerful non-proliferation tools were officially dealt the death knell. It was an extraordinary reversal of twenty-five years of non-proliferation foreign policy—enacted by a Republican-controlled Congress and a Democratic President. What message were we sending to other nuclear wannabes, like Iran, North Korea and Iraq? And what message were we sending to the world? Here we were preaching the importance of preventing the spread of nuclear weapons around the world and, simultaneously, we were encouraging our 'pet' ally, Pakistan, to have them. As my Native American friends in South Dakota say, we were speaking with a 'forked tongue'.

The mess in Pakistan is a prime example of the Octopus's bungling of foreign policy. A tough sanctions regime ensures congressional engagement in US foreign policy, but the Brownback Amendment amounted to congressional abdication of its responsibilities in foreign affairs. Congress should have been and should be much more involved. I predict that in the long run, we will look back upon our closeness to Pakistan as a foreign policy disaster. If we had listened to the desk officers and foreign policy experts in the State Department during the last twenty years instead of the generals in the Pentagon and those associated with the Octopus, we would have been much better off. The result is that we have allowed a corrupt Pakistan, which is feudal in nature and whose elected government has little control over the country, to possess nuclear weapons. It is a disaster, with worse still to come.

27

The Aftermath of the Pressler Amendment

'There's not a Pakistani junior officer that doesn't know who former Senator Pressler is, and there's not a junior officer in the U.S. military that knows who Senator Pressler is.'

—Navy Admiral Michael Mullen, former chairman of
the joint chiefs of staff, quoted as saying in 2008[1]

It continues to amaze me how famous, or infamous, I have become in India and Pakistan as a result of the Pressler Amendment—far more famous than I am in the United States. To this day, if I am riding in a cab in New York or Washington and my driver is of Indian or Pakistani descent and he overhears my name in a cell-phone conversation, he will either be very friendly to me or tell me what a bad man I am! Recently, I was going through customs to enter India, and the young inspector looked at my passport and said, 'Are you *the* Senator Pressler of the Pressler Amendment?' I said 'yes', and he gave me a salute. I asked him how someone so young could know about the amendment and he told me there was a question about the Pressler Amendment in the Indian Administrative Services exam. For several years, when

I served on the board of directors of Infosys Ltd, they conducted a survey and I was cited as the third most admired man in India (after at least one cricket player!).

Today, the Pentagon still makes the absurd claim that the Pressler Amendment caused our present poor relations with Pakistan. Moreover, the Octopus delights in saying that I am an ineffective character in the United States, as Admiral Mike Mullen alleged in 2008.

My critics say that the Pressler Amendment alienated us from Pakistan's leaders at a time when we needed to engage with them, leaving us with little leverage over them. But I'm more of a purist when it comes to non-proliferation. I felt we needed to stay strong and consistent in our message to Pakistan and hold them accountable for their deception and lies—then and now.

Today, by all accounts, Pakistan has more than a hundred nuclear warheads. While India's conventional forces are five times as large as Pakistan's, the two countries' nuclear arsenals are almost at parity. The head of the US Central Command, General Joseph Votel, testified before Congress in March 2017, warning about the escalating arms race in South Asia. He fears that the border skirmishes or terrorist attacks increase the frightening potential of miscalculation by both countries that could lead to a nuclear showdown.[2]

Unlike India, Pakistan has a central government of only marginal competence that cannot consistently exert its authority over or maintain order in certain of its regions. The country harbours known jihadi organizations and allows known jihadi sympathizers to reside within the ranks of its military and the ISI.

First and foremost, US policymakers have a responsibility to our taxpayers, and in the face of evidence that taxpayer money was being used to pursue a nuclear weapons programme, the Pressler Amendment was a compelling case for responsible governance.

Second, the use or withholding of US assistance can be a critical point of leverage to achieve important foreign policy objectives. The Pressler Amendment *was* that leverage. If the Pressler Amendment had continued to be enforced, it is the opinion of many that Pakistan would have run out of money and would have been forced to shut down its programme.

The failure of various presidential administrations to enforce the Pressler Amendment is an example of how the Octopus can prevent congressional action. They do it by stalling, by 'lawyering around' the law, by mincing the law's language, and by employing legions of lobbyists to work against Congress. Since I had served in the legal adviser's office in the State Department as a young foreign service officer, I knew exactly what was going on. I just did not seem to have the power to do anything about it. The problem was that I was too much of a nice guy who did not retaliate sharply. I just did not feel that was the right thing to do.

My main supporter on the other side of the aisle was Senator John Glenn. In fact, I have frequently said that the Pressler Amendment should have been called the Glenn Amendment, since he was such a driving force on nuclear non-proliferation. Senator Glenn originally became famous as an astronaut, the first American to orbit the earth in 1962. He was a man of strong character, deep religious values, and resilience. His road to the Senate was marked by a lot of stumbles, only being elected on his third attempt. He was always very generous in giving me credit for the Pressler Amendment. In fact, when we travelled together to the Verkunde Conference in 1986 (now called the Munich Security Conference), he introduced me to the world leaders in the audience, saying, 'Senator Pressler is one of the few people who has actually sponsored a non-proliferation measure that counts.' He gave impassioned speeches about the need to keep the sanctions against Pakistan, but he was not a sharp-elbowed politician and nor was I. We were just two Boy Scouts who got rolled in the process.

The dangers of the Pakistan nuclear weapons programme are many: their nuclear weapons are routinely moved around the country over dangerous and treacherous roads in unmarked vehicles with few defences. There is evidence that the fifteen-or-so facilities housing their nuclear weapons have been targeted by militants—including the 2007 suicide bombing on a bus carrying workers to the Sargodha air base and the 2008 Taliban suicide bombing of a weapons depot called Wah Cantt in the Punjab province outside Islamabad.[3] A Pakistani bomb could be easily stolen by terrorists, it could be transferred to Iran, or it could be taken over by a militant group during regional unrest. This should make us all scared.

The security of Pakistan's nuclear weapons is suspect, even though Pakistani leaders insist their programme is safeguarded. Speaking to the *Atlantic* magazine in 2011, former Pakistani President Pervez Musharraf said, 'I think it's overstated that the weapons can get into bad hands.' He further wondered why the world is not worried about the security of *India's* nuclear programme. 'No one ever speaks of the dangers of a Hindu bomb,' he said.[4]

And still, US aid to Pakistan continues to flow. After the 11 September 2001 attacks on the World Trade Center and the Pentagon, we once again turned on the aid spigot to ensure Pakistan's cooperation with us in the War on Terror. After intense lobbying by the Pakistanis, President George W. Bush agreed in 2005 to sell to the Pakistani military an unlimited number of F-16s—plus reconnaissance drones, Cobra attack helicopters, C-130 Hercules transport aircraft, a navy frigate and other arms to help them in the fight against terrorists. But these arms seemed better suited to fight a conventional war with a neighbour than to root out domestic terrorists among its own ranks.

At the time, the State Department said that the move would help purge the 'bitter legacy' of the Pressler Amendment.[5] (The State Department seemed to love to 'bad-mouth' the Pressler Amendment!) And, of course, diplomats and military officials all claimed the aid would encourage Pakistan to expel the terrorist network within Pakistan. But Osama bin Laden was found living at a stone's throw from a Pakistan military academy in 2011! The Afghan Taliban chief Mullah Akhtar Mansour was killed by a drone strike in Balochistan in May 2016. And the ISI and the Pakistani military continue to protect the Afghan Taliban operating within the country's borders.

According to Matthew M. Aid's 2012 book, *Intel Wars: The Secret History of the Fight against Terror*, US intelligence experts were reluctant to admit that the ISI and the Taliban were collaborating.[6] But the evidence kept mounting and, in 2008, they determined that the ISI was providing training, money and logistical support to the Taliban. Furthermore, a December 2010 National Intelligence Estimate claims that Pakistan continues to harbour every major terrorist group that the United States deems an enemy. The northern Pakistan region remains a lawless 'Wild West' where the Pakistani Taliban and other homegrown terrorists roam without much interference. Some experts claim that the Pakistani government has all but lost control over vast swaths of this northern territory of Pakistan.[7] So much for eliminating the terrorists that are using sovereign Pakistani territory to breed, train and grow their ranks.

It seems that our rationale for continuing to provide aid to Pakistan during the War on Terror is similar to our rationale for providing aid during the Cold War, and it is equally flawed. In each case, we have subsidized this unstable and corrupt government's nuclear arsenal because we believed its leaders were helping us fight the Soviets and, now, terrorists.

Where does this aid—more than $25 billion since 2002—that we continue to give to Pakistan end up? Why is the country still experiencing such widespread poverty and high unemployment and inflation rates? Are we pouring money down a drain? What happens if Pakistan becomes a failed state? What happens to Pakistan's nuclear weapons if the government implodes? *Why do we continue to treat Pakistan like an ally?*

Although sidelined from the role of policymaker since leaving the US Senate twenty years ago, I have not been silent on the issues that matter to me. I was offered several lucrative positions that would have allowed me to cash in on my legislative experience and contacts. A lobbying firm wanted to pay me $1 million to help dismantle the Telecommunications Act of 1996, and four different countries— including India—wanted me to lobby for them as a foreign agent.

I turned down all these opportunities. Not surprisingly, I wanted to keep my independence.

Instead, I embarked on a teaching career which has taken me all over the world. I have served as an outside consultant and on the boards of directors or advisers to several for-profit companies, including Infosys Ltd, the Philadelphia Stock Exchange and a major US railroad. But the majority of my time has been spent teaching undergraduate and graduate students compressed courses (one to two months) on political science, public administration, international relations, ethics and comparative government. Over the last two decades, I have taught at twenty-one universities as a Fulbright professor and as a Distinguished Visiting Faculty member in Europe, Asia, the Middle East, South Asia and the United States. I relish the interaction I get to have with these young minds and I cherish the opportunity to imbue them with my idealistic view of the world and the importance of public service and ethical leadership.

As a member of the board of directors for Infosys Ltd, I have been able to travel back to India several times a year where I have maintained personal relationships with many current and former Indian government leaders, including Prime Ministers Narasimha Rao, Manmohan Singh, Atal Bihari Vajpayee and Narendra Modi; the economist Montek Singh Ahluwalia; former parliamentarian Murli Deora (until his untimely death); and former Infosys executives Nandan M. Nilekani and N.R. Narayana Murthy. During my tenure on the board of directors of Infosys, I was instrumental in assisting the company's efforts to get listed on the New York Stock Exchange.

Continuing my lifelong passion for veterans, I serve on the board of directors for the Jericho Homeless Veterans Projects in Harlem and the Bronx, and have been appointed to several presidential commissions, including the Military Compensation and Retirement Modernization Commission.

Now as an observer of my country's diplomatic and military relationship with South Asia for the last two decades, I continue to be disappointed. I'm frustrated by the increasing power of the Octopus and how much the arms trade dominates the United States' foreign policy agenda, I'm frustrated by continued American intervention overseas in costly and endless wars, and I'm frustrated by how little the average citizen in both the United States and places like India, Pakistan and Afghanistan can do about it. I wanted to do something more than just complain. So, against all odds, I decided to jump into the arena one more time and run for public office again, in 2014.

28

My Last Stand against the Octopus: Another Senate Campaign in 2014

'Pressler is right: He's a long shot. But his authenticity and candid comments could spice up an otherwise boring race. With polls reporting record dissatisfaction with the federal government, his candidacy could test whether voters would ever actually turn to an independent candidacy as an outlet for their frustration.'

—*National Journal*, November 2013[1]

Curiously, a movie release helped me make my decision to run for the US Senate again after almost two decades out of office. In 2013, *American Hustle* hit the movie theatres—with a big Hollywood promotional campaign and multiple Academy Award nominations. I played a real-life role in the subject of this movie, ABSCAM, and suddenly, my phone was ringing off the hook with calls from national media wanting my comment on an event that had given me my fifteen minutes of national fame in 1979.

In the three decades since ABSCAM, I've watched Washington slip into an ethical abyss. We continue to embark on foolish democracy-building military campaigns overseas—especially in the Middle East and South Asia. Nuclear non-proliferation efforts have totally failed in this region.

I was—and still am—angry, disgusted, heartbroken and just downright mad about the dysfunction of the two political parties in Washington, D.C. The Republicans and the Democrats in Washington are more loyal to their political parties than they are to their voters—a big reason why more and more voters do not identify with either major party. I wanted to break the stranglehold of the insane partisan fighting that is dragging our nation down.

So, as I approached my seventy-first birthday and reflected on a life of public service—two tours of duty in Vietnam, three years in the State Department, four years in the House of Representatives, and eighteen years in the Senate—I decided to try once more to do something about it.

I am still the moderate, independent centrist that I was in Congress, but the Republican Party has moved far to the right—now neither party works well with the other. Both the Republicans and Democrats are locked into a 'lobbyist-controlled spending and taxing' cycle. And they are both mired in poisonous partisan fights where nothing is resolved. I wanted to break that stranglehold.

An open Senate seat in 2014 in South Dakota presented a rare opportunity for an Independent to run. I also knew that I could have a very good chance of winning the Republican primary, and may have won, but then I would be committed to joining a traditional congressional caucus. (Congress has many caucuses or groups that represent a specific interest and to pursue common legislative objectives, i.e., the Senate Republican Conference, the Senate Democratic Caucus, Congressional Black Caucus or the Congressional Hispanic Conference.) That option was not at all appealing to me. If elected, I wanted to be truly independent in Congress, able to vote with either caucuses and not obligated to either party or any interest group. I wanted to be able to work with both sides. Indeed, a core group of Independents in Congress could be part of the solution—a group of policymakers that finally ends that bickering and stands up to the Octopus.

Currently, one of the most influential men in the US Senate is Senator Angus King of Maine, an independent and fiscal moderate who has been able to work with both parties. He was my model and later endorsed me. South Dakota needed a powerful Independent US senator to speak for its citizens on state and national matters. The prospect of being freed from the strings of a political party was a dream.

To 'test the waters' on a potential Independent candidacy, I began reaching out to some colleagues and former advisers to get their feedback—and a reality check. From these conversations, I slowly developed the idea to run an experimental, idealistic campaign. I was determined to keep my budget small and produce only positive ads and messaging. I would not respond to any attacks against me. Pledging to serve only one six-year term, I vowed not to raise any money once elected because I would not want to get back into the big fundraising efforts that US senators have to make. The need to constantly raise funds makes you beholden to the Octopus. Since senators spend up to half their time raising money, it really distracts them from the business of legislating. I would only go back into the Senate if I could have six years without having to raise a dime for the next term.

As I began to share my unofficial intentions with more and more people, word started to spread around political circles that I was considering a candidacy. I was trying to do on a smaller scale what President Trump succeeded in doing on the national level in the 2016 presidential election. He ran as an independent-minded candidate, but instead he hijacked the Republican Party to win it. He outmanoeuvred them all. My campaign was a long shot, but many of my friends told me it was worth a try. As my campaign manager Don Frankenfeld wrote to me in an email, 'Running for Senate in 2014 would be a noble, patriotic sacrifice, but a quixotic effort that might—if everything fell together in just the right way—lead to success.'

Public service in the US and India are thankless jobs and the odds of winning in any given election are slim. A lot of very fine people who run for office in both countries are defeated. For example, Nandan M. Nilekani, former CEO of Infosys Ltd, and later head of one of the national agencies in India, was responsible for distributing identity cards to a large number of India's citizens. Despite this major achievement and his proven dedication to public service, he was humbled at the polling stations. Nilekani ran for Indian Parliament from his hometown in Bengaluru. He was probably one of the most accomplished people by way of résumé and character in the entire Indian campaign that year. Good people can run but forces outside their control can trump good candidates. Running for office is a scary and daunting task. Nilekani was exceedingly skilled in the high-stakes game of global corporate politics, but he was no match for the rough and tumble of Indian parliamentary politics. He was too nice a guy to fight back as hard as he probably should have. In many ways, he was a lot like I am.

So, as I mulled my options in late 2013, I caught a lucky break when *American Hustle* was released in mid-December. There was immediately a lot of publicity and Oscar buzz surrounding this film, and that created new interest in the ABSCAM scandal—more than thirty years later. All of a sudden, national media were calling me to talk about my involvement in ABSCAM and how I was the only elected official to turn down the bribe. The timing of the movie's release was unrelated and coincidental to my planned Senate campaign announcement, but the film helped reintroduce me to a national audience.

I knew the Republican Party would consider me a 'spoiler'. I was not at all deterred. I was seventy-one years old, still healthy, and still eager to contribute to my nation. After all, throughout my life, I have always opted for public service. Idealism and my faith in God have driven my commitment to my career and my activities. This decision was just one more example.

Accordingly, between Christmas and New Year's Eve in 2013, I held a series of press conferences across my state to formally announce my independent candidacy for the US Senate. I dove back into the fray.

Rabbit in a Firing Range: The Octopus Takes Its Best Shot

'In an era of homogenized, data-driven campaigns, a quirky and unpredictable contest has emerged in South Dakota, confounding operatives and experts and potentially deciding who controls the United States Senate after the midterm elections. A race that most had thought was safely Republican is suddenly the focus of national attention, thanks to the surprisingly successful candidacy of former Senator Larry Pressler, a Republican who is running as an independent.'

—*New York Times*, 13 October 2014[1]

I had forgotten how exhausting the tempo of a campaign can be, but it sure felt good to be back in the game again. Every day, I awoke early and visited local coffee shops and diners to shake hands and talk with voters on their way to work.

It is probably hard for readers in India to visualize a US Senate campaign. Usually there are candidates running from the two major national political parties, the Republicans and the Democrats. I decided to go outside that party structure and run as an Independent, so I had to do some real 'retail' politics with no organizational or financial support from the national parties.

Each day during my 2014 campaign, I would field calls from local and statewide media, in between attendance at multiple business, civic and community events around the state. My wife, Harriet, and I would get in the car and just drive and drive and drive. It would take about two weeks to get all the way around South Dakota—stopping along the way. I was sleeping about three or four hours every night. It was exhausting. Yet it was a renewal of sorts for me because I could sense I was getting traction with voters.

How did I know? Because of the bipartisan voter feedback I was receiving. In my travels around the state, I spoke to voters from the heart, talking about how hard it was to run as an Independent and how much had changed in the two decades since I had last campaigned for office. I told them that although I served in combat in Vietnam, I was not a defence 'hawk', meaning the Octopus was not supporting me. Moreover, I had come to see many of our conflicts overseas as a waste of American blood and treasure. We were not the policemen of the world. I explained that one of my many teaching assignments since leaving the Senate was as a Fulbright professor in Italy. There, Harriet and I observed that we still had fifty-nine base sites—many of them obsolete military installations from World War II.[2] In my opinion, these bases should be closed and these troops should be returned to the United States. It would be better to spend money at home on education, deficit reduction, senior citizens, roads and tax relief. I believe our fiscal deficit is the largest threat to our economy and our national defence.

The PBS *NewsHour's* host Judy Woodruff, Fox Business Network's Lou Dobbs, and MSNBC *Hardball's* Chris Matthews were some of the first national network hosts to call me and invite me to appear on their shows. Others followed over the next few months. Despite the conventional wisdom that the presumptive Republican nominee was unbeatable, the reaction I was receiving from the media indicated that people really wanted a horse race—not a coronation.

We launched a statewide advertising campaign and assembled a comprehensive biographical ad. This two-minute montage of photos from my career showed me with many historical leaders: former Presidents John Kennedy, Richard Nixon, Lyndon Johnson, Jimmy Carter, Ronald Reagan, Bill Clinton and George Bush; the United Kingdom's Queen Elizabeth; former Cuban President Fidel Castro; Indian Prime Minister Rajiv Gandhi; and former Egyptian President Hosni Mubarak. We wanted to appeal to those younger South Dakota voters who were too young to remember the last time I was the state's US senator. It resonated. To differentiate me from the other candidates, we described my two decades of experience working for South Dakota and the nation. That worked too. We started running that ad as soon as it was ready and I had people on the street telling me that, while they didn't know me earlier, they were backing me in the upcoming election.

Then, on 8 October 2014, with four more weeks of hard campaigning ahead of me, a new poll came out that changed everything. That poll and all subsequent polls showed me leading the race. However, the hard lesson I learnt was that most people who claim to be 'Independents' with a capital 'I' actually vote as Republicans or Democrats when they enter the voting booth. Some have even called it the 'myth of the Independent voter'.[3] That's why President Donald Trump was smart to run on the Republican ticket and enlist the power structure of the national party and the party base of supporters, even though he advocated many independent ideas. Indian politicians could learn from Trump as well: working within the framework of national parties like the Congress and the BJP are still probably the best means to make progress for India.

I gave numerous media interviews over the course of the next few days and the resulting headlines were telling. The *Washington Post* said, 'A surprise in the South Dakota race?' The *Atlantic* wrote, 'The Rise of the Independents?' That Sunday, the *New York Times* ran a front-page story that read, 'Senate Contest in South Dakota Is Free-for-All'. The *National Journal* said enthusiastically, 'The Improbable

Career of Cowboy Poetry Aficionado, Senate Candidate Larry Pressler'.

My potential election to the US Senate in 2014 had major national implications. In those heady days in early October when I was leading in the polls, several political scientists and historians called me to discuss my candidacy. They felt that we were on the verge of something new and big in the United States. Why? Because, if the nation could elect four Independents to the Senate that year, the Independent senators could create their own, albeit small, Independent caucus.

With forty-eight Republicans and forty-eight Democrats in the Senate, we four Independents could have been the tiebreakers on any highly divisive issue. Theoretically, we could have controlled the leadership outcome and voted to elect Maine Senator Angus King the Senate majority leader. Our small but powerful Independent caucus could have indeed started a 'third way'.

It felt like we were on the verge of something very big, and we were.

CNN's Dana Bash travelled from Washington to South Dakota to attend several campaign events—including my cowboy poetry reading, held in a loud and boisterous sports bar/restaurant in mid-October. She was one of several reporters who travelled to cover my campaign. The *Times of London* even sent a correspondent across the pond to write a story about me.

CNN's Bash called the poetry reading 'an off-beat event befitting an unusual candidacy'.[4] (Much later, she told me this event was her favourite of the entire 2014 election season.) But it made sense to me. Cowboy poetry grew out of the campfire tradition of storytelling and singing songs about ranch and farm life, but some of the poetry's messages also reflected those of my campaign.

As a member of the South Dakota Badger Clark Poetry Society, I enjoy these poetry reading events on a regular basis. Badger Clark, known as a cowboy poet, was the Poet Laureate of South Dakota in the 1930s. Earlier, he also read to President Calvin Coolidge in his 'summer White House' in Custer, South Dakota. At this campaign event, I also read the classic 'Homecoming Queen' by M.J. McMillan, about a pretty young girl with promise who becomes a bitter waitress by the time she is forty: 'Waitin' tables and cryin' the blues. / Don't judge her too harshly till you've had the chance to walk a few miles in her shoes.'

It seems that people in the country like the comfort of poetry more than urban dwellers do. The lyrics of country Western songs are basically poetry. It might seem strange to Indians that a political candidate would hold poetry readings as part of his campaign, but these would attract fairly large crowds and also some news coverage. I have noted that in the south of India at political events, there are frequently poems or readings from some of the sacred texts.

It did not take long for the national political party operatives and the special-interest groups from around the country to start invading South Dakota. When they got a whiff of my surge in the polls, they got scared. They descended on my state. The barrage began.

Within thirty-six hours of the 8 October poll publication, the first attack ads appeared on television and radio. My campaign expected some of this, but we could never have imagined the number, the severity, the inaccuracies, the hate and the spitefulness of the attacks. Usually, a candidate is attacked by the left or the right. I was attacked by everyone. Both the National Republican Senatorial Committee and the National Democratic Senatorial Committee, both the uber-liberal donor George Soros and the super conservative Koch brothers, and both the National Rifle Association (NRA) and gun-control groups spent money in my state to defeat me. It was an ugly blitzkrieg—the Octopus at work again. It was evident that what they were really afraid of was having a real Independent in the Senate. It would upset the Octopus and its grip on the power structure in Washington.

Each group doubled or tripled its spending before the end of the campaign. Their sole objective was to defeat Independent Larry Pressler. They cared nothing about my philosophy or where I stood. Very few of these groups have connections to South Dakota, nor do they care about South Dakotans and the real issues my state faces. They simply wanted to preserve their respective party's numbers in the Senate. Period.

The Republicans and the Democrats have powerfully entrenched special-interest groups that support them. In this campaign, they were deployed into action. I answered calls from friends who said they received conflicting mailings—on the same day—from the NRA and gun-control groups. One mailer said I planned to give everyone guns. The next mailer, allegedly from a local pheasant and duck hunters' association but in reality produced by the NRA, said I planned to take away everyone's guns. It was a constant armada of false attacks. I felt like a rabbit in a firing range—with shots coming from all sides and every angle.

And then there were the strange, ghostly spam emails. Thousands of them started flooding my inbox starting in mid-October and they jammed my server, essentially shutting down my Internet service for two weeks. Big campaigns have the money to disable smaller opponents in this way. The content was identical in each one and it was mean-spirited and personally invasive. For example, one subject line read: 'Please don't play spoiler. Drop out.' Other messages said I was too old to run or that my campaign finance reports were inaccurate or that a personal scandal about me was about to be revealed. Each one was signed by a different person. It was creepy. I suspect the people were fictitious and computer-generated. But given the fact that they all had identical content, I knew there was some campaign entity creating and disseminating them. Without significant technical support, I could not respond adequately. It shows you how sinister the Octopus can be.

Despite the challenges I faced in responding to my critics, I was still racking up endorsements almost on a daily basis. The retired FBI agent who had led the ABSCAM 'sting' operation, John Good, came out of the blue to publicly endorse me. Angus King, the Independent senator from Maine, announced on 28 October that he was supporting me.

On 1 November, my state's largest newspaper, the *Sioux Falls Argus Leader*, endorsed me. Over the next few critical days before the election, all the rest of the major newspapers in my state endorsed me. And South Dakota veteran journalist Steve Hemmingsen, in his first-ever political endorsement, issued a statement: '. . . The gridlock in Washington has gone on long enough, and Larry Pressler, as an Independent U.S. senator, could be a major wedge in breaking that two-party logjam. Vote for Larry Pressler.'[5] He is an immensely popular figure in South Dakota and his words carried a lot of weight in my state.

Despite all this good news, I feared that the repeated attacks against me coming from all sides were crowding out my very positive message and my very productive campaign. The drumbeat of negative ads seemed to be quickening—with no balanced response.

On the eve of the election, I watched with disgust as major false, negative ads appeared on television almost every fifteen minutes, accusing me of not supporting Social Security, or some other such distorted and untrue allegation. The ads were broadcasting outright lies about my positions and deceiving the voters. This is why good people don't run for office. As I went to bed that night, I prayed that the citizens of South Dakota would look past this obnoxious clutter and make rational decisions in the voting booth the next day.

My mood on election day was bittersweet. The truth was that my campaign had probably been lost over the previous few weeks in the wake of the bombardment from all sides. I was probably doomed from the day I surged in the polls. The political parties' leadership just could not take the chance of having a real Independent in the Senate. They could not imagine not having their marionettes at their disposal.

Shortly after the polls closed at 8 p.m., all the national media called the election and announced that the Republican candidate was the winner. Only slightly more than half the eligible voters turned out at the polls. The following day, a radio announcer opined that I won all the debates and got all the endorsements, but not enough votes.

I knew the odds had been against me, but the polls had seemed so promising. Although I had run five victorious campaigns during my career, I had lost before. My political nemesis, Democratic senator Tim Johnson, narrowly defeated me in 1996 in a sharply fought and very costly campaign—the most expensive campaign in South Dakota's history at the time. But I moved forward then and I didn't look back. In fact, I even voted for and endorsed Senator Johnson in 2008. So, I knew that I would move forward once again. But I will admit that I was smarting and felt a bit bruised by the process.

It is my observation that a person's success should be judged by how he handles defeats and setbacks in life. Everybody has successes and stumbling blocks, though we usually only hear about the successes. But dealing with the defeats, great or small, is more important. In the prayer 'Our Father', the sentence that says 'Thy will be done . . .' is my refuge. This prayer has taught me to trust in God and move on after a setback.

Part of the reason I ran in 2014 was to get off my duff and take some action. Clayton Christensen, who brought me to the Mormon faith, gave a speech to the Harvard Business School graduating class in 2010. He titled it: 'How to Measure Your Life'. It had a profound impact on me. Clayton adheres to his religion's ideal of living by a strong work ethic. He advised these ambitious graduate students to work with a higher purpose in mind. He talked about how work should be done in the service of others—even in a business setting. He talked of measuring the value of life by broader things than just money earned. He talked of serving others. His thinking was one of my inspirations for running again—after so many years on the political sidelines.

I strongly believe that we all have to be politically active. That might involve running for office, it might involve volunteering for a political campaign, or it might involve attending a political meeting to truly understand the issues affecting everyday folks, instead of just relying on thirty-second campaign ads. My pet peeve is the uneducated and apathetic voter—someone who determines how he will vote by sitting in an armchair with a beer in one hand and a TV remote in the other, listening uncritically to negative ads.

I regard a vote as a sacred right, just as I regard public service as a sacred obligation. Public service to me means service to God and mankind. I believe that public service is among the highest callings, and politics is part of that. Most people who run for office lose, but their campaigns can have a positive effect on issues. I'm confident mine did.

Despite defeat at the polls, we succeeded in my 2014 campaign because we set a new standard for decency and clean campaigning. We succeeded because I followed my calling to run and did absolutely everything I could to win. I was satisfied that I had followed my innermost spiritual drives.

Maybe I was ahead of my time. Maybe I envisioned something that is not yet apparent to our country. But I know I was a catalyst for change and I'm confident our country will solve its problems. And by losing in 1996 and 2014, I won so many other things. So many opportunities for teaching and travel, so many friendships, and so many experiences outside of elected office were afforded me when I lost. So, I never complain as God always seems to bring me new challenges.

In general, I admire the way President Jimmy Carter has spent his post-presidency years. He has continued to serve as a diplomatic emissary for several presidents, and has devoted himself to several charitable causes. He is a fine example of austerity and common sense. Most other presidents enrich themselves after leaving office.

Abraham Lincoln lost his Senate race to Stephen Douglas, but the Lincoln–Douglas debates set a new national standard for Senate races. I would not dream of placing myself anywhere near the stature of Abraham Lincoln or Stephen Douglas, but I think in a small way my campaign as an Independent in 2014 had an impact far beyond winning or losing. I was able to speak out freely on issues without fear or party constraint. It was liberating. I was freed from the demands of the Octopus, even if its tangled tentacles strangled my campaign.

I'm reminded that the four political figures etched on Mt Rushmore in South Dakota were all Independents at some point in their careers. They took political risks and unpopular positions to benefit our great nation—not to advance their reputations or to line their pockets. They were committed public servants and knew how to cross vast party chasms and create progress. We, as a nation, should still be able to produce public servants like that. I know we still can.

I could have made a small fortune lobbying, but I chose public service instead. This decision has come at a financial cost to my family. My wife, Harriet, and I now live on my government pension, some social security benefits, a small veteran's disability income, and our retirement funds. (I spent almost $500,000 on my 2014 senatorial bid, so the retirement fund has dwindled!) My disability income is for my exposure to Agent Orange in Vietnam and for symptoms of PTSD from my experiences there. Unlike many other former senators, I will not be leaving behind a large estate. But that is fine with me and our daughter. I have had a great life and I am not complaining to my God. I would still highly recommend the public service route to young people in both India and the United States—that is, service to others over self-enrichment.

As I now look back on my 2014 campaign, I recognize it as one of the happiest times of my life. My campaign chairman had told me at the beginning of the campaign that the journey was more important than the destination. I know my campaign has inspired other Independents to try to get elected. I know I demonstrated how an honest, issues-oriented campaign can resonate with voters. I know that a low-budget campaign can be successful. I know I took the high road when the Republican and Democratic parties didn't. I know I put up a good fight against the Octopus. Even though it prevailed in this election, I will keep up the fight. I know I followed my heart, and it set me free.

30

Observations and Prescriptions for the Future

'Free at last, free at last! Great God Almighty, Free at last!'

—African American spiritual song

There is an assured type of freedom that humans experience when they reach a certain age in life. You could say that those of us approaching our twilight years do not care what other people think. We do. But, rightly or wrongly, we also feel somewhat emboldened to share our hard-earned wisdom. At age seventy-five, although in excellent health, I do not plan to run for office again. I feel free to say whatever I want.

My professional legacy in the area of foreign policy is one that history will have to decide. This book, and my career in the Senate, began with a commitment to reform and an avowed opposition to the spread of nuclear weapons—especially in the South Asian region. *On this issue, I consider myself largely a failure.* Despite my best efforts, Pakistan has a robust nuclear weapons programme. The *Wall Street Journal* estimated in March 2017 that India and Pakistan each have more than 100 nuclear warheads that can be delivered from land, air or sea.[1] Pakistan's arsenal could be easily hijacked by the large number of terrorists hiding there in plain sight. This should keep all world leaders up at night.

As a student of history, I think it is useful to study the past in order to forecast the future. In strategic planning classes, examples of 'alternative history' can sometimes be useful. Alternative history is a genre of storytelling where crucial moments of history unfold with different results. For example, what if Neville Chamberlain had said 'no' to Hitler in 1938? Would there have been a World War II? Many historians believe that Hitler could have been contained early on. The unfortunate Neville Chamberlain gets the blame and his example is used by interventionists to this day.

Likewise, what if the Pressler Amendment had continued to be enforced as it had been for a few years during the George H.W. Bush administration? I contend that there was a very good chance that the Indian subcontinent would be nuclear-free today.

Consider the different standards the US government has set with various countries regarding the possession of nuclear weapons. As this book points out, the Octopus actually encouraged the development of nuclear weapons in Pakistan, yet we invaded Iraq partly because Iraq possessed nuclear weapons grade 'yellowcake', or 'urania'. Why the double standard?

The point I am making is the US government had enough carrots and sticks to control the spread of nuclear weapons in the 1980s and '90s. If we had applied the Pressler standards everywhere, we would not have many of the problems we now have throughout the world. *It is my contention that—if we had continued to apply the Pressler Amendment standards in the Indian subcontinent and elsewhere—the world would have been a much safer place, the Indian subcontinent would have been nuclear-free, and we would not have fought the Iraq war.*

Thus, the Pressler Amendment was poised to play a much bigger role in nuclear non-proliferation goals worldwide than it ultimately did. For some reason, as Senator Glenn pointed out in many speeches, the various US presidential administrations just refused to obey US laws. Current policymakers, especially the Trump administration, could learn much by studying exactly what happened with the Pressler Amendment.

Paradoxically, though I fought against the spread of nuclear weapons, it does not follow that I am against the peaceful use of nuclear energy. Indeed, I will devote whatever remaining energy I have to advocate for the implementation of the US–India nuclear agreement. In addition, I intend to remain steadfast in my support for better US–India relations and to pursue opportunities to broaden areas of collaboration and cooperation between these two great democracies. This book ends with some of my observations on these issues—a recap of the recommendations I have made in earlier chapters.

Get Lobbyists and Influencers Out of the Fundraising Chain

In this book, I have added a new word to the lexicon of our national and international debate: the 'Octopus', that ubiquitous creature that spreads the money and makes the decisions in the murky depths of Foggy Bottom. I have illustrated how the Octopus has taken over a big chunk of the role of formulating foreign policy in the United States. Foreign policy is supposed to be made by the President, the secretary of defense, the secretary of state, congressional committees, and judicial interpretation. Our Constitution placed all the powers for formulating foreign policy in the President, the Congress and the courts. Of course, there has been some debate—Alexander Hamilton argued that the President had inherently a full panoply of rights in foreign affairs. James Madison argued that these powers were more meant for Congress to wield. But they both concluded that setting foreign policy springs from our Constitution and is one of the principal roles of the federal government. Sadly, the leadership of the federal government has almost completely relinquished this responsibility. Today, it is the Octopus and all its slimy money and tentacles that make the back-room deals dominating my country's foreign policy agenda. I go into this period of semi-retirement with the satisfaction of having fought the good fight, and doing what I could to oppose the Octopus and its influence on domestic and international relations. However, it did put an end to my years of public service and sent me to the political graveyard. The Octopus may have nailed my political coffin shut, but as long as I have a spiritual pulse, I intend to continue the fight.

Unfortunately, I have concluded that we must live with the Octopus. It is a permanent force in foreign policy. And, as long as we have the threat of terrorism anywhere in the world, we will have to spend a lot of money on national defence and homeland security. But we must try to channel it to be a force for good. The major antidote to the Octopus dominating foreign policy is the broad engagement of people at the grass-roots level. We must somehow get informed and conscientious voters participating in campaigns and elections. The voter turnout in the 2016 US presidential election was 55 per cent, the lowest in twenty years. India's record is not much better: 66 per cent in the 2014 General Election. Involved voters who reward leaders for policies centred on human development, and punish leaders for policies bogged down by arms sales, are the ethical and effective methods of combating the Octopus in the long term.

To reduce the power of the Octopus in the United States and the world, we have to choke off its main sources of energy, which are money, and lobbyists. How about a programme that prohibits lobbyists and influencers from raising money for candidates, PACs and independent expenditures? My friend, Tom Patton, a prominent Washington, D.C., lawyer, recommends passing a law that restricts lobbyists and influencers from raising money for political candidates. They should be prohibited from being 'in the fundraising chain'— or orchestrating these campaigns. This would mean broadening the definition of lobbying to include anyone who is paid to influence public policy, and it could be accomplished by passing a statute— not a constitutional amendment. Lobbyists and influencers would still lobby on the merits of legislation, but they would not be able to raise money to influence legislators.

Create a 'Super US–India Alliance'

Today, the state of India–US relations has become almost entirely that of a military relationship. The War on Terror, the fight against Islamic militants worldwide, is consuming the foreign policy agendas of both the US and India, and dominating bilateral dialogue of both countries. With the dark shadows of 9/11 and the Mumbai attack still looming large on our collective consciousness, America and India are forced to engage together and with all our shared allies in this fight. The military relationship the US has with India is one of necessity. We share a commitment to democratic values in a continent where democracy is scarce. We also share a fear of China's increasing aggression and are committed to developing a strong, joint naval posture to counter this threat. But the alliance between our two nations could be much, much more than a military one.

We must decisively choose India as our nation's most favoured ally in the world—on a par with the special relationships we have with Israel and the United Kingdom. The world's largest democracy deserves a special relationship with the US and a favoured status— with free trade agreements and massive foreign development aid.

Harness the Octopus to Accelerate the US–India Nuclear Agreement

India, the United States and the United Nations must do much more to educate their populations on the significant benefits that nuclear power can bring to their everyday lives: more reliable electricity, more household and business productivity, and cleaner air. The governments of the US and India can use France as a model. They must also engage academia, religious leaders and the charities that work with the poor to help them understand the benefits and alleviate their fears and misconceptions about nuclear power.

But the most potent, potential, untapped advocate is the Octopus. This might seem to contradict my convictions about the corruptive influence of the Octopus, but I do think the US and the Indian governments should harness its power to help with the implementation of the civil nuclear deal. While Bhopal is very much on the minds of many Indian policymakers, numerous organizations committed to India's economic and social progress must push back much more forcefully against the anti-nuclear movement—with the skills of lobbyists, think tanks, religious institutions, academia and the media. The insurance and liability issues are real and a formidable challenge. All with an interest in all facets of the US–India relationship—including, yes, ironically, the Octopus—should be engaged in overcoming these obstacles, using the power of its money and influence. The Octopus is standing to profit the most from the increased military sales afforded by the US–India nuclear deal. I firmly believe that the Octopus can and should do much more to promote the peaceful use of nuclear energy in India.

Declare Pakistan a Terrorist State

Pakistan should be treated like North Korea—like a rogue state. The only reason Pakistan is not a totally failed state is that countries like China and the United States continue to prop it up with massive amounts of foreign aid. Unless Pakistan changes its ways with respect to terrorism, it should be declared a terrorist state. Several leading foreign policy experts besides me have urged as much. Indeed, the first Bush administration seriously considered doing so in 1992.[2] Pakistan's leaders have essentially blackmailed us into providing aid for the War on Terror with threats to cease assistance in rooting out terrorists in Afghanistan. Meanwhile, we know full well that Pakistan harbours terrorists, and many military leaders believe terrorists have infiltrated Pakistan's ranks. We let Pakistan use US taxpayer money to build their nuclear weapons programme. Why do we now let them use US taxpayer money to harbour terrorists? Without our money and military supplies, Pakistan would be powerless. Why do we continue to call Pakistan an ally? Why do we continue to be blackmailed?

Enact More Pressler Amendments

I believe the Pressler Amendment *would have been enforced earlier* if President Reagan had not been suffering from the early symptoms of Alzheimer's during his second term, if he had not been unduly influenced by staff who were beholden to the Octopus, and if Senator Glenn and I had not been significantly distracted by domestic issues. Senator Glenn, in particular, spent nearly eighteen months during this time frame defending himself against what I consider a very unfair ethics charge called the Keating Five matter. This involved a savings and loan scandal in the United States. Finally, I believe the Pressler Amendment also would have survived if not for the stupefying intransigence of the Clinton administration. Would it have been better had the Clinton administration put pressure on Pakistan to suspend its nuclear programme rather than put pressure on Congress to roll back the Pressler Amendment? I believe so and I still believe that President Clinton caved in to pressure from Pakistan because he was laying the groundwork for payments and contributions for his highly lucrative Clinton Foundation. Qatar, Saudi Arabia and many Muslim-dominated countries wanted Pakistan to have a bomb. It is the only way I can explain his complete reversal on nuclear non-proliferation and the Pressler Amendment.

Was the Pressler Amendment worth the effort? Some might say no, as Pakistan ended up with a nuclear bomb, but I say the basic strategy of both the Pressler Amendment and the Glenn Amendment—to leverage US financial assistance and cooperation to achieve nuclear non-proliferation goals—was successful. Moreover, the ripple effect was tangible: countries like Brazil and South Africa had considered pursuing nuclear programmes when these amendments were being debated and enforced, but they backed down, fearing a strong pushback from the United States. During the presidency of George W. Bush, the Libyan government, valuing US assistance and cooperation in the face of internal insurgencies, rolled back its nuclear programme. Even the controversial Iran nuclear agreement and the US–India civil nuclear agreement, imperfect though they may be, have the fingerprints of the Pressler and Glenn Amendments. The IAEA inspections are much more thorough because of the rigour of the Pressler and Glenn debates.

The Pressler Amendment is also wrongly blamed for political instability in Pakistan during its enforcement period. That is just nonsense—there was just as much instability in Pakistan before the Pressler Amendment. Critics will say that, during that time, Iran and Saudi Arabia started fuelling sectarianism in Pakistan. The truth of the matter is that the Pressler Amendment *did* slow down Pakistan's nuclear ambitions, and I think the public attention forced Pakistan to be much more careful and transparent.

I issued an early warning call about the threat of an 'Islamic bomb', and I was roundly criticized for being unduly concerned about Islamic fundamentalism and the terrorists' ambitions to build a Muslim caliphate. It was considered politically incorrect then to talk about the danger of any Islamic state having nuclear weapons or to publicly warn about the threat of an Islamic caliphate—or 'confederation', as I termed it in 1992. It turns out I was pretty prescient.

The underlying policy objectives at the heart of the Pressler Amendment clearly have had a long-lasting impact, even if inconsistently enforced. Like anything in government and public affairs, with the pull-and-push of numerous interests in a complex geopolitical landscape, it takes years of hard work and confrontation to achieve sometimes limited, but useful, results.

On some days, when I reflect on that era, it is clear to me that the whole Pressler Amendment effort was very much like the nearly fatal Apollo 13 space mission—a successful failure! You could say it was, like Apollo 13, a failed mission because it does not exist any more. However, the Pressler Amendment was a mission that had a number of positive consequences and even today offers some potent reminders. I believe both Pakistan and India have more limited and controlled nuclear weapons programmes than they would have were it not for the debate and sanctions of the Pressler and Glenn Amendments.

Second, while the ultimate outcome of the Pressler Amendment was not to my liking, the debates Senator Glenn and I had with our colleagues, on and off the Senate floor, served to invigorate Congress as a major player in US foreign policy during and after the Cold War. The debates on the Pressler Amendment were some of the more interesting and passionate dialogues I ever experienced with my Senate colleagues. Mine was certainly not a lonely voice, thanks to skilful and thoughtful debaters like Senators Glenn and Cranston. These debates are an essential part of a representative democracy.

While the President of the United States may be our commander-in-chief who has a number of institutional advantages in setting US foreign policy, that does not and should not preclude Congress from its responsibility in shaping US foreign policy. The decades-long battles over the Pressler Amendment encapsulate the three great powers of the US Congress: the powers of debate, legislation and, of course, the purse.

In recent years, Congress has struggled to find its footing as a legislative body, which also includes its role in shaping US foreign policy. Congress needs to get back in the business of being at times a complementary voice to the President's and at other times a competing voice to the President's on foreign policy. We need many more tools like the Pressler Amendment. They could make the world a safer place.

In spite of all this, those of us who are non-proliferation purists must keep on fighting. Struggle! Struggle! We make progress one step at a time—sometimes two steps forward followed by one step back. But we should never stop trying to move the human race inches forward. God apparently did not intend that all human achievement would be clearly recognized. It is mostly smaller victories that improve humanity.

Appendix

A Timeline of Pakistan's Nuclear Ambitions[1]

1955 – The Pakistan Atomic Energy Commission is established.

1965 – Pakistan's Atomic Energy Commission begins operation of its first research reactor (PARR) at Rawalpindi, under IAEA safeguards. Minister of Foreign Affairs Zulfikar Ali Bhutto says, 'If India builds the bomb, we will eat grass or leaves, even go hungry. But we will get one of our own. We have no alternative.'

1972 – Pakistan completes the Karachi Nuclear Power Plant (KANUPP) with plans to operate it under IAEA standards.

1976 – The Symington Amendment is passed, requiring cut-off of US economic and military aid to countries obtaining enrichment or reprocessing technology. Dr A.Q. Khan founds the Engineering Research Laboratories (ERL) at Kahuta.

1977 – The Glenn Amendment is passed, requiring cut-off of US economic and military aid to countries that deceptively import nuclear reprocessing technology. President Carter suspends US military and economic aid to Pakistan because of the country's attempts to acquire reprocessing technology.

1978 – General Mohammed Zia-ul-Haq says, 'China, India, the USSR, and Israel in the Middle East possess the atomic arm. No Muslim country has any. If Pakistanis had such a weapon, it would reinforce the power of the Muslim World.'

1979 – US economic and military aid is terminated because of Pakistan's importation of enrichment technology for the Kahuta plant.

1979 – Soviet troops invade Afghanistan in December.

Early 1980s – Multiple reports emerge in the media that Pakistan has obtained bomb-grade enriched uranium from China.

1981 – Pakistan violates US nuclear export laws by seeking to obtain inverter components used in gas centrifuge enrichment activities, via Canada, and zirconium, a nuclear fuel-cladding material, from New York. An Associated Press story cites a State Department cable: 'We have strong reason to believe that Pakistan is seeking to develop a nuclear explosives capability ... Pakistan is conducting a program for the design and development of a triggering package for nuclear devices.'

1982 – European press reports that Pakistan is employing Middle East intermediaries to acquire bomb parts (13-inch 'steel spheres' and 'steel-petal shapes').

1983 – Declassified US government reports conclude: 'There is unambiguous evidence that Pakistan is actively pursuing a nuclear weapons program ... We believe the ultimate application of the enriched uranium produced at Kahuta, which is unsafeguarded, is clearly nuclear weapons.'

1984 – President Zia claims Pakistan has a modest uranium enrichment capability intended for 'nothing but peaceful purposes'. More reports emerge that China is helping Pakistan with the enrichment. The *Washington Post* cites court records to report that a federal grand jury had indicted three Pakistanis for trying to ship parts for nuclear weapons to Pakistan. The *New York Times* publishes an interview with Dr A.Q. Khan in which he says Pakistan could enrich uranium and produce its own bomb if necessary.

1985 – The Pressler Amendment is passed, cutting off all aid to Pakistan unless the President can annually certify to Congress 'that Pakistan does not possess a nuclear explosive device and that the proposed United States assistance program will reduce significantly the risk that Pakistan will possess a nuclear explosive device'. The Solarz Amendment is also passed, cutting off all aid to countries that illegally export or attempt to export nuclear-related materials from the US.

1986 – The *Washington Post* reports that Pakistan has 'detonated a high explosive device between September 18 and September 21 as part of its continuing efforts to build an implosion-type nuclear weapon' and has produced uranium enriched to a 93.5-per cent level.

1987 – Pakistani native Arshad Pervez is arrested in Philadelphia for attempting to illegally purchase and export 'maraging steel', a key material used in gas centrifuge enrichment technology to make nuclear weapons. *London Financial Times* reports US spy satellites observing construction of a second uranium enrichment plant in Pakistan. Dr A.Q. Khan admits to a reporter that 'what the CIA has been saying about our possessing the bomb is correct'. President Zia tells *Time* magazine that 'Pakistan has the capability of building the Bomb. You can write today that Pakistan can build a bomb whenever it wishes. Once you have acquired the technology, which Pakistan has, you can do whatever you like.'

1988 – The *New York Times* reports that US government sources believe Pakistan has produced enough highly enriched uranium for four to six bombs. President Zia tells a Carnegie Endowment delegation that Pakistan has attained a nuclear capability 'that is good enough to create an impression of deterrence'.

1989 – Multiple reports emerge that Pakistan is modifying US-supplied F-16 aircraft for nuclear delivery purposes. An article in *Defense &*

Foreign Affairs Weekly states that 'sources close to the Pakistani nuclear program have revealed that Pakistani scientists have now perfected detonation mechanisms for a nuclear device'. UK press reports that Pakistan and Iraq are cooperating on a nuclear programme. Prime Minister Benazir Bhutto vows to a joint session of Congress: 'I can declare that we do not possess, nor do we intend to make a nuclear device. That is our policy.'

1990 – *U.S. News* reports that Pakistan has recently 'cold-tested' a nuclear device and is now building a plutonium reactor, while it is also engaged in nuclear cooperation with Iran. President George H.W. Bush invokes the Pressler Amendment, cutting off all aid to Pakistan.

1991 – The *Wall Street Journal* reports that Pakistan is buying the nuclear-capable M-11 missile from China.

1993 – *New Yorker* reporter Seymour Hersh reveals a narrowly avoided nuclear catastrophe that had been kept largely under wraps for three years. The article details a 1990 nuclear standoff between India and Pakistan, which was only averted through diplomatic intervention.

1995 – The 1993 World Trade Center bombing mastermind Ramzi Yousef is arrested in Islamabad. The Brown Amendment is enacted, which gives the President the power to waive for one time the Pressler Amendment certification.

1998 – India successfully conducts five underground nuclear tests on 11 May. Pakistan conducts six underground nuclear tests on 28 and 30 May. The Brownback Amendment is adopted, giving the President the opportunity to issue a one-time waiver of the sanctions required under the Glenn, Symington and Pressler Amendments.

2005 – President George W. Bush agrees to sell to the Pakistani military an unlimited number of F-16s.

2011 – Osama bin Laden is assassinated in Abbottabad by US Navy special forces. He is found living in a walled compound near a Pakistan military academy.

2016 – Obama administration agrees to sell sixteen F-16s to Pakistan with US taxpayer subsidies. Congress approves the sale without US subsidies, citing concerns over Pakistan's assistance to the Afghan Taliban. Later that year, the US denies $300 million of military aid to Pakistan after Secretary of Defense Ashton Carter declines to give a certification to Congress that Pakistan is taking sufficient action against the Haqqani terrorist network, as required by the Fiscal Year 2015 National Defence Authorization Act (NDAA).

Notes

Chapter 1: Growing Up in the Nuclear Age

1. Hans J. Morgenthau, *Politics Among Nations* (New York: Alfred A. Knopf, 1949).

Chapter 2: The Octopus

1. President Dwight D. Eisenhower's final address to the nation, 17 January 1961, https://eisenhower.archives.gov/research/online_documents/farewell_address.html.
2. Bret Baier, *Three Days in January: Dwight Eisenhower's Final Mission* (New York: William Morrow and Company, 2017).
3. Andrew J. Bacevich, *Washington Rules* (New York: Metropolitan Books, 2010), 15.
4. Ben Freeman and Lydia Dennett, 'Loopholes, Filing Failures and Lax Enforcement: How the Foreign Agents Registration Act Falls Short', Project on Government Oversight, 16 December 2014, http://www.pogo.org/our-work/reports/2014/loopholes-filing-failures-lax-enforcement-how-the-foreign-agents-registration-act-falls-short.html.
5. Joel Brinkley, 'Edward von Kloberg III, Lobbyist for Many Dictators, Dies at 63', *New York Times*, 4 May 2005, http://www.nytimes.com/2005/05/04/politics/edward-von-kloberg-iii-lobbyist-for-many-dictators-dies-at-63.html?_r=0.

6. Ibid.
7. Ibid.
8. Philip Shenon and Anne E. Kornblut, 'Lobbyist Paid by Pakistan Led U.S. Delegation There', *New York Times*, 8 May 2005, http://www.nytimes.com/2005/05/08/politics/lobbyist-paid-by-pakistan-led-us-delegation-there.html.

Chapter 3: India Learns to Use Washington's Revolving Door

1. Michael Forsythe and Veena Trehan, 'Friends in high places help India; Corporate America steps up lobbying for nuclear accord', *International Herald Tribune*, 18 July 2006, 17.
2. Mira Kamdar, 'Forget the Israel Lobby. The Hill's Next Big Player Is Made in India', *Washington Post*, 30 September 2007, http://www.washingtonpost.com/wp-dyn/content/article/2007/09/28/AR2007092801350.html.
3. Jie Zong and Jeanne Batalova, 'Indian Immigrants in the United States', Migration Policy Institute, 6 May 2015, http://www.migrationpolicy.org/article/indian-immigrants-united-states.
4. Elizabeth Bumiller, 'Backing an Iraqi Leader Again, This Time for a Fee of $300,000', *New York Times*, 29 October 2007, http://www.nytimes.com/2007/10/29/washington/29blackwill.html.
5. Steven Mufson, 'New Energy on India: Companies and Lobbyists Throw Support Behind U.S. Participation in the Country's Nuclear Sector', *Washington Post*, 18 July 2006, https://www.washingtonpost.com/archive/business/2006/07/18/new-energy-on-india-span-classbankheadcompanies-and-lobbyists-throw-support-behind-us-participation-in-the-countrys-nuclear-sectorspan/c8f3f94d-6b19-4c5f-a000-05724839c463/?utm_term=.34ede62cd6fa.

Chapter 4: Lobbying 'Light': The Increasing Influence of Public Relations Firms and Think Tanks

1. *U.S. & Politics,* https://www.nytimes.com/video/us/politics/100000004514485/elizabeth-warren-on-think-tanks.html.

2. Binoy Prabhakar, 'Flacking for Gujarat, Washington lobby Apco also deflects flak for Narendra Modi', *Economic Times*, 8 December 2012, http://economictimes.indiatimes.com/news/politics-and-nation/flacking-for-gujarat-washington-lobby-apco-also-deflects-flak-for-narendra-modi/articleshow/17527297.cms.

3. As recently as 2016, APCO Worldwide, a global public relations agency, was registered as a lobbyist with the clerk of the US House of Representatives and the secretary of the Senate, http://lobbyingdisclosure.house.gov/, http://www.senate.gov/lobby.

4. APCO has registered as a foreign agent for various governments with the Department of Justice, as recently as April 2017: https://www.fara.gov/quick-search.html.

5. Anand Giridharadas, 'Lobbying in U.S., Indian Firms Present an American Face', *New York Times*, 4 September 2007, http://www.nytimes.com/2007/09/04/business/worldbusiness/04outsource.html.

6. Laura Barron-Lopez, 'Former EPA leader: "Irresponsible" for US to halt nuclear power', *Hill*, 24 October 2014, http://thehill.com/policy/energy-environment/221787-former-epa-chief-irresponsible-if-us-takes-nuclear-power-off-the.

7. https://www.thenation.com/article/secret-donors-behind-center-american-progress-and-other-think tanks-updated-524/

8. Eric Lipton and Brooke Williams, 'How Think Tanks Amplify Corporate America's Influence', *New York Times*, 7 August 2016, https://www.nytimes.com/2016/08/08/us/politics/think-tanks-research-and-corporate-lobbying.html?_r=0. See also, Eric Lipton, Nicholas Confessore and Brooke Williams, 'Think Tank Scholar or Corporate Consultant? It Depends on the Day', *New York Times*, 8 August 2016, https://www.nytimes.com/2016/08/09/us/politics/think-tank-scholars-corporate-consultants.html.

9. There have been several articles in the *Washington Post* examining the cosy relationship between think tanks and their corporate donors: Dan Morgan, 'Think Tanks: Corporations' Quiet Weapon', *Washington Post*, 29 January 2000, https://www.washingtonpost.com/archive/politics/2000/01/29/think-tanks-corporations-quiet-weapon/3d0ccef7-9c46-418d-a2fe-

35bfd6c1119e/?utm_term=.ab5161ca8d8c. See also, Tom Medvetz, 'The myth of think tank independence', *Washington Post*, 9 September 2014, https://www.washingtonpost.com/news/monkey-cage/wp/2014/09/09/the-myth-of-think-tank-independence/?utm_term=.da0f4bedd55f.

10. Secretary of State John Kerry, 'India: 2020 Program'. Remarks made at the Center for American Progress on 14 July 2014.

11. Ken Silverstein, 'The Secret Donors behind the Center for American Progress and Other Think Tanks', *Nation*, 22 May 2013, https://www.thenation.com/article/secret-donors-behind-center-american-progress-and-other-think-tanks-updated-524/.

12. The Brookings Institution opened the New Delhi–based Brookings India in January 2013, citing 'India's growing importance on the world stage as the world's largest democracy and a rising power with one of the fastest growing economies'. The press announcement also said 'the establishment of Brookings India has been made possible by the generous and visionary support of the Brookings India Initiative Founders Circle', https://www.brookings.edu/news-releases/brookings-to-open-brookings-india-in-new-delhi/.

13. Raj Nambisan, 'The "world's best" think tank pegs tent. "It's about time"', 18 March 2013, http://www.dnaindia.com/money/interview-the-world-s-best-think tank-pegs-tent-it-s-about-time-1812402.

Chapter 5: F-16 Jousting: How One Firm Worked for Both India and Pakistan

1. Letter from Senator Robert Corker to Secretary of State John Kerry protesting the proposed sale of eight F-16 Block 52 aircraft to Pakistan, 9 February 2016.

2. Dana Priest and William M. Arkin, 'A hidden world, growing beyond control', *Washington Post*, 19 July 2010, http://projects.washingtonpost.com/top-secret-america/articles/a-hidden-world-growing-beyond-control/.

3. Dana Priest and William M. Arkin, 'National Security, Inc.', *Washington Post*, 20 July 2010, http://projects.washingtonpost.com/top-secret-america/articles/national-security-inc/.

4. Bruce Riedel, 'How Pakistan may test the Trump administration', 17 January 2017, https://www.brookings.edu/blog/markaz/2017/01/17/how-pakistan-may-test-the-trump-administration/.

5. C. Christine Fair and Sumit Ganguly, 'An Unworthy Ally', *Foreign Affairs*, September–October 2015, 160–70.

6. 'Report of the Attorney General to the Congress of the United States on the Administration of the Foreign Agents Registration Act of 1938, as amended, for the six months ending December 31, 2015', Department of Justice, https://www.fara.gov/reports/FARA_DEC_2015.pdf.

7. 'FBI affidavit—Syed Ghulam Nabi Fai (2011.07.18)', Scribd, https://www.scribd.com/doc/102696647/FBI-affidavit-Syed-Ghulam-Nabi-Fai-2011-07-18.

8. Center for Responsive Politics' Open Secrets database, https://www.opensecrets.org/lobby/clientsum.php?id=D000000104&year=2017.

9. 'The Government of Pakistan—F-16 Block 52 Aircraft', Defense Security Cooperation Agency press release, 12 February 2016, http://dsca.mil/major-arms-sales/government-pakistan-f-16-block-52-aircraft.

10. Department of Justice, https://efile.fara.gov/pls/apex/f?p=171:200:15268156911970::NO:RP,200:P200_REG_NUMBER,P200_COUNTRY:5926,INDIA.

11. Press release issued by the Office of Senator Rand Paul on 25 February 2016, https://www.paul.senate.gov/news/press/sen-rand-paul-introduces-joint-resolution-of-disapproval-to-halt-arms-sales-to-pakistan.

12. Annie Gowen, 'As Trump vows to stop flow of jobs overseas, U.S. plans to make fighter jets in India', *Washington Post*, 5 December 2016, https://www.washingtonpost.com/world/asia_pacific/as-trump-vows-to-stop-flow-of-jobs-overseas-us-plans-to-make-fighter-jets-in-india/2016/12/05/a4d3bfaa-b71e-11e6-939c-91749443c5e5_story.html?utm_term=.fd1453edd19f.

13. Press release issued by Senator Bob Corker, 10 March 2016, https://www.corker.senate.gov/public/index.cfm/news-list?ID=7FA590FA-6369-423D-A1A5-F8A0391094B4.

14. K. Iqbal, 'F-16's impact on Pak-US relations', *Nation*, 16 May 2016, http://nation.com.pk/columns/16-May-2016/f-16-s-impact-on-pak-us-relations.

15. Hussain Nadim, 'Losing friends in Washington DC', *Express Tribune*, 25 March 2016, https://tribune.com.pk/story/1072857/losing-friends-in-washington-dc/.

Chapter 6: The Untapped Potential of the India–United States Civil Nuclear Agreement

1. Andy Mukherjee, 'A nuclear-powered India would charge up global trade', *International Herald Tribune*, 3 March 2006, http://archive.li/zcCIR.
2. Annie Gowen, 'India's huge need for electricity is a problem for the planet', *Washington Post*, 6 November 2015, https://www.washingtonpost.com/world/asia_pacific/indias-huge-need-for-electricity-is-a-problem-for-the-planet/2015/11/06/a9e004e6-622d-11e5-8475-781cc9851652_story.html?utm_term=.f888627c62dd.
3. Ministry of Power, Government of India, http://www.cea.nic.in/monthlyinstalledcapacity.html.
4. Chelsea Harvey, 'Air pollution in India is so bad that it kills half a million people every year', *Washington Post*, 11 May 2016, https://www.washingtonpost.com/news/energy-environment/wp/2016/05/11/air-pollution-in-india-is-so-bad-that-it-kills-half-a-million-people-every-year/?utm_term=.a267108f8c78.
5. 'How Clean Is Nuclear Power', MEGA Uranium Ltd, http://www.megauranium.com/uranium_industry/clean/.
6. Ministry of Power, Government of India, http://www.cea.nic.in/monthlyinstalledcapacity.html.
7. Ritika Katyal, 'India census exposes extent of poverty', CNN, 3 August 2015, http://www.cnn.com/2015/08/02/asia/india-poor-census-secc/.
8. Rai Atul Krishna, 'Nearly 70% of Bihar struggles below the poverty line', *Hindustan Times*, 24 August 2015, http://www.hindustantimes.com/india/nearly-70-of-bihar-struggles-below-the-poverty-line/story-0pXcpPLFb5WDy7f4y3Oy5H.html.
9. Subrata Ghoshroy, 'Taking stock: The US–India nuclear deal 10 years later', *Bulletin of the Atomic Scientists*, 16 February 2016.
10. 'Trade in Goods with India', United States Census Bureau, http://www.census.gov/foreign-trade/balance/c5330.html.

11. Subrata Ghoshroy, 'The Real Story Behind the U.S. –India Nuclear Deal', Alternet, 16 October 2008, http://www.alternet.org/story/103313/the_real_story_behind_the_u.s.-india_nuclear_deal.

12. 'US submits list of 10 defence items for transfer to India', *Free Press Journal*, 3 October 2013, http://www.freepressjournal.in/business/us-submits-list-of-10-defence-items-for-transfer-to-india/239050.

13. Gil Plimmer and Victor Mallet, 'India becomes biggest foreign buyer of US weapons', *Financial Times*, 23 February 2014, https://www.ft.com/content/ded3be9a-9c81-11e3-b535-00144feab7de.

Chapter 7: The Obstacles to the Nuclear Agreement and the Complicated History between the US and India

1. Robert D. Blackwill, 'The United States, India and Asian Security'. Presented to the Institute for Defence Studies and Analyses' Fifth Asian Security Conference, New Delhi, 27 January 2003, https://www.mtholyoke.edu/acad/intrel/bush/blackwill2.htm.

2. 'India To Test Long Range Submarine Launched Nuclear Missile Next Week', Defenseworld.net, 23 January, 2017, http://www.defenseworld.net/news/18300/India_To_Test_Long_Range_Submarine_Launched_Nuclear_Missile_Next_Week#.WIkiwIWcFPY.

3. For a brief summary of President Obama's US–India Strategic and Commercial Dialogue (S&CD), which kicked off in January 2015, see: https://www.state.gov/p/sca/ci/in/strategicdialgue/. See also, https://www.commerce.gov/tags/us-india-strategic-and-commercial-dialogue-scd.

4. The Institute of World Politics, http://www.iwp.edu/.

5. Mandakini Gahlot, 'Obama, India's Modi cite nuclear investment breakthrough', *USA Today*, 25 January 2015, https://www.usatoday.com/story/news/world/2015/01/25/obama-india-arrival/22307343/.

Chapter 8: Galvanizing Grass-roots Support for the US–India Nuclear Agreement

1. William F. Vendley, 'The Recovery of Transcendence in Political Order: The Role of Multi-religious Cooperation', UNESCO conference in Paris, 2005.

2. The case studies on the role of churches in effecting policy and state changes in the Philippines and in South Africa originate in *Religion: The Missing Dimension of Statecraft* by Douglas Johnston and Cynthia Sampson (Oxford: Oxford University Press, 1994).

3. George Pratt Shultz, *The Church as a Force for Peaceful Change in South Africa* (Washington, D.C.: Bureau of Public Affairs, United States Department of State, 1986), 2.

Chapter 9: The Roots of My Independence

1. Dan O'Brien, *Buffalo for the Broken Heart: Restoring Life to a Black Hills Ranch* (New York: Random House, 2002), 171.

Chapter 11: Debut on the International Stage

1. The Cecil Rhodes Trust: http://files.rhodesscholarshiptrust.com/governancedocs/WillandCodicils.pdf.

Chapter 12: Stirrings of War: Discussions on the Vietnam Draft

1. Hamilton Gregory, *McNamara's Folly: The Use of Low-IQ Troops in the Vietnam War* (West Conshohocken, Pennsylvania: Infinity Publishing, 2015).

Chapter 14: A Lonely Vietnam Veteran at Harvard Law School

1. 'The Root of Student Unrest', *Boston Globe*, 7 May 1969, A18.

Chapter 15: Getting Elected to the House and Senate

1. Donald Loren Hardy, *Shooting from the Lip: The Life of Senator Al Simpson* (Brilliance Audio, 1 May 2013).

Chapter 16: The 'ABSCAM' Scandal

1. Martin Schram, 'Sen. Pressler: He Spurned the "Arabs"', *Washington Post*, 4 February 1980, https://www.washingtonpost.com/archive/

politics/1980/02/04/sen-pressler-he-spurned-the-arabs/d88b54da-963f-4780-b7d7-dc60cabf34b6/?utm_term=.f868cd579c62.

2. Alan Ehrenhalt (ed.), *Politics in America: The 100th Congress* (Washington, D.C.: Congressional Quarterly, Inc.) 1389.

3. 'Excerpts from ruling by federal judge upholding the ABSCAM convictions', *New York Times*, 25 July 1981, http://www.nytimes.com/1981/07/25/nyregion/excerpts-from-ruling-by-federal-judge-upholding-the-abscam-convictions.html?pagewanted=all&mcubz=0.

Chapter 17: The Making of the Pressler Amendment

1. This is Senator Pressler's recollection of comments made by President Ronald Reagan during White House meetings on nuclear non-proliferation.

2. George Crile, *Charlie Wilson's War: The Extraordinary Story of How the Wildest Man in Congress and a Rogue CIA Agent Changed the History of Our Times* (New York: Grove Press, 2003).

Chapter 18: The Immediate Impact of the Pressler Amendment

1. 'Pakistan–United States: Dynamics of the Relationship, An Intelligence Assessment', prepared by the US State Department's Office of Near Eastern and South Asian Analysis, September 1985, http://nsarchive.gwu.edu/nukevault/ebb531-U.S.-Pakistan-Nuclear-Relations,-1984-1985/documents/doc%2016%209-1985%20%20 US%20Pakistan%20dynamics.pdf.

2. Rone Tempest, '2 Reagan Aides Arriving in India to See Gandhi', 16 September 1985, http://articles.latimes.com/1985-09-16/news/mn-22010_1_india-and-pakistan.

3. Elaine Sciolino, 'Zia Hopes To Ease Friction With India', *New York Times*, 21 October 1985, http://www.nytimes.com/1985/10/21/world/zia-hopes-to-ease-friction-with-india.html.

4. 'Pakistan Has "Produced an Atomic Weapon"', Defense Intelligence Agency cable to [excised location], 'Pakistan-China: Nuclear Weapons Production and Testing', 7 December 1985, Secret, excised copy, https://www.documentcloud.org/documents/347038-doc-19-12-7-85.html.

5. 'South Asia After Indira Gandhi', a report prepared for the US Senate Foreign Relations Committee by Senator Claiborne Pell, 1985, and transmitted to the US Senate Foreign Relations Committee.

6. Senator Pressler's 'Foreign Trip Report' prepared for Senator Richard Lugar, chairman of the Senate Foreign Relations Committee, 18 February 1985.

7. Voice of America News, 12 January 1985.

8. 'New Documents Spotlight Reagan-era Tensions over Pakistani Nuclear Program', National Security Archive, George Washington University, 27 April 2012, http://nsarchive.gwu.edu/nukevault/ebb377/.

9. Ibid.

10. Bob Woodward, 'Pakistan Reported Near Atom Arms Production', *Washington Post*, 4 November 1986, https://www.washingtonpost.com/archive/politics/1986/11/04/pakistan-reported-near-atom-arms-production/acd69089-dff0-424c-ba59-bd3fcac02b76/?utm_term=.94031da7381b.

11. Rone Tempest, 'Bomb Project Could Lead Congress to Cut Off Aid: Pakistan's Nuclear Secret Goes Public', *Los Angeles Times*, 24 March 1987, http://articles.latimes.com/1987-03-24/news/mn-249_1_nuclear-weapons.

12. 'New Documents Spotlight Reagan-era Tensions over Pakistani Nuclear Program', National Security Archive, George Washington University, 27 April 2012, http://nsarchive.gwu.edu/nukevault/ebb377/.

13. 'Pakistan and the F-16s', testimony by Senator Larry Pressler to the US Senate (Congressional Record, 28 June 1995, S9229-9230), https://www.gpo.gov/fdsys/pkg/CREC-1995-06-28/html/CREC-1995-06-28-pt1-PgS9227.htm.

14. John H. Cushman, Jr, 'Pakistan's Nuclear Effort Worries US', *New York Times*, 6 March 1987, A3.

15. Statement by Senator John Glenn, 'U.S. Assistance to Pakistan before the Senate Foreign Relations Committee', 23 March 1987, John H. Glenn Archives, Ohio State University Libraries.

16. 'Pakistan's Illegal Nuclear Procurement Exposed in 1987', National Security Archive, George Washington University, 27 April 2012, http://nsarchive.gwu.edu/nukevault/ebb446/.

17. Memo from Kenneth L. Adelman for the undersecretary of state for political affairs on 'The Pakistani Procurement Cases', 23 July 1987, http://nsarchive.gwu.edu/nukevault/ebb446/docs/8.pdf.

18. Memo from Kenneth Adelman for the President on the 'Certification on Pakistan', 21 November 1987, http://nsarchive.gwu.edu/nukevault/ebb446/docs/20.pdf.

19. Memo from President Reagan to the Speaker of the House, 17 December 1987, enclosing presidential determination, http://nsarchive.gwu.edu/nukevault/ebb446/docs/24%20Reagan%2017%20Dec%2087.pdf.

20. 'White House Statement on Continuation of Military Aid to Pakistan', 15 January 1988, *Public Papers of the President of the United States, Ronald Reagan, 1988*, Book I (Washington, D.C.: Government Printing Office, 1990), 46.

Chapter 19: The Enforcement of the Pressler Amendment

1. Seymour Hersh, 'On the brink of nuclear war: How Pakistan came close to dropping the bomb—and how we helped them get it', *New Yorker*, 29 March, 1993, 56.

2. Speech made by Prime Minister Benazir Bhutto to a joint session of the US Congress (Congressional Record, 9 June 1989, S6472).

3. Senator John Glenn's statement to the US Senate (Congressional Record, 16 November 1989), 29419.

4. C. Uday Bhaskar, 'The Forgotten India–Pakistan Nuclear Crisis: 25 Years Later', 18 May 2015, http://thediplomat.com/2015/05/the-forgotten-india-pakistan-nuclear-crisis-25-years-later/.

5. 'Letters to Prime Minister Bhutto, President Ghulam Ishaque Khan, and Prime Minister Singh'—memo for National Security Advisor Brent Scowcroft from the State Department, 13 August 1990, obtained from the George Washington University National Security Archives.

Chapter 20: The Fallout from the Enforcement of the Pressler Amendment

1. John Stackhouse, 'Cutoff of U.S. aid hurts Pakistan's poor the most', *San Francisco Examiner*, 15 March 1992, A7.

2. Adrian Levy and Catherine Scott-Clark, *Deception: Pakistan, the United States and the Global Nuclear Weapons Conspiracy* (London: Atlantic Books, September 2007), 161–62.

3. Ibid., 197.

4. Ibid., 203.

5. Letter from President Bush to Congress, reproduced in the US Department of State dispatch, 12 April 1991, 278–79.

6. 'Keep the Pressure on Pakistan's Bomb Program', *Christian Science Monitor*, 1 July 1991, http://proxygw.wrlc.org/login?url=http://search.proquest.com.proxygw.wrlc.org/docview/291193666?accountid=11243.

Chapter 21: Stepping into the Line of Fire

1. 'Scene-setter for Senator Pressler's Visit to Pakistan', US State Department message, 8 January 1992.

2. Ibid.

3. Catherine Collins and Douglas Frantz, *Fallout: The True Story of the CIA's Secret War on Nuclear Trafficking* (New York: Simon & Schuster, 2014), 132–33.

4. 'Is it too much to expect normal good manners?', *The Muslim*, 13 January 1992.

5. 'The fundamentalist peril', Middle East News Network, 13 January 1992.

6. 'The Islamic genie is out of the bottle', Middle East News Network, 15 January 1992.

7. Leon T. Hadar, 'The "Green Peril": Creating the Islamic Fundamentalist Threat', Cato Institute, 27 August 1992, https://www.cato.org/publications/policy-analysis/green-peril-creating-islamic-fundamentalist-threat.

8. Transcript of 13 January 1992 press conference by Senator Larry Pressler—unclassified message from the American Embassy in Islamabad, 13 January 1992.

9. Ashley Parker, 'Spending Cuts Put Damper on Trips by Lawmakers', *New York Times*, 21 March 2013, http://mobile.nytimes.com/2013/03/22/us/politics/spending-cuts-put-damper-on-trips-by-lawmakers.html.

10. Jeffrey R. Smith, 'Pakistan Official Affirms Capacity for Nuclear Device', *Washington Post*, 7 February 1992, A18.

Chapter 22: The Octopus Strikes Back

1. Murray Waas and Douglas Frantz, 'Despite Ban, US Arms Are Sold to Pakistan', *Los Angeles Times*, 6 March 1992, WA1, http://articles.latimes.com/1992-03-06/news/mn-3321_1_arms-sales.

2. Letter from Secretary of State James Baker to Senator Larry Pressler, 12 March 1992.

3. Letter to Senator Larry Pressler from Janet G. Mullins, assistant secretary of state for legislative affairs, 21 April 1992.

4. Letter to Senator Larry Pressler from Janet G. Mullins, assistant secretary of state for legislative affairs, 30 July 1992.

5. 'Interpreting the Pressler Amendment: Commercial Sales to Pakistan', a hearing before the Committee on Foreign Relations, United States Senate, 30 July 1992.

6. Ibid.

7. Ibid.

8. Ibid.

Chapter 23: The Battle for the Pressler Amendment Continues

1. Steven A. Holmes, 'Clinton Plans Change in the Law Banning Military Aid to Pakistan', *New York Times*, 27 November 1993, 5, http://www.nytimes.com/1993/11/27/world/clinton-plans-change-in-the-law-banning-military-aid-to-pakistan.html.

2. Strobe Talbott, *Engaging India* (Washington, D.C.: Brookings Institution Press, 2004), 37.

3. Jeffrey R. Smith, 'Clinton Moves to Ease Pakistan Nuclear Curb', *Washington Post*, 25 November 1993, A59.

4. Letter to President Bill Clinton from Senator Larry Pressler, 23 November 1993.

5. Larry Pressler, 'Nonproliferation—The Pressler Amendment', *Washington Post*, 14 December 1993, A24, https://www.washingtonpost.com/archive/opinions/1993/12/14/nonproliferation-the-pressler-amendment/1562bf06-f317-4154-a839-ddd0d58fa9ee/?utm_term=.f85553b6cb94..

6. "'A Trip Report Summary" of an Official Trip by Senator Larry Pressler: South Korea, Burma, India (Bombay and New Delhi), Pakistan (Islamabad and Karachi), Kuwait and Austria (Vienna), December 1993' (Congressional Record, 8 February 1994).
7. Ali Sarwar Naqvi, 'Discard The Pressler Amendment', *Washington Post*, 21 December 1993, A22, https://www.washingtonpost.com/archive/opinions/1993/12/21/discard-the-pressler-amendment/c9532c96-bd8c-4d1e-ae31-8e3a504e33ed/?utm_term=.29f800529bf4..
8. Letter from President Bill Clinton to Senator Larry Pressler, 27 December 1993.
9. Letter from Senator Larry Pressler to President Bill Clinton, 8 March 1994.
10. Larry Pressler, 'US Non-Proliferation Policy and South Asia', Congressional Record, 5 August 1994, S10843.

Chapter 24: On the Home Front: Domestic Legislative Achievements

1. Senator Pressler's recollection of President Clinton's comments at the 28 February 1996 signing ceremony.

Chapter 25: The Clinton Administration Weakens the Pressler Amendment

1. 'Clinton: Pakistan Should Get Its F-16s Or Get Its Money Back', *St. Louis Post-Dispatch* (Missouri), 12 April 1995.
2. Dana Priest, 'U.S., Pakistan to Renew Talks; Perry Vows to Improve Military Relations Despite Congressional Ban', *Washington Post*, 11 January 1995, A15, https://www.highbeam.com/doc/1P2-815737.html.
3. 'Clinton: Pakistan Should Get Its F-16s Or Get Its Money Back', *St. Louis Post-Dispatch*, Missouri, 12 April 1995, https://www.newspapers.com/newspage/142412288/.
4. R. Jeffrey Smith and Thomas Lippman, 'Pakistan Building Reactor That May Yield Large Quantities of Plutonium', *Washington Post*, 8 April 1995, A20.
5. 'Clinton: Pakistan Should Get Its F-16s Or Get Its Money Back', *St. Louis Post-Dispatch* (Missouri), 12 April 1995, 5A.

6. 'Against Brown Proposal to Weaken US Nuclear Sanctions on Pakistan', remarks by Senator John Glenn and Senator Hank Brown (Congressional Record, 20 September 1995), S13956–13971.

7. Press Release issued by the Ministry of External Affairs, External Publicity Division, Government of India, 22 September 1995.

Chapter 26: The Death of the Pressler Amendment and the Success of the Octopus

1. Letter from Senator John Glenn to President Bill Clinton, 12 February 1996, John H. Glenn Archives, Ohio State University Libraries.

2. Strobe Talbott, *Engaging India* (Washington, D.C.: Brookings Institution Press, 2004), 37.

3. Kiyotaka Shibasaki, 'Bhutto: N-Program up to India', *Daily Yomiuri*, 4 January 1996, 1.

4. Thomas W. Lippman and Paul Blustein, 'U.S. Clears Pakistan Deals', *Washington Post*, 17 April 1996, A28.

5. 'Pakistan welcomes $465m arms delivery', *Australian*, 2 September 1996, 9.

6. The US Bureau of Labor Statistics cited the South Dakota unemployment rate from June 1996 as 2.8 per cent.

7. Strobe Talbott, *Engaging India* (Washington, D.C.: Brookings Institution Press, 2004), 2.

8. Maimuna Ashraf, 'Finest-hour at Chagai: From obscurity to history', http://foreignpolicynews.org/2015/05/27/finest-hour-at-chagai-from-obscurity-to-history/.

9. Lanny Davis, 'America can't afford breach with Pakistan', 29 June 2011, *Hill*, http://thehill.com/opinion/columnists/lanny-davis/169143-america-cant-afford-breach-with-pakistan.

Chapter 27: The Aftermath of the Pressler Amendment

1. 'Resentment among younger Pak armymen towards US hurting war-on-terror', ANI, 25 November 2008, http://zeenews.india.com/news/south-asia/resentment-among-younger-pak-armymen-towards-us-hurting-war-on-terror_486284.html.

2. Saeed Shah, 'India and Pakistan Escalate Nuclear Arms Race', *Wall Street Journal*, 31 March 2017, https://www.wsj.com/articles/india-and-pakistan-escalate-nuclear-arms-race-1490983537.

3. Ibid.

4. Jeffrey Goldberg and Marc Ambinder, 'The Ally From Hell', *Atlantic*, December 2011, https://www.theatlantic.com/magazine/archive/2011/12/the-ally-from-hell/308730/.

5. C. Christine Fair and Sumit Ganguly, 'An Unworthy Ally', *Foreign Affairs*, September–October 2015, 164.

6. Matthew M. Aid, *Intel Wars : The Secret History of the Fight against Terror* (London: Bloomsbury Press, 2012), 112, 189.

7. Ibid., 120.

Chapter 28: My Last Stand against the Octopus: Another Senate Campaign in 2014

1. Alexa Roarty, 'Former Republican Senator Making His Comeback as an Independent', *National Journal*, November 2013, https://www.nationaljournal.com/s/66708/former-republican-senator-making-his-comeback-independent.

Chapter 29: Rabbit in a Firing Range: The Octopus Takes Its Best Shot

1. Jonathan Martin, 'Senate Contest in South Dakota Is Free-for-All', *New York Times*, 13 October 2014, https://www.nytimes.com/2014/10/14/us/politics/senate-contest-in-south-dakota-is-free-for-all.html?_r=1.

2. David Vine and Tomdispatch, 'The Pentagon is turning Italy into a military base', *Salon*, 4 October 2013, http://www.salon.com/2013/10/03/the_pentagon_is_turning_italy_into_a_military_base/.

3. Bruce E. Keith, David B. Magleby, Candice J. Nelson, Elizabeth Orr, Mark C. Westlye and Raymond E. Wolfinger, *The Myth of the Independent Voter* (Berkeley: University of California Press, 1992).

4. Dana Bash and Adam Levy, 'Larry Pressler stumps through cowboy poetry circuit', CNN, 16 October 2014, http://www.cnn.com/2014/10/16/politics/cowboy-poetry-south-dakota-senate/.

5. Steve Hemmingsen, 'Pressler for Senate', quoted by Senator Larry Pressler, Facebook post, 1 November 2014. In addition, he recorded a campaign advertisement for Senator Pressler: https://www.youtube.com/watch?v=CQJ1hEpGy0E.

Chapter 30: Observations and Prescriptions for the Future

1. Saeed Shah, 'India and Pakistan Escalate Arms Race', *Wall Street Journal*, 31 March 2017, https://www.wsj.com/articles/india-and-pakistan-escalate-nuclear-arms-race-1490983537.
2. Bruce Riedel, 'How Pakistan may test the Trump administration', 17 January, 2017, https://www.brookings.edu/blog/markaz/2017/01/17/how-pakistan-may-test-the-trump-administration/.

Appendix: A Timeline of Pakistan's Nuclear Ambitions

1. Excerpted and abridged from these two sources: Warren Donnelly, 'Pakistan and Nuclear Weapons', Environment and Natural Resources Policy Division, Congressional Research Service, 24 March 1987, and 'From Myth to Reality: Evidence of Pakistan's "Nuclear Restraint"', Congressional Record, 31 July 1992, S11068.

* * *

To view some of the historical documents referenced in this book, please explore the Larry Pressler Papers, housed at the University of South Dakota Archives and Special Collections, and read excerpts of which are available online at the Digital Library of South Dakota: http://www.usd.edu/library.

Index

Abramoff, Jack, 17–18
ABSCAM (Arab scam), 109–13,
    203, 206, 213; corruption
    probe, 111
Adelman, Kenneth, 133–34, 139
Afghanistan, xviii, xx–xxi, 6, 36,
    53, 95, 121–23, 126–27, 133,
    136, 143, 147–48; Islamic
    fundamentalism and, 163;
    Pakistan policy on, xix; policy
    to support resistance of, 6;
    Soviet invasion of, xviii,
    xx–xxi, 6, 121–22, 126–27, 133,
    141, 143, 148, 156; terrorism
    and, 53, 223; US assistance to
    rebels of, 6; wars in, xviii, 95,
    147
Aga Khan, Yasmin, 123
Agent Orange, 89–90, 217
Ahluwalia, Montek Singh, 82–83,
    119, 155, 158, 201
aid and assistance, xii; disbursement
    of, xvii; to Pakistan, xiii, xv,

xvii–xviii, 6, 54, 120, 127–29,
    133, 139–40, 193–94, 199–200
al-Qaeda, xx–xxi, 123, 160, 188
American International Group
    (AIG), 21
American Soybean Association, 152
Anderson, Elmer, 72
APCO, 24–25; its International
    Advisory Council (IAC), 25;
    Vibrant Gujarat and, 24
Apollo 13 space mission, 225
Aquino, Benigno, 63
Armacost, Michael, 130, 138
Armitage, Richard, xxi
arms control, 116, 118, 124, 131;
    Reagan and, 5
Arms Export Control Act of 1976,
    39
arms trade, 50, 56, 202
Association of Physicians of
    Pakistani Descent of North
    America (APPNA), 192
Aziz, Sartaj, 155, 162